Continuity and
Management

Continuity and Change in Public Policy and Management

Christopher Pollitt

Research Professor in Public Management, Public Management Institute, Katholieke Universiteit Leuven, Belgium

Geert Bouckaert

Director, Public Management Institute, Katholieke Universiteit Leuven and President, European Group for Public Administration, Belgium

Edward Elgar
Cheltenham, UK • Northampton, MA, USA

Published by
Edward Elgar Publishing Limited
The Lypiatts
15 Lansdown Road
Cheltenham
Glos GL50 2JA
UK

Edward Elgar Publishing, Inc.
William Pratt House
9 Dewey Court
Northampton
Massachusetts 01060
USA

Paperback edition 2011

A catalogue record for this book
is available from the British Library

Library of Congress Control Number: 2009930878

ISBN 978 1 84844 308 2 (cased)
ISBN 978 0 85793 543 4 (paperback)

Typeset by Servis Filmsetting Ltd, Stockport, Cheshire
Printed and bound by MPG Books Group, UK

Contents

Preface   vi
Acknowledgements   viii

1   Theory and method in comparative studies of organizational
    change   1
2   National reforms: the Belgian and English regimes   22
3   National reforms: hospitals   32
4   National reforms: police   50
5   National reforms: intersectoral comparison   71
6   What happened locally? Hospitals   81
7   What happened locally? Police   101
8   Reflections on theories of change   135
9   Reflections on doctrines of comparison   170
Appendix: The Brighton–Leuven project   195

References   198
Index   211

Preface

This book sprang originally from a simple source. As we worked together on earlier academic projects we also talked about our national differences – of custom, language and, inevitably, public policymaking. Eventually opportunities presented themselves (with a little help, as usual) and we were able to tailor at least some of our curiosities into the shape of a joint academic project. And now, three years later, we have a book that compares the police service with the hospital service, Leuven with Brighton, Belgium with England, and 'then' (1965) with 'now' (more than 40 years later years). It focuses on similarities as well as differences, and on continuities as well as changes. It examines the national level and the local. It also interrogates a range of contemporary academic approaches to policy analysis and international comparison. If we have done our job properly, readers should be able to get at least a flavour of that original fascination that prodded us to begin. How can two countries, so close to each other geographically and historically, be so different? Then (after some more detailed observation) are they really so different, or is that just a superficial stereotype?

When would-be authors approach publishers with propositions for academic books the publishers always ask 'Who is this for?' Our answer on this occasion is, first, advanced students of public management and public policy, and second, their professors. Both these groups, however, already have a lot of reading to do, so the obvious further question is why they should add this book to their existing burdens. Here the answer is a little more complicated. Obviously *Continuity and Change in Public Policy and Management* should be of special interest to those who have a particular focus on Belgium and England, or on hospitals or the police. However, we have tried to make its relevance go far beyond these (worthy and legitimate) special interests. Our aim has been to make the book relevant for anyone who has a general interest in the study of comparative public management and policymaking. We have attempted to achieve this broad relevance by using the particular chosen topics as vehicles with which to examine the usefulness of some much more general theories and models of the policy and management. We have tried to make these larger sets of ideas 'work' with a lot of detailed material, and have reflected at length on the successes and limitations of this application.

Much of the public management and public policy literature falls into a few well-recognized subsets. There are books on 'theory'. There are case studies, often of currently fashionable policies. There are a few histories, looking back over decades. There are methods texts, which discuss the properties and limitations of different ways of gathering and manipulating data. One reason why we hope that the present work will be of wider usefulness and interest is that it offers all these things together. It engages with theory, it provides new and original case studies, it spans 40 years of history and it contains considerable discussion of sources, tools and methods. Indeed, teachers could use it as a core book for a course that sought to integrate these different aspects of the subject (we hope they will).

As we write this preface the mass media are full of claims that we are on the verge of a new era in public policymaking. We have a global economic crisis that seems to be prompting hitherto unthinkable degrees of government intervention in the business sector. We have a new American President who has achieved remarkable popularity through an extended, cleverly nuanced exposition on the theme of 'change'. We have a recently enlarged European Union which is attempting to play a larger part as a global actor, well beyond its existing competencies in trade and agriculture. In both Belgium and England – our two focal countries – we can witness high levels of public discontent with contemporary governments, and a sense that the way policymaking is done itself needs to be transformed. Much is to be gained, we would suggest, from detailed, longer-term studies of such apparent turning points and new departures. *Continuity and Change* is our attempt to provide such an analysis.

Christopher Pollitt
Geert Bouckaert

Leuven, January 2009

Acknowledgements

Our biggest acknowledgement must go to a large but individually anonymous group – the senior police officers, hospital doctors and managers, civil servants and politicians who agreed to talk to us and provide us with material for our study. Many individuals have been generous with their time and trusting in their confidences, and all for no obvious reward other than helping a couple of academics pursue their particular research interests. We are very grateful, and much enjoyed (most of) our interviews.

Second, Christopher Pollitt wishes to acknowledge the financial assistance provided by the Hans Sigrist Stiftung (University of Bern). The award of the 2004 Hans Sigrist prize made all sorts of research trips and investigations that much easier. Subsequently the Belgian side of the research was greatly facilitated by the award of a Katholieke Universiteit Leuven Senior Visiting Research Fellowship during part of 2006.

Third, we have chalked up a number of debts among our academic colleagues. These are of various kinds – offering information, providing contacts, reading through drafts, and so on. Since 2005 these debts have become so extensive that we can here only register some of the larger red entries on our personal accounts. They comprise debts to Professor Sue Balloch (Brighton University), Professor Paul Collier (Monash University), Professor Steve Harrison (University of Manchester), Professor Michael Hill (Queen Mary's College, London), Dr Jeroen Maesschalck (Katholieke Universiteit Leuven) and Professor Peter Squires (Brighton University). Naturally, they are free of responsibility for the results.

Finally, we thank our secretaries – Inge Vermeulen and Anneke Heylen – who have not merely tidied up our drafts and worked magic with our many travel claims, but have also converted some pretty ragged-looking hand-drawn maps and diagrams into neat, electronic form.

1. Theory and method in comparative studies of organizational change

1.1 INTRODUCTION

This book presents a comparative analysis. It is comparative in at least four senses:

- It compares public policymaking and management in two countries, England and Belgium.
- It compares two major public services, hospitals and the police.
- It compares shifts in national policies with what was actually happening in two specific localities (and is thus, in current parlance, a study in 'multilevel government').
- It compares developments over time (diachronic comparisons).

We hope that readers will find each and all of these comparisons intrinsically interesting, but here at the outset we must warn that none of the four are straightforward. As we shall see, there are many obstacles and difficult choices involved in each of these comparisons, and the voluminous literature on public policy and management shows quite clearly that there is no academic consensus on the best way to make them. Because of this, the discussion within our book will alternate frequently between two (mutually dependent) levels: first, that of actually comparing 'things' (political systems, hospital financing systems and so on); and second, ways of making those comparisons – how does one do it? To give readers a framework for the substantive descriptions and discussions that come later, this first chapter will concentrate on the 'how' question, and will briefly introduce some of the main issues. Right at the end of the book (Chapter 9), when the substantive analyses are complete, we will return to these questions of theory and method, to review what we have learned.

1.2   SOME KEY ISSUES IN COMPARISONS OVER TIME

Some fundamental issues underlie any attempt to compare policies and organizational practices over time. Among these are the following: what do we mean by 'policy'? Which of the many aspects of 'policy' are we going to concentrate on? (In practical terms there are usually far too many to cover them all: political maneouvres and agenda setting; the role of the media; pressure groups and lobbying; the patterns and respective powers of relevant formal organizations such as ministries and agencies; acts of leadership; accidents; organizational standard operating procedures; changes in the economic situation; social and demographic changes, and so on.) Then, how do we conceptualize time? At what points do we start and stop the historical clock, and how do we justify cutting history into the particular period we have chosen? How do we define and recognize change? All these questions apply even if the object of the research is change in one sector in one country. But if, as here, the aim is to compare more than one sector and more than one country, then an additional set of questions spring into existence. There is a need to justify the particular selection of these two (or three, or six) countries and these particular localities and these two policy fields. And, last but not least, there is the problem of finding a theoretical approach and conceptual framework that can accommodate and give order to diversity, similarity and change without grossly distorting any of them.

It would be easy to spend the whole book wrestling with these preliminary questions (indeed, many whole books have been just so preoccupied: see, for example, Gerring, 2007; Hill and Hupe, 2002; Kay, 2006; King et al., 1994; Peters, 1989; Sabatier, 1999; Yanow and Schwartz-Shea, 2005). However, that is not at all our intention. We started this work out of an old-fashioned interest in what had happened on the ground, and that remains our central focus. So while we recognize and accept that we have to deal with these fundamental issues, our strategy is to get them over with fairly quickly (and return to them at the end). Naturally, one cost of such an approach is that we have to skim the surface of a number of complex issues of theory and method. We can only plead that it is better to acknowledge such issues, however briefly, than to ignore or conceal them. Certainly we make it clear throughout that any idea that analytic comparisons can be made by just looking at the facts and 'telling it like it is/was' is naive and passé. Comparative policy studies are always 'constructed' – fashioned by the author(s). That is not a radical relativist position: it is not at all to say that any one construction is as good as any other. But it is to presuppose a certain obligation on the constructors that they will show something of what they have done to fashion their final product, faults and all. And that is an obligation that we will seek to fulfil.

1.3 WHAT DO WE MEAN BY 'POLICY' AND WHICH ASPECTS ARE WE FOCUSING UPON?

Public policy is, at its most simple, a choice made by government to undertake some choice of action. (Howlett and Ramesh, 2003, p. 3)

This is not a bad start, but readers should be aware that there is a 40-year-old debate about the definition of public policy, and that the above is but one candidate, and a very simple, possibly oversimple, one at that (see also Dye, 1972; Hill and Hupe, 2002). Hogwood and Gunn found at least ten meanings, including policy as an expression of general purpose, policy as specific proposals, policy as a programme and policy as formal authorization (Hogwood and Gunn, 1984, pp. 13–19). In some ways it is easier to pronounce upon what a definition of policy should not say than on what it should. Thus, we should be careful that our conceptualization of policy does not:

- Imply that policymaking is always an instrumental-rational business, with clear goals, objectives, calculations of cost and benefit and so on. As Wildavsky wrote a long time ago, policy objectives are frequently multiple, confusing and vague (Wildavsky, 1979, pp. 41–61). Policies come out as uneasy compromises as often as they do as clear visions.
- Imply that policymaking proceeds in neat stages ('formulation, implementation, evaluation', or various more elaborate versions – see Hogwood and Gunn, 1984; Howlett and Ramesh, 2003; Hill and Hupe, 2002).
- Assume that what finally gets done (if anything) closely matches the policy as originally announced (Hill and Hupe, 2002)
- Imply that policy usually flows from the head of a single minister, or group, because more usually it arises from interaction between different groups and interests
- Assume that policymaking always or even usually begins at the top and flows down organizational hierarchies. It may equally well be 'bottom-up', 'middle-up', 'middle-down' or some other combination.
- Assume that all the main participants have the same view of either what the problem is or, indeed, what the policy itself is (Colebatch, 1998). Different participants often construct their own images and understandings of what the policy is and is about (see the discussion of social constructivism under 1.10, below). Shared goals are nice to have, and may be worth working hard towards, but they are by no means always essential for a policy to exist.

- Assume that policies either clearly succeed or clearly fail. More typically they will appear to have a spectrum of effects, some intended and some unintended, some large and many marginal. Furthermore, some effects may be doubtfully attributed to the policy (that is, analysts cannot be sure that the policy has actually 'caused' these effects). Other effects may actually result from the policy but be mistakenly attributed to other developments.

But if we manage to avoid all these negatives, is there anything more positive we can say about what policy is? In his classic, Heclo gives us an initial location:

> the term policy is usually considered to apply to something 'bigger' than particular decisions but 'smaller' than general social movements (Heclo, 1972, p. 84)

Parsons takes us a little further:

> Above all, the modern meaning of the word . . . is that of policy as a rationale, a manifestation of considered judgement . . . A policy is an attempt to define and structure a rational basis for action or inaction. (Parsons, 1995, p. 14)

And Hill and Hupe take us further still:

> While policy refers to a purposive course of actions, this does not exclude the possibility that purposes may be defined retrospectively. Policy arises from a process over time, which may involve both intra- and inter-organizational relationships. Public policy involves a key, but not exclusive, role for public agencies. (Hill and Hupe, 2002, p. 4)

Taken together, therefore, these are some of the core features of the animal 'public policy'.

1.4   WHAT DO WE MEAN BY 'TIME', AND HOW HAVE WE CHOSEN OUR PERIOD?

We see time not just as unvarying and impersonal 'clock time', but as something which is constructed and used by different societies in different ways in different periods (Elias, 1992; Nowotney, 1994; Pollitt, 2008). Thus attitudes to time themselves vary over time and from culture to culture. There is, for example, a widespread perception in North America and Western Europe that the 'pace of life', very much including politics and public policymaking, has accelerated during the past few decades

(Whipp et al., 2002). There is also said to be a change in the way many of us regard the future. Forty or 50 years ago it tended to be thought of as a space in which things would improve – there would be economic growth, technological progress, social betterment. Politicians held out brave visions of a better world tomorrow. More recently, however, the future seems to have become a more troubling and threatening space – populated with demographic crises, new epidemics, disastrous climate change and other frightening prospects (Nowotney, 1994).

The period covered by this book stretches for four decades, from the mid-1960s to 2005. No choice of period is perfect for all analytical purposes, but we would claim that our selection does have some logic.

To begin with, 40 years should be enough to allow us to see some of the 'longer waves' in policy development, patterns that are not so visible if one confines oneself to the common three to five years' study of some attention-grabbing contemporary policy and where it immediately came from (Pollitt, 2008). One leading policy scholar has declared that 'a number of recent studies suggest that time periods of twenty to forty years may be required to obtain a reasonable understanding of the impact of a variety of socio-economic conditions and the accumulation of scientific knowledge about a problem' (Sabatier, 1999, p. 3).

Second, the 1965–2005 period covers a development from high modernism (with the 1960s in many ways the acme of hopes for rationalist policymaking) to sceptical postmodernism (with the governments of today apparently wrestling with 'wicked', won't-be-solved problems, declining public trust in governments and the dwindling and disappearance of the grand reform programmes and major ideological controversies which are said to have characterized the 1960s).

Third, particularly in our local case studies (Chapters 6 and 7), the 40-year span means that we have been able to interview and/or engage in first-hand correspondence with some of those who were involved. This gives us an extra source of data – particularly valuable for discovering what expectations and frames of reference were entertained by key decision-makers at the times that policies shifted. For obvious reasons this valuable source dries up as one pushes further into the past.

1.5   HOW DO WE CONCEPTUALIZE 'CHANGE'?

We are well aware that there is a vast literature, spanning public and private sectors, on 'change management'. This literature includes lengthy debates about what counts as change and what does not, and what the differences are between ordinary, continuous change and 'discontinuous change' (that is, innovation) (Osborne and Brown, 2005, pp. 4–7). In the last few years this debate has been paralleled by a similar set of definitional manoeuvres about what is and is not an 'innovation' (for example Hartley, 2005). To be candid, we find much of this slightly overdone. The word 'change' denotes an exceedingly common, everyday concept, and there is something faintly absurd about academics spending page after page trying to turn it into a precise technical term, or rather an entire family of technical terms. The everyday concept contains several notions – that of time passing (from before the change, through the change until after the change) and of one entity or system moving between different states. Thus change is change in something, and the something endures its change ('John is much changed since I last met him'). A country may change its electoral system from first-past-the-post to proportional representation, but it is still the same country and it still has an electoral system. Similarly, the UK in 1948 underwent a huge change in its hospital system, moving from a mixed system of public and private hospitals to one where almost all hospitals were owned and managed by the central state. Yet we can still refer to the UK hospital system, both before and after; we are not talking about something being entirely replaced with something else from a completely different category.

What we wish to be able to do is to distinguish different scales of change in the two public services that we have chosen to study. We want to be able to say 'this was a big change, but that was only a small one', and be able to justify the distinction. This is not entirely straightforward (although perhaps not as difficult as some of the change management literature makes it out to be). Fortunately the policy literature has some helpful suggestions. Think, for example, of an annual budget. It changes all the time, but usually only incrementally – this programme gets 2 per cent more than last year, that programme gets 3 per cent less, and so on. A bigger change may come if there is a fiscal crisis and the government is suddenly obliged to reduce public spending by 20 per cent over three years – although even this may be achieved through the usual procedures. But still deeper forms of change involve altering the procedures, techniques and categories of the budget – this actually affects the dynamics of the fiscal debate and the structure of the budget. So the budget categories may be changed from line items to programmes, and the accounting system from cash to accruals (Pollitt and Bouckaert, 2004, Chapter 4). These are big changes. Yet there is an even more profound form of change, and that is when policymakers actually begin to think about the budget in a different way, to see it as something different from what they thought it was before. Previously, perhaps, it was thought of in the traditional way, as an annual process for allocating public expenditure to approved activities. But now there is a new paradigm: a budget is viewed as both a macroeconomic tool (to promote growth) and/or as a framework for allocating resources to policy fields, and/or as a way of managing public services for higher performance ('performance budgeting') (Rubin, 2000). The budget has changed its meaning and even the criteria for the 'success' or 'failure' of a budget have therefore shifted. Here we are drawing on an influential analysis of different levels of policy change by Hall (1993):

- First level of change: changes in the levels set for specific policy instruments (for example grants for x are increased from 20 to 30 per cent; the percentage of police allocated to anti-terrorist duties is increased from 5 per cent to 12 per cent).
- Second level of change: shifts in the types of policy instruments actually used (for example the Conservative government's introduction of market mechanisms partly to replace organizational hierarchies in the National Health Service (NHS) after the 1989 White Paper, *Working for Patients* (Department of Health et al., 1989)).
- Third level of change: change in the overall policy paradigm (for example if some British government were to reconceptualize the NHS as no longer a universal service, but rather as a residual service for people who could not afford to purchase private health care insurance).

This kind of conceptual scheme is helpful in ordering our data, but it does not eliminate the fact that grading some particular policy change 'big' or 'small', or 'paradigmatic' or 'incremental' is ultimately a matter of judgement by observers, and not all observers are likely to agree among themselves. There is thus an inescapably socially constructed dimension to policy change – and we will have to return to this at various points in the book. When a public service closes local offices and shifts to a Web-based service, the managers of that service may see it as a medium-sized technical change, improving the overall quality of service and lowering costs. A busy professional woman may see it as a very minor change – it is handy that the service is now available 24/7 from any Internet connection. An 80-year-old man who has never owned or operated a computer may see it as a radical change, and a very unwelcome one, in that it effectively greatly reduces and complicates his access to the service.

The other limitation to note in Hall's three-level scheme is that it is focused on policy change. As we will see later, policy changes, while important, are not the only source of change in public sector organizations. We will introduce a more general classification of change (that is, not only policy-inspired change) in section 1.10 below.

1.6   WHY HAVE WE SELECTED THESE TWO POLICY FIELDS?

There are several reasons why the hospital sector and the police make for interesting comparisons. To begin with, and most obviously, they are both public services of great importance to many, many citizens – they are each an accepted and continuous part of everyday life in a civilized society. Second, although they may appear to be very different, one from the other (in the sense that hospitals are to do with 'caring' and the police are to do with 'controlling') the fundamental political and organizational challenges which the two services face are in other ways very similar. Among these shared features are the following.

In practice there is no end to the demands on both services. They could always do more. Society contains unmeasurably vast and varied amounts of 'crime' and 'ill health' (the inverted commas are merely intended to signal that there are important conceptual debates to be had about both these terms, although this book is not really the place for them). Therefore prioritizing, or to use an unfashionable but accurate term, 'rationing', hospital and police services is permanently on the agenda (for both managers and politicians). Who is going to get how much of which type of service? Are we going to have more policemen on the street, reassuring local citizens and maintaining daily order, or are we going to have more specialist, high-tech police tracing terrorist suspects or combating computer fraud and identity theft? Should the new hospital money go for advanced neurosurgery to help children born with rare brain disorders, or should it be deployed to shorten the queues of elderly waiting for routine but highly effective joint replacement or cataract surgery?

Both services are highly diverse and unstandardized, in the sense that they provide not one service but many, calling for a fantastic range of different skills. It would take more than one book simply to describe every major activity taking place within a big hospital or a police force during a single week. Thus managers are not managing one production line process, but rather wrestling with a great range of different tasks and processes. The same police force may be working on a major incident such as an airliner crash or a bomb explosion at the same time as they are sitting discussing relations between different ethnic groups with local leaders of those groups, and tracing a gang that is stealing high-price cars. A hospital is dealing with a footballer's broken leg in Accident and Emergency while elsewhere in the building a heart is being transplanted and low-birth-weight babies are being intensively monitored in their cots. For a large part of the time managers are trying to manage highly skilled professionals. This gives an added dimension of complexity to the management task because such professionals normally demand and require large areas of discretion in which to exercise their skills. What is more, their professional associations tend to be strong and well organized, as anyone who has ever had to negotiate with medical associations or police unions will confirm. These factors have implication for the ways in which new policies descending from 'above' may be responded to.

Both services are also having to cope with rapidly changing technologies that may have major impacts on how their work is organized and, indeed, on what work they can actually undertake. For the police the advent of advanced information and communication technologies (ICTs) have brought them the ability to check number plates, identities, local crime trends and many other things almost at the touch of a button. The patrolling 'bobby', locus of a historically high level of discretion and independence, used to be only occasionally in touch with 'the police station'. Now he or she is in constant, instant touch and is visible on the screens in the central operations control room. In the investigation of crimes, forensic technologies such as DNA analysis have revolutionized what can be discovered and proven to the satisfaction of the courts. In the hospital, new technologies permit doctors and nurses to diagnose and treat conditions that would have gone unnoticed, or which would have remained essentially untreatable even a decade or so ago. The implications of this constant technological advance for budgets, for training, for rationing decisions and for management itself are enormous.

In addition to coping with changing technologies, both services are directly affected by changing social habits and norms. Changing diets and exercise regimes lead to new patterns of disease. The ever-developing 'consumer society' and 'globalized economy' provoke new patterns of crime. Both services have had to begin to come to terms with serving multi-ethnic, multicultural communities, where different social groups may have differing values and norms in relation to both 'health' and 'crime'. Shifting social norms have also led to far more questioning of 'the experts'. Both doctors and the police can expect to be questioned and criticized by their 'clients' (let alone the mass media) far more than would have been usual in the 1950s or even 1960s. Records seem to show that, in the UK at least, the number of occasions when citizens have been prepared to use physical violence towards health staff or police officers has increased markedly.

Both services are labour intensive, and involve a lot of face-to-face interaction with citizens. They are largely (though by no means exclusively) 'people services'. Unlike some parts of the public services, therefore, most citizens think they know something about hospitals and the police. This helps to make and keep them in the public and political eye.

Because of their direct implications for our health and safety, and the sometimes dramatic nature of their interventions, both services have long been major foci for the purveyors of popular culture. The number of TV series about hospitals or police services are legion. The TV and newspaper coverage of high-profile crimes and health miracles and scandals is endless. Top doctors and police officers have become regular performers on the TV news. Thus both services have a strong public image – or rather, images – and in subtle and important ways these images shift over time (McLaughlin, 2007; Van den Bulck, 2002; Van den Bulck and Damiaans, 2004).

Thus there are a number of dimensions on which we can compare the responses of the two services to broadly similar challenges. Whilst it remains true that they are different from each other in important respects, they are not so different as to make comparison fanciful or pointless. Their similarities mean that we can consider them not as 'most similar' but as 'fairly similar', or similar enough to make differing patterns of development thought-provoking and stimulative of further analysis.

1.7   WHY HAVE WE SELECTED THESE TWO COUNTRIES?

In a very general sense, Belgium and England are similar. Both are advanced industrial economies; both have a heritage of now-much-declined heavy industry (coal, steel, heavy engineering); both were until recently colonial powers; both are liberal democracies and, of course, both are geographically situated in north-west Europe, as close neighbours. However, the institutional structures of England and Belgium are very different. The UK is frequently cited as a political system which is unitary, centralized and majoritarian (Pollitt and Bouckaert, 2004, pp. 292–6). It tends to produce strong, one-party central governments which are able to impose their legislative programme on the legislature without too much difficulty. Belgium, by contrast, is a federal, decentralized and multiparty polity. Much of its recent political history has centred around a series of constitutional reforms designed to give greater autonomy to the three regions (Flanders, Wallonia, Brussels) and three language groups (Dutch, French, German) (De Winter et al., 2006; Pollitt and Bouckaert, 2004, pp. 216–20). Getting major reforms through the complex, decentralized, multiparty Belgian political system is fiendishly difficult (Witte et al., 2000, pp. 293–7).

Therefore one of our reasons for selecting Belgium and England, in combination with the hospital service and the police, is that while the two services share some important characteristics and the two countries are neighbours and subject to many of the same socio-economic pressures, the institutional structures are so different. This provides an interesting test: if policies are mainly determined by broad socio-economic circumstances and/or by the technical characteristics of the service, then we might expect roughly similar policies to emerge in these two countries. If, however, institutional frameworks have a significant effect, then the expectation would be for greater differences between policies in England and in Belgium. This is rather a crude test, and our analysis is about much more than just this 'big picture' similarity or difference, but one factor behind the selection of these two countries was our interest in exploring the influence that their hugely contrasting governmental institutions might have on what kind of policies got made, by whom and with what effect.

1.8 WHY HAVE WE SELECTED THESE TWO LOCALITIES?

First, one might ask, why address the local level at all? The answer is that it has been clear from many studies in many countries that national policies are not simply implemented, formulaically, by regional and local authorities: they are frequently reinterpreted, modulated, adapted, diluted or even resisted (for example Hill and Hupe, 2002, pp. 127–33; Pollitt et al., 1998). Thus, at the very least, a rounded understanding of the policy process requires attention to local implementation as well as national promulgation. Beyond this, however, local authorities and organizations have, in varying degrees, their own powers of policymaking. One central question for subnational government scholars has long been the degree of independence or autonomy a given authority or organization possesses from the national government. Whilst constitutional and legal provisions tell an important part of this story they usually do not tell it all. Dynamic, shrewdly led local authorities or local organizations may be able to make themselves more room for policy maneouvre than unimaginative, sluggishly led authorities or organizations, even where both inhabit the same legal framework. Thus our comparison of Brighton and Leuven enables us to observe degrees of policy dynamism and degrees of policy autonomy, and thus contribute to the current debates on multilevel governance (Bache and Flinders, 2004)

Second, why choose these two particular cities? Sheer convenience was one reason for selecting Brighton and Leuven. Each of us was well enough connected in these two cities to be able to gain access to key people and papers without too much difficulty (and with a lot of generous help). Convenience, of course, is not academically respectable as a criterion for social science research design, but it has its advantages nonetheless.

Convenience was not the only factor, however. We were looking for large towns or small cities that possessed both advanced hospital facilities and fairly sophisticated police forces. We did not want capital cities, which tend to have their own particular dynamics and preoccupations, especially for the police, but also to a significant extent for hospital services. On the other hand we did not want remote cities or those wrestling with hard cases of industrial decline – we wanted reasonably prosperous, reasonably cosmopolitan places that were regular players in national and regional policies and were not strikingly unusual along some significant dimension. Brighton and Leuven both fitted these specifications.

1.9   A PRELIMINARY NOTE ON CASE STUDIES

England and Belgium are our two country case studies. Brighton and Leuven provide us with two local case studies. The case study is a very commonly used approach in the social sciences in general, and in public policy and public management in particular. Yet its status and purpose remain contested. At one extreme, case studies may be frowned upon as one of the weakest research strategies. From this perspective they are 'soft', qualitative investigations which are vulnerable to all sorts of biases and which, at best, can be thought of as 'small N' research – a poor cousin of the 'large N' statistical analysis of whole populations of policies or countries that we should really be pursuing if we want to do serious science (King et al., 1994). At the other extreme, case studies are seen as a highly valuable and rather flexible research strategy that can be used for a variety of important purposes, including testing theories, tracing key causal processes and mechanisms and 'congruence analysis' (Blatter, 2007; Blatter and Blume, 2007).

One's perspective on case studies depends to a considerable (though not absolute) degree on one's theoretical affinities and orientation. These orientations are discussed in the following section. Therefore, at this early point, we will not go any further into the case study debate. Rather we will proceed with our study, including the elaboration of its theoretical framework and the delivery of our case studies, and then return, in the final chapter, to the debate about the potential of this approach. Since we have chosen to make case studies an important part of our own work it will not come as a surprise to readers to be forewarned that we find them very useful.

1.10 CHOICE OF THEORETICAL APPROACH AND CONCEPTUAL FRAMEWORK

It is a common observation in social science texts that theory is central and unavoidable, because one cannot have an explanation without, explicitly or implicitly, a theory (or theories). Even to describe a social or political entity requires categories and concepts, which may be theory-linked, but to explain – to answer a 'Why?' question – is said always to presuppose an underlying theory.

So far, so good. The problem is that what constitutes a theory is a controversial issue, and one that, over the past three decades or so, has become if anything even more, rather than less, vigorously contested. The relevant arguments are often philosophically both complex and profound, and we can do more here than briefly to sketch our own position, and how it relates to some of the other main 'camps'.

For one group, a theory is formal, explicit and of general application. When x and y occur, then z always follows, or follows with a high and measured probability. Lower-level hypotheses are derived from higher-level theoretical generalizations (at the highest level termed 'covering laws'), and the academic then tests these hypotheses against specially collected evidence to see if they hold. The model for explanation is a set of beliefs about how the natural (or 'hard') sciences (physics, biology and so on) are supposed to generate their explanations (though many social scientists and some natural scientists have doubted whether this is really how most natural scientists proceed). The language is that of 'covering laws', 'variables' and 'falsifiable hypotheses'. The preferred methods are experimental or quasi-experimental, quantitative wherever possible. One underlying assumption is that the social world is regular and repetitive – if only we can find the patterns and mechanisms then we will be able to apply them to a wide range of circumstances. This position is often referred to as the 'hypothetico-deductive approach' or as 'nomothetic' (Kay, 2006, pp. 17–28). In political science and policy studies it is most closely approximated by economics-derived approaches, especially rational choice theory (John, 1998).

This particular model of what social science can be or should aspire to be has never been the only perspective on offer, but over the past few decades it has come under sustained attack from many quarters. Within the particular field of policy studies a squadron of alternatives have sailed forth – historical institutionalism, social constructivism, complexity theory and postmodernism, to mention but a few. Some of these challenge the very idea that there could be general laws and invariant 'variables' (pointing, among other things, to the startling lack of any discovered laws or closely modelled political relationships, despite well over half a century of nomothetic political science). These critics argue instead that policymaking and implementation is highly context-dependent, and that the same policy instruments or techniques will be differently conceived, differently received, differently 'played' and differentially 'successful' according to the local culture(s), dominant frames of reference, patterns of institutions, preceding histories, chance events and so on. Furthermore, the actors in the policy process are highly reflexive: that is, they are constantly looking at what they have done, what happened last time, what their opponents seem likely to do next, and so on, so that they learn (or mislearn) and adapt their behaviours rather than repeating them whenever similar situations recur. Indeed, one internationally influential work described the ideal professional as a 'reflective practitioner' (Schön, 1999). In other words, the socio-political world is just too complex, too dynamic and reactive, and too variable to be captured by general models or physics-type formulae. The most we can hope for are a few guiding concepts and frequently recurring processes or mechanisms that are moderately 'portable' (that is, they will travel limited distances over space and time and are not totally unique to one particular context). Thus some generalizations will still be possible, but always cautious and related to a limited range of contexts. Kay calls this wing of policy scholars 'idiographic' (picture-making), but we prefer to call it simply 'post-positivist', because this group contains within itself a range of positions on how far generalized explanations are possible (some being quite optimistic in this regard, while others are against all 'grand narratives'). Post-positivists are very diverse, minimally united by their critique of the hypothetico-deductive approach. Chapter 9 is the place where we go further into these epistemological and ontological debates.

Meanwhile, through the central chapters of this book we will usually ally ourselves with this 'post-positivist' wing. We will do this without retreating to a wholly relativist or postmodernist position. For the most part our approach falls within the grouping usually labelled as 'historical institutionalist' (HI). Kay puts his position in a way that appeals to us too:

> relying on thick, contextual and historical description structured by general concepts or portable metaphors is not a failure of formal modeling, but rather the appropriate response to what cannot be formalized into a model; nor is it amenable to explanation by general testable theory. (Kay, 2006, p. 42)

However, we resist those puritanical colleagues who demand that every scholarly project must begin with a formal declaration of fidelity to a singular, 'branded' theoretical position. Our association with historical institutionalism (itself quite a loose grouping) is a rough-and-ready one, and where we see advantage in borrowing from other theoretical traditions, we will not hesitate to do so (while giving consideration to the mutual compatability of the different approaches). Indeed, our reading of the policy studies literature leads us to suppose that some of the most intriguing and enduring works have been theoretically rather promiscuous, mongrel-like affairs, and we would be happy to be counted in their company. What is more, while we cannot avoid choosing between different theoretical approaches, we certainly have no wish to volunteer as foot-soldiers in the social sciences' 'paradigm wars'. Thus it is not a prime part of our mission to attack or undermine those colleagues who use more hypothetico-deductive approaches. We may not think that these approaches will work very well with the questions and subject matters which we are addressing in this book, but that does not mean that we believe they are useless or should be abandoned. On the contrary, from time to time the findings of such 'hard-edged' approaches have been both convincing and extremely interesting, and, where we are aware of that, we shall mention it.

It remains therefore to say something more about the nature of the historical institutionalist approach. What are its key assumptions, insights and limitations? At this initial stage we will pick out just five, although our discussion of these will develop further as the book goes on, and we may identify additional characteristics later.

First Point

'History matters': what happened before often affects what happens later (Pollitt, 2008; Tilley, 2006). For example, the choice of a particular kind of constitution has many effects on what can and cannot be done subsequently (of course, the constitution can be overthrown or amended, but in most countries this is not an everyday occurrence, and for most practical purposes governments and parties can only act as the constitution permits them to act, more or less). The question 'What is history?' has no single, simple answer (Pollitt, 2008, Chapter 2) but for our purposes it can be considered as a form of scholarly description and analysis which uses a narrative form to focus on the sequence of developments over time, and which has developed specific and meticulous techniques for identifying, classifying and interpreting various sources of data about the past. History is not theory-free, but the approach to theory is principally inductive and inclusive. That is, explanations are produced by constructive attention to many details and aspects and there is a willingness to try out a range of competing explanations before selecting the one that seems to do the best job of synthesis. The synthesized narrative is created by the historian, not simply revealed as some pre-existing, underlying reality. Unlike

nomotheistic social science there is subsequently no compulsion to gener-
alize the explanation to many other situations, and no requirement that the
form of the explanation must be capable of yielding predictions about the
future (although many historians would hold that limited generalizations,
for example about political revolutions or peasants' revolts, are possible,
and would also accept that the past can yield at least some pointers for the
future). A proper historical explanation should include the antecedents to
the present situation, and an understanding of actors in relation to 'where
those actors have come from'.

Second Point

'Institutions matter': since a constitution is one form of institution, the
above example works for this point too. By assuming that institutions
matter, HIs do not assume that institutions never change, but they do
assume that the course of events is not simply the outcome of the exercise
of choice by thousands or millions of freely and rationally choosing individuals. Institutions (that is, collectivities) exercise influence of various
kinds, including the ability of certain institutions to shape and guide individuals in the formation of their preferences, and of others to normalize
or prohibit certain forms of action. It is very unlikely to be an accident
that all the countries which pushed furthest and fastest with New Public
Management (NPM) reforms had majoritarian political systems (Pollitt
and Bouckaert, 2004). 'Institutions' would include, for example, constitutions, budget rules, planning and personnel systems and organizational
standard operating procedures (SOPs). There has been much learned discussion about how to define an institution, but we cannot hope to replay
all that debate here. We will therefore simply state that, for the purposes of
this book, 'institutions' are structured sets of rules and norms that endure
over time. A slightly more elaborate version of this came recently from the
fathers of the new institutionalism, James March and Johan Olsen:

> An institution is a relatively enduring collection of rules and organized prac-
> tices, embedded in a structure of meaning and resources that are relatively
> invariant in the face of turnover of individuals and relatively resilient to the
> idiosyncratic preferences and expectations of individuals and changing external
> circumstances. (March and Olsen, 2006, p. 3)

Networks of institutions tend to develop their own particular logics, thus:

> Understanding path dependency requires an understanding not just of politi-
> cal institutions but of the political economy of a policy arena as a whole. It
> means understanding the interactions of political and economic actors within

the parameters established by public policy. Those interactions follow a logic as actors respond rationally to the incentives they face. And that logic is shaped not only by the policy parameters but also by the microeconomic and techno-logical characteristics of the particular arena. (Tuohy, 1999, p. 261)

Third Point

Having an 'institutionalist' perspective does not imply that agents are no more than the slaves of institutional structures. One unfortunate tendency in the 'paradigm wars' is for advocates of one position to stereotype rival paradigms, especially in terms of their location on the 'structure–agency' dimension. Thus 'institutionalist' theories are often accused of exclud-ing or having no concept of the choices and actions of individual agents, whereas individualist theories such as rational choice are correspondingly accused by institutionalists and structuralists of having no concept of structure. For the record, therefore, we perhaps need to say that we do have a strong concept of agency, and, as our empirical work will show, we acknowledge that agents can play a catalytic role in modifying and, occa-sionally, transforming institutions. We follow Hay and Wincott:

> Change is seen as the consequences (whether intended or unintended) of stra-tegic action (whether intuitive or instrumental) filtered through perceptions (however informed or misinformed) of an institutional context that favours certain strategies, actors and perceptions over others. (1998, p. 955)

Strategic action (with all the caveats included in the above quotation) takes place within institutional contexts but also reshapes those contexts. As Hay and Wincott suggest, strategic action has both direct effects (for example direct organizational restructuring to achieve 'decentralization') and learning effects (for example where the consequences of attempted change makes the actors involved realize that some aspect of their insti-tutional framework is more or less strong than they realized) (Hay and Wincott, 1998, p. 956).

Fourth Point

Developments over time often exhibit certain patterns (Pollitt, 2008; Zerubavel, 2004). Consider Table 1.1., which we have developed from work by two leading HIs (Streeck and Thelen, 2005). This offers four possible patterns (the labels are ours). In the first (box A) small, frequent changes in process lead to small, frequent changes in results. One might call it 'Tortoise' change – regular but small steps forwards (or backwards, or sideways – the Tortoise does not necessarily move in a single direction).

Table 1.1   Patterns of institutional change: the 'BEST' schema

		Result of change	
		Within path/incremental	Radical/transformation
Process of change	Gradual	A. Classic incrementalism *TORTOISE*	B. Gradual, but eventually fundamental change *STALACTITE*
	Abrupt	C. 'Radical conservatism' – rapid return to previous ways *BOOMERANG*	D. Sudden, radical change *EARTHQUAKE* (punctuation)

Note: BEST = Boomerang, Earthquake, Stalactite, Tortoise.

Source: Developed from Streeck and Thelen (2005), p. 9.

This is quite a stable situation over time, and much of the classic literature on incrementalism addresses change of this type (Lindblom, 1959, 1979). Incremental change is relatively predictable, at least in the sense that the participants do not usually have to worry about sudden, radical shifts. One of the best-known examples comes from Wildavsky's seminal work on budgeting in 'advanced' Western states (Wildavsky, 1986). Let us say that the English health service gets 2 per cent more in this year's budget but the police get 3.5 per cent. However, next year, or the year after, the health service will get a slightly bigger margin of growth than the police, and so the relative budget shares of the two services will not change very much over time.

In the second type (box B) the process of change is again gradual, but here the direction of change is constant, so the 'increments' build up, one upon the other. One might call it 'Stalactite' change, in the sense that, without anything dramatic happening, eventually water slowly dripping in the same direction cumulates in a major new feature. It is not always remembered that Lindblom himself recognized that such a unidirectional process could eventually lead to 'a drastic alteration of the *status quo*' (Lindblom, 1979, p. 517). In the case of Belgium, for example, it could be argued that a series of incremental transfers of competencies from the national level to the regional level eventually reached the point where there was a de facto federal system.

Box C denotes a pattern of change which we think is only rarely acknowledged in the policy literature, but which may be rather more common in the real world. The process of decision appears to be radical. The claims and intentions of policymakers indicate that a major step is being taken. Yet, within a few years, the policy system in question has slipped back to something more like its former self – 'business as usual' has quietly reasserted itself. We call this 'Boomerang' change – it is as if the policy suddenly flies out to a distance from the launch, but then curves back towards its point of departure (always raising the question of what forces are producing this return). An example from England might be the periodic announcement by government that the police service is going to put much greater emphasis on 'community policing' and 'getting bobbies back on the beat'. This populist policy has experienced several incarnations during our 40-year period of study, but somehow the shift towards the community always seems to get blunted and diminished by other pressing demands – serial killers, terrorism, gun crime or whatever. The police officers who had been assigned to community duties are suddenly needed back in some specialist unit or operation, to fight high-profile crimes. This is certainly not to say that nothing has happened, simply that, on the ground, what has happened can, after a first flush of enthusiasm, look more like a modest course adjustment than a major new direction.

Box D is the kind of change which has attracted most attention both from policy scholars and from the mass media: the 'great leap forward', or 'Earthquake' as we call it. The policy process announced radical change and the results showed a correspondingly dramatic, and enduring, impact. The moment represents a full stop to the previous policy trajectory and the beginning of a new one – literally, a 'punctuation', to use the terminology of those who embrace the now quite fashionable concept of path-dependency (Pollitt, 2008, pp. 40–51). Policy scholars have thus written of 'punctuations' and 'windows of opportunity', quite short periods of time when such major changes can occur quite suddenly (Baumgartner and Jones, 1993, 2002; Kingdon, 1995; Pierson, 2004). Usually these upheavals result from a combination of circumstances and pressures rather than from one, big cause. Often (but not always) there will be a major external shock – an economic crisis, or a technological breakthrough or a political collapse. But endogenous developments can also be significant. Whatever the combination, when the 'window' for radical change opens, fortune favours those who are organized and have some sort of prepared ideas for what to do instead of the status quo. A Belgian example might be the local government reorganization of 1975, which reduced 3000 cities and municipalities to 589 within a short space of time. For some analysts this path-and-punctuation (or quiet periods periodically disturbed by Earthquakes) has become the central picture of how big changes occur. We will test that claim.

These, then are four broad possible patterns of change – the BEST typology, as we will call it, reading the four cells anticlockwise from the bottom left-hand cell. We will inspect our two countries and two services to see whether one or more of these categories fits the chronologies that we will set out. But these are not the only patterns that may interest us. A number of previous works in the fields of public policy and management have found policy 'cycles' or alternations or other sequences (Pollitt, 2008, pp. 21–4). What is more, there may be different temporal patterns at different levels in the policy system – for example, cycling between centralization and decentralization at the national level while there is simultaneously some quite significant Earthquake or 'punctuation' happening in one or more specific localities. In the chapters to come we will search for, and find, a range of patterns, and patterns within patterns.

Fifth Point

Both our histories and our institutions are 'socially constructed', in the sense that their forms depend on the choices of their writers, founders and reformers, and those choices, in turn, very probably have something to do with the beliefs and interests of the relevant actors. This means that they are constantly reconstructed too, which is one reason why social constructivists have difficulty with positivistic treatments of social phenomena that assume that a 'parliament' or an 'election' or even a 'hospital' or a 'profession' means the same thing over long time periods, or all over the world. On the contrary, say the social constructivists, scholars should always pay careful attention to how these concepts are articulated in any given context (time, place, culture). Even such apparently 'hard' management technologies as performance indicators are best understood as socially defined (Moynihan, 2008). Furthermore, the patterns we see over time are themselves socially constructed:

> One of the most remarkable features of human memory is our ability to mentally transform essentially unstructured series of events into seemingly coherent *historical narratives*. We normally view past events as episodes in a story (as is evident from the fact that the French and Spanish languages have a single word for both story and history . . .) and it is basically such stories that make these events historically meaningful. (Zerubavel, 2004, p. 13)

This is not to say that any story is as good as any other, or that factual accuracy is not a crucial part of the historian's craft. But it is to say that there is always more to it than a simple reflection of the 'facts'. That is one reason why the histories of particular periods and events are being constantly rewritten and reinterpreted.

Sixth Point

HIs sometimes have trouble with using their temporal and institutional patterns as explanations. As many but not all HIs have realized, they need something else, 'behind' or 'beneath' the patterns to actually power an explanation. Thus, for example, to say that something is 'path-dependent' is not to explain why it remains fairly stable over time. It merely describes a pattern of development – stable, moving down the same, constant track. To explain why this happens requires the theorist to spell out some process(es) or mechanism(s) which holds things in this steady direction (Kay, 2006; Pierson, 2004). Such processes may be difficult to observe, and/or there may be so many candidate processes that it is hard to decide which to include in the explanation and which to leave out. Some theorists have attempted to classify these processes, but there is no generally accepted categorization in use (Pollitt, 2008, pp. 43–4). Whilst some theorists have taken an essentially economistic approach (for example Arthur, 1994, identifies large sunk costs, learning effects and network effects) our own belief is that a broader spectrum needs to be considered. Thus cultural and political mechanisms need to be added to those which operate through the assumptions of economic rationalism. At all events, identifying and evaluating key processes of positive and negative feedback to policymakers and implementers is a crucial part of the construction of a convincing and well-grounded analysis of policy change. This point connects strongly with the third point (above). Actors with strategies are often those who, by understanding underlying processes, are able to seize upon 'windows of opportunity' for significant change (Kingdon, 1995).

We have now spent enough time on the sketch map. It is time to start the journey.

2. National reforms: the Belgian and English regimes

2.1 BRITAIN AND BELGIUM: SIMILARITIES AND DIFFERENCES

Before moving to an account of specific national policies towards the police services and the hospital sector, we will first take a broader look at the policy context and regime in each country. This is intended to provide readers with a framework within which the policies themselves can be analysed and understood.

We will approach this task in a 'nested' fashion, beginning with the most general and impressionistic, then moving steadily 'inwards' towards more analytic and specific features. Thus we begin with general, popular stereotypes (this section), then shift to broad categorizations of the political systems in each country (section 2.2), then sketch a historical narrative for the two policy sectors that particularly interest us (section 2.3). We will then be ready to turn to specific accounts of sectoral polices in Chapters 3 and 4.

This chapter is therefore concerned with institutional frameworks (the 'statics' in one sense, although these institutions are actually in a process of constant evolution, as will be seen), and in subsequent chapters we will move to the 'dynamics' of policy.

Let us begin, therefore, with the popular stereotypes – or at least, first, the stereotypes from a British perspective. One might sum this up in the intendedly humorous English taunt, 'Can you name three famous Belgians?' The implication is that most British people could not, and that they could not because Belgium does not produce famous people, unlike Britain. (As many commentators have pointed out this is a deeply misleading quip, since, despite the country's modest size and population, there have actually been many internationally famous Belgians.) The further implication is that Belgium is a small and not very interesting country – not to be compared with the important, dynamic UK. The Belgians themselves have some wry stories, such as the one that tells that Belgium is such a complex country that only two constitutional lawyers understand it – one from the north and the other from the south. And they disagree.

To some extent there has been a softer, more nuanced echo of this stereotype in the academic literature on public policy and management. To begin with, Belgium is often completely absent from comparative texts – it seems to appear much less often than other small countries such as Denmark or Sweden or the Netherlands. In addition, when it does appear, it is usually labelled as a slow-mover, a polity which is so institutionally complex and so locked into elaborate consensualist processes by its internal linguistic divisions that it finds it hard to act dynamically or decisively. (For a range of internal views by Belgian scholars, see the very useful November 2006 special issue of *West European Politics*, including article titles such as 'Does Belgium (still) exist?' Billiet et al., 2006). Thus, in mainstream comparative politics texts, Belgium is (or at least used to be) deemed to be highly consensualist and corporatist, almost in the opposite corner from the UK in most diagrammatic representations (Lijphart, 1984, 1999). And in comparative public management texts we see the same thing: in general Belgium comes over as slow-moving, incrementalist and conservative, whereas the UK has been one of the most consistently radical 'core New Public Management' states (Pollitt and Bouckaert, 2004).

More recently, however, a different perspective has appeared. From this alternative point of view Belgium appears relatively stable in policy terms, whereas the UK can be seen to be in the grip of 'hyper-modernism' and 'hyper-innovation' – a frenetic urge to interfere and reform which carries many costs as well as benefits (Moran, 2003; Pollitt, 2007, 2008). A third view might be that, while Belgium has been slow-moving with respect to policymaking, it has witnessed a surprising amount of constitutional reform and change in the system of political parties over the 40 years of our study (Deschouer, 2006; De Winter et al., 2006).

There is no short answer to these stereotypes. Through the remainder of this book, beginning in this chapter, we will begin to unpick the various elements, accepting some, qualifying others and reframing or rejecting the remainder.

2.2 THE POLITICAL SYSTEMS OF ENGLAND AND BELGIUM

England and Belgium are both liberal democracies, but of fundamentally different types. The UK political system is majoritarian and adversarial. The norm in the House of Commons is two and a half constantly fighting parties – visitors from continental Europe are frequently surprised and dismayed by the undignified rhetorical brawling and name-calling that takes up a good deal of the Commons' time, and most of the televised 'highlights'. The Belgian system is multiparty and consensual (though decreasingly so). Deals and negotiations have usually been the order of the day. Since the 1960s this system has undergone considerable fragmentation, and its previous relative stability has been lost:

> The absence of integration between the Flemish- and French-speaking parties, the importance of the community cleavage at the level of party elites, and the observed divergences in the weight of other cleavages at the level of the lectorate all point to the fact that, despite state and electoral reforms, the polities of the two main regions have increasingly diverged and now display deeply entrenched differences. (De Winter et al., 2006, p. 933)

Thus Belgium is now a heavily decentralized federal system with a rather weak and divided central executive. Many powers have been devolved to the three main subnational governments: Flanders, Wallonia and Brussels. Linguistic cleavages have been extremely important: Dutch is spoken in the north (and may there be termed Flemish); French is spoken in the south; and the capital, Brussels, is officially bilingual (French and Flemish). In the east of the country there is an area in which German is the dominant language. Thus there are six governments in all (federal plus three regions plus three language communities – although the Flemish language community and the Flanders regional government merged in 1980). Constitutionally these different governing authorities are equal – there is not a hierarchical relationship between them as there is between central and local government in Britain.

The UK, by contrast, has usually been seen as a heavily centralized state, with an extremely strong central executive, which dominates local authorities to a degree which would be unusual elsewhere in Europe. (Since the late 1990s this picture has been considerably modified by the constitutional reforms which have led to Scotland and Wales forming their own elected assemblies and governing executives. However, this book concentrates on England, and that remains a highly centralized entity, where the short-lived Social Democratic Party (1981–88) was the only major break in the party system.) The famous comparative political scholar Arendt Lijphart classifies the UK as 'majoritarian/unitary/centralized' and Belgium as 'intermediate/decentralized/federal' (Lijphart, 1984, p. 219 and 1999, pp. 110–11).

There is also a difference between the two countries in respect to the relationships between ministers and civil servants. In Belgium most of the policymaking is done by ministers and the political advisers in their cabinets. The upper levels of the civil service are highly politicized, while the middle and lower levels comprise a highly regulated and closed career system (De Winter and Dumont, 2006, pp. 969–71). About three-quarters of senior civil servants are party members. Since the late 1990s efforts have been made to break away from the cycle of political appointments at the highest levels, and to give civil servants both a bigger policymaking role and more room to manage in a professional way, but progress has been slow. The biggest reform at the federal level – the 'Copernicus' initiative from 2000 – made some significant changes, but the original intention to transfer much policy formulation from ministerial cabinets to more professional policy units staffed by civil servants was soon dropped (Brans et al., 2006). In its 2007 review of the Belgian system of public management the Organisation for Economic Co-operation and Development (OECD) concluded that:

> Personnel management systems are indeed highly regulated in Belgium, leading to high transaction costs, to major difficulties in the delegation of authority to managers and in the implementation of performance-based management, as well as in the management of the size of the workforce. (OECD, 2007, p. 11)

In short the (many) political parties remain the kernel of the Belgian system, controlling both policymaking and many public appointments. They have their own ways of evading bureaucratic congestion:

> governments have developed inventive ways of bypassing too burdensome regulation, notably by increasing the use of contractual staff and politicizing the workforce, and, by doing so, have added to governance problems . . .
>   Belgium appears to be a special case among OECD members regarding the large and increasing extent to which governments use (supposedly 'temporary' or 'mission specific') contractual staff. (OECD, 2007, pp. 12, 21)

By contrast the British civil service has traditionally played an important part in policymaking, yet has taken great pains to remain politically neutral (Steen et al., 2005). Since the 1980s temporary political advisers have begun to play a larger role in policymaking than hitherto, but never organized on the Continental cabinet model, and never to the exclusion of the permanent civil service. At lower levels in the civil service the terms of employment have become much more like those prevailing in the rest of the labour market and there is not now any equivalent to the framework of special statutory protections enjoyed by their Belgian counterparts. It would be quite mistaken, however, to see the British civil service as relatively unchanging over our 40-year period of study. Whilst the ideal of political impartiality has survived, albeit somewhat bruised and reinterpreted, in other respects both the culture and the specific procedures of the civil service have changed a great deal. Indeed, Moran (2003) argues that there has been a fundamental shift from a 'club culture' that survived into the 1970s to a 'new regulatory state' which grew up during the 1980s

Table 2.1   Some measures of political system differences

	UK	Belgium
Average effective number of political parties represented in the lower houses of parliaments following elections, 1945–96[1]	2.11	4.32
Proportion of time when cabinet was single party, 1945–96	100%	8.3%
Index of executive dominance[2]	5.52	1.98

Notes:
1. This is not the same as the number of self-defined parties. For details of measurement see Lijphart (1999), pp. 74–7.
2. Lijphart's Index of Executive Dominance is a complex measurement, and its full derivation is too complex to spell out here. Essentially it is related to two different measures of the average durability of cabinets in each country, where longer duration is taken as a sign of a strong executive, and produces a higher index number. For details see Lijphart (1999), pp. 129–39.

Source: Lijphart (1999), pp. 76–7, 110–11, 132–3).

and 1990s. The gentlemanly club culture was the stagnating residue of a nineteenth-century political and social settlement, a matter of informal, semi-private coordination between elites. The new regulatory state emerged from the political, economic and social crises of the 1970s. It was marked by a hyperactive process of institutional upheaval, with organizational restructurings, remodelling of the public service professions and the vigorous creation of formal frameworks of targets and criteria by which to steer other social actors. Whether or not one accepts the full thrust of Moran's analysis it is undeniably the case that, first, there have been many, many reforms and, second, that the informal and even amateur style of the senior civil service of the 1950s and 1960s has been replaced by a much more formal and managerial image (Bovaird and Russell, 2007; Pollitt and Bouckaert, 2004, pp. 292–9).

Some of the differences in political systems can be represented in tabular form. Table 2.1, extracted from Lijphart (1999), shows some important dimensions. Table 2.2 summarizes some of the key differences in the nature of executive government.

2.3   POLICE AND HOSPITAL POLICIES: A COMPARATIVE OVERVIEW

In both countries and both sectors the pace of policymaking seems to have quickened in the second half of our period (1985–2005) as compared

Table 2.2   The nature of executive government: some key Anglo-Belgian comparisons

Aspect	Belgium	England
1. Type of government	Consociational	Majoritarian
2. Party system	Increasingly fragmented and regionalized	Except for 1981–88, just two main parties, and one lesser one (in England)
3. Structure of executive	Federal: increasingly decentralized	Unitary: increasingly centralized
4. Civil service role in policymaking	Limited – policies hatched in ministerial cabinets and party fora	Extensive, though weakened by the growth of political advisers from 1980 onwards
5. Politicization of public service appointments	Extensive	Limited
6. Extent of civil service reform	Major initiative from 2000 (Copernicus) but faded considerably after a few years	Continuous reform from the early 1980s, peaking 1995–2004

with the first (1965–85). However, that acceleration appears to have been far greater in England, with respect both to the police and the hospital system. Table 2.3 sets out the barest bones of the story, to be filled out in subsequent chapters.

The table already hints at, but does not fully register, the greater degree of 'activism' in English policymaking. For the police, for example, in the Belgian case one could refer to 'the' (singular) 'police reform' and most people would understand that you were referring to the police reorganization of 1998–2002. But if you mentioned 'the police reform' in England it would make no sense, and your respondent would almost certainly reply by asking which reform you meant.

It was not only that more measures and decisions were taken in England, it was that many of these were more aggressively implemented than in Belgium. For example, by the late 1990s, performance indicator systems in both the English police and the English hospital system had real 'bite', in the sense that senior managers could be (and sometimes were) dismissed for missing targets, and performance failures led to rapid, intrusive central intervention. By contrast the Belgian hospitals had no national performance measurement system, although indicative targets had been formulated for certain dimensions (for example average lengths of stay). Certainly the

Table 2.3   Comparative overview of policy developments in England and Belgium, 1965–2005

Period	England/Police	Belgium/Police	England/Hospitals	Belgium/Hospitals
1965–75	Little structural change. Some specialization. Growth of mobile patrol. Growing concern with police corruption and handling of suspects.	Growth in numbers. Some centralization and specialization. Growth of mobile patrol.	1960s saw the first coordinated attempt to build new hospitals since the founding of the National Health Service (NHS) in 1948. The first major organizational restructuring of the NHS took place in 1974.	First hospital plan, with indicative targets for each region (1966). Gradual extension of health care insurance to new groups. 1973 Hospital Act indicated that no federal subsidies would be made available unless new hospital development fitted with the federal plan.
1975–85	Early 1980s saw major anti-police riots by ethnic minorities in South London. Led to major reforms to improve community policing. Police and Criminal Evidence Act, 1984, codified police powers and procedures. Miners' strike (1984–85) drew police into political controversy.	Drastic mergers of local authorities, resulting in matching reduction in the number of police forces. Several notable police failures to solve headline crimes. But no fundamental reform.	New national formula for allocating resources to different areas – based on mortality and morbidity, not historical spending levels (1976). First national performance indicators (1983). Government announced that every unit, district and area would henceforth have general managers (1983). NHS Management Board set up at national level.	Rapid growth in hospital beds, leading to government attempts (from 1982) to restrain this.

Table 2.3   (continued)

Period	England/Police	Belgium/Police	England/Hospitals	Belgium/Hospitals
1985–95	Growth of a strong emphasis on 'value for money', including the first set of performance indicators. More urban unrest. Major restructuring 1993–94, involving a strengthening of central (Home Office) control. Further specialization.	The 'Pentecost Plan' (1990) signalled a shift towards community policing. Rise of far right political parties helped force the political system to move towards, but not yet implement, reform Also during this period came the demilitarization of the Rijkswacht/ Gendarmerie (federal police).	Intensification of reform. Considerable further strengthening of hospital managers and of performance measurement systems. 1989 White Paper allowed hospitals to become trusts (public corporations) and obliged them to compete in a 'provider market' to win contracts from health authorities.	Faced with rapidly rising expenditures, the federal government strove to minimize hospital admissions. Target lengths of stay were introduced from 1990. New regulation of mutualities health care expenditure (1994).
1995–2005	Further growth of specialized units, both at national level and within particular forces. Intensification of performance measurement regime and 'targetry'. First National Policing Plan announced in 2002.	Dutroux Affair prompted unprecedented popular unrest over the criminal justice system. Fundamental police restructuring legislation in 1998, strengthening local police forces and introducing a more managerial approach. Integration of specialized forces into the new federal police system.	From 1997 the New Labour government swung away from and then back towards market mechanisms as a way of forcing greater productivity and customer responsiveness on hospitals. Further intensification of performance measurement regimes and yet further strengthening of managers. New organizations set up to regulate clinical practice and oversee doctors.	In the face of rapid expenditure rises, the federal government introduced DRG (prospective) reimbursement system for hospital pharmaceuticals (1996). First moves to limit the number of doctors. Rationalization of expensive medical equipment per region. Some hospital mergers.

national government would not think of marching into a major hospital, replacing its leaders and imposing a 'rescue plan' (as occurred in the period from 2001 in England). Nor was there any system by which the police reported to the government and public against a set of quantified targets. There was – from 2001 – a national security plan cascading down to local plans, but it was of a loose and general nature compared with the more elaborate, specific, quantified English National Policing Plans and their local counterparts (see, for example, Home Office, 2004). Or again, consider the emphasis on 'community policing', which emerged in both countries during the 1980s. Whilst it was much debated, and often appeared in the rhetoric of policy documents, there was no Belgian equivalent to the way in which, in England, community aspects of policing were made the subject of direct and publicly reported-upon targets and performance measures – for example a Public Service Agreement target to increase the proportion of citizens in each area who thought that the police in their area were doing a good or excellent job (Home Office, 2004, pp. 14–16). Whilst local safety plans (*veiligheidsplannen*) became an important tool in Belgian police administration from the turn of the century on, and whilst these plans often contain quantitative data about the recent past, they do not commit themselves to future targets to remotely the same extent as their English equivalents (see, for example, Politie PZ Leuven, 2005).

Nevertheless, even if the speed and forcefulness of reform differed on the different sides of the Channel, there are some recognizable similarities in the general direction of travel. In both countries 'management' has come strongly to the fore. At the beginning of our period this would not have been a concept that was particularly prominent in the discussion of the organization of hospitals or police forces. Long before the end, however, it was almost universally believed that these organizations had to be 'managed', and that 'management' was something that needed to be systematically taught and learned. Management courses directed specifically to hospitals staff and police were launched at universities and professional training institutions. In both countries it had become normal for both hospitals and police forces to have regularly updated plans, with objectives and targets (or, at least, statements of aspiration).

Another common feature was the way in which rising healthcare expenditure drove central government towards steadily more detailed intervention in the workings of the hospital system. In England, of course, this started from a different point, since the government owned most of the hospitals and directly employed their staffs. In Belgium too, however, despite the non-profit, non-governmental status of most hospitals, much of the cost of expansion and increasing technological sophistication was borne by the federal authorities. And in the mid-1980s there was a serious

financial crisis in many municipalities when they became liable for the deficits of public OCMW/CPAS (Openbaar Centrum voor Maatschappelijk
Welzijn/Centre Public d'Aide Sociale) hospitals. So, despite starting
'further back' in terms of control, the Belgian government tried various
forms of indicative planning and norm-and-quota and limit setting to
restrain and guide the expansion of hospitals.

There were also some common elements to the evolution of the police
services in the two countries, despite very different organizational histories
and frameworks. In Belgium, as in England, our 40-year period saw the
police become a more specialized, high-tech operation. Police cars made
the first impact on the traditional 'bobby on the beat', and they were followed by computers, mobile phones, closed-circuit television (CCTV),
DNA testing and many other developments. It is not much use sending
a generalist police constable out to deal with Internet crime, complicated
fraud, budding terrorist cells or cross-border people trafficking. Officers
have to be given specialist training for such assignments, as increasingly
they also need to receive training for victim support, crime scene management and riot control. Furthermore, as in many other countries, the forms
that police filled in whenever they recorded a crime became more elaborate
and formulaic and 'feeding the database' became a more prominent part
of everyday police activities (Ericson and Haggerty, 2002).

Yet at the same time both countries experienced strong political and
popular demands for more emphasis on 'community policing' that would
be responsive to the particularities of specific communities and localities.
Later on we may see how difficult success in this area is to achieve, but
for the moment we may simply note that this was a recurrent response to
violent street crime and local breakdowns of public order (especially where
the latter had an anti-police, ethnic minority dimension, as they did on a
number of occasions in England).

In the next two chapters, maintaining our comparative focus, we will
extend this analysis by moving deeper into the specifics of each policy
sector.

National reforms: hospitals

3.1 INTRODUCTION

Chapter 2 provided a very brief, high-level introduction to policymaking in England and Belgium. In this chapter and the next we will dive deeper into our two selected policy sectors – hospitals in this chapter and the police in Chapter 4. The first step is to identify the main institutional players in national policymaking (section 3.2) and after that we will set out the English and Belgian policy chronologies for the period from 1965 to 2005 (section 3.3). After that we begin the analysis of change and continuity, similarities and differences.

3.2 KEY INSTITUTIONS IN HOSPITALS POLICY

3.2.1 English Hospitals

The main players in England over the whole period were central government, the medical profession (both locally, in the hospitals, and centrally, through its national representative associations) and the hospitals themselves. However, the balance between these three has certainly shifted more than once, and arguably an important new player has emerged since the mid-1980s, in the shape of professional National Health Service (NHS) managers. Local governments have never had any serious influence over the development of NHS hospitals, except insofar as they can limit infrastructural developments through their use of land use planning legislation.

An authoritative recent textbook divides the key developments in formal organization into the following phases (Harrison and McDonald, 2008):

- 1948–79, 'The illusion of hierarchy'. Hospitals were supervised by regional boards that were in turn responsible to the Ministry of Health. From the outset the Minister therefore had a strong responsibility for the whole NHS. In practice, however, the medical profession dominated many of the boards and committees and there were few attempts to exert central authority. The first attempt to plan a hospital building programme came in the early 1960s. Serious government attempts at resource redistribution did not begin until the mid-1970s. The first major reorganization took place in 1974, and aimed at strengthening the chain of command and creating a hierarchy of plans – local–regional–national. Academic research mainly suggested that NHS managers (then called 'administrators') had little power in this system – for the most part they acted as 'diplomats and housekeepers', attempting to bring the various professional groups to consensus and seeing to financial and procedural propriety.

- 1979–90, 'The emergence of hierarchy'. From 1984 the government insisted on the insertion of a cadre of general managers at every level. Furthermore, with 'efficiency' as a major political preoccupation, the ministry intervened with new systems of performance measurement and budgetary control. At first, the medical profession locally seemed able to resist serious incursions into its autonomy, but it was certainly under pressure.

- 1991–97, 'Constructing markets'. The Conservative government's White Paper of 1989 ushered in an unprecedented (and wholly untested) 'internal market' within the NHS. Hospitals, under managerial chief executives, were now classified as 'providers', who had to 'sell' their services to district health authorities ('purchasers'). Almost all hospitals now became 'trusts' – self-governing public corporations run by boards. Relationships between them and the purchasing authorities were supposed to be via contracts. This reform was initially strongly resisted by the medical profession, but it was faced down by a strong and determined government. In practice, however, in most places the market never became very competitive, and local relationships 'were more usually based on collaboration than competition' (Harrison and McDonald, 2008, p. 92). Paradoxically, the internal market seems to have led to more central control, as the government intervened constantly to prevent competitive processes leading to hospital closures or other negative headlines. Furthermore, it represented a significant additional increment of managerial power vis-à-vis the doctors. It was managers who were the primary conduit for government interventions, and managers who understood the arcane new procedures of accruals accounting and contracting.

The authors do not assign a title to the most recent period, since the arrival of the New Labour government in power in 1997. In keeping with the maelstrom of reforms since then we are tempted to call it:

- 1997–2005, 'New Labour's re-disorganization'. The new government initially made some show of moving away from market mechanisms, but within five years it was moving back towards them again. Throughout this period there was a hectic rate of institutional change, with countless new organizations being invented at local, regional and national levels, on the purchasing 'side', the provider 'side' and especially in the shape of new national regulatory agencies (see Pollitt, 2007 for details). The role of managers in all this was further strengthened and they became, in the words of one professor of healthcare policy '"change junkies" – able to deliver whatever structures or systems their political masters and mistresses demand' (Hunter, 2006, p. 209). In 1998, for the first time, trust chief executives (most of whom were managers with no clinical training) became formally responsible for the clinical as well as the financial performance of their organizations. Doctors, meanwhile, became subject to tighter and tighter guidance and regulation in their practice of medicine – mandatory clinical audit, retraining programmes, a proliferation of guidelines and protocols and the appearance of a National Institute for Clinical Excellence (NICE) which appraised the effectiveness and cost-effectiveness of specific clinical interventions and then gave authoritative advice to the NHS on what should and should not be available.

Yet this story of growing, government-backed managerial power should not be read as an inevitable progress or finished accomplishment. The struggle is unfinished, and the medical profession is far from helpless. The growing authority of managers may be plotted as a kind of asymptotic curve, where they seem to approach the axis of control but can never reach it. The government's preferred model of 'clinical governance' has been very slow in arriving, and seems to be open to a wide variety of local interpretations (Salter, 2006). The medical profession is able to resist, dilute, delay and reshape the government's various initiatives. It continues to deploy medical expertise 'as a scarce political resource which the profession naturally employs as a bargaining counter in its dealings with the state' (Salter, 2006, p. 272).

3.2.2 Belgian Hospitals

The main characteristics of the Belgian health care system date from decisions taken after the Second World War, when a compulsory public health insurance system was set up, based on the principles of:

- independent medical practice;
- free choice of health care provider by the patient;

- fee-for-service payment of providers, with reimbursement (European Observatory on Health Care Systems, 2000).

About 70 per cent of Belgian hospitals are private, non-profit establishments (Eeckloo et al., 2004). The other hospitals include public hospitals which are owned by public municipal welfare centres (CPAS/OCMW) or by provinces, the state or intermunicipal associations. There are nine university hospitals which can charge a higher per diem fee than other hospitals. To operate and run a hospital accreditation must be obtained from the Flemish, French or German-speaking community governments. However, the criteria for accreditation are set by the Ministry of Public Health, service by service. Patients are free to choose which hospital they will attend and – a crucial difference with England – there is no formal primary–secondary–tertiary referral system. In most hospitals the doctors are self-employed (although not in the academic hospitals). The system as a whole is complex, and only the briefest account is appropriate here (Figure 3.1).

Financially, health care is primarily a federal responsibility, although since the 1980s the communities have had increasing responsibilities, especially of a regulatory nature. In 1980 the Ministry of Public Health merged with the Ministry of the Environment, and in 1995 it grew again, via a merger with the Ministry of Social Security. Within the enlarged ministry there remain, however, separate ministers of Public Health and Social Affairs (usually from different political parties).

The ministry supervises the National Institute for Sickness and Invalidity Insurance (INAMI/RIZIV), which manages the health insurance system. This is a non-governmental body which is actually accountable to the Minister of Social Affairs rather than the Minister of Public Health. Its medical division includes representatives of employer and employee organizations, mutualities (see below), health care provider organizations, pharmacists and allied health professions.

The mutualities provide the actual insurance policies which cover the bulk of health care expenditure. Belgians choose which mutuality to join. They are private, legally independent, non-profit organizations. Legally, they are the primary providers of the statutory health insurance programme. Originally – and still, though to a diminishing extent – the biggest mutualities were ideologically based, with links to the christian democrat, socialist and liberal 'pillars' in Belgian society.

Last, but not least, the Order of Physicians registers doctors for practice and has judicial powers to impose penalties on its members, up to and including striking them from the practice register.

During 1970–2000 'the number of personnel in most health care

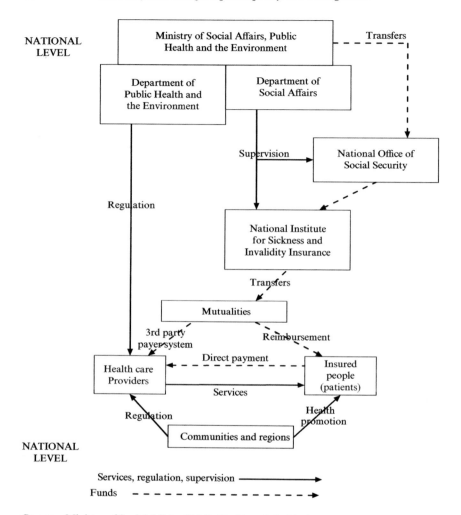

Source: Ministry of Social Affairs, Public Health and the Environment – see European
Observatory on Health Care Systems (2000), p. 10.

Figure 3.1   Organizational chart of the Belgian health care system

professions in Belgium doubled or even tripled . . . due mainly to the lack of
control over the supply side of the market (there was until recently no limit
on the entry of trainees into these professions)' (European Observatory on
Health Care Systems, 2000, p. 51).

Hospital funding is provided by two parallel systems, one for non-medical activity (for example nursing, hotel costs) and one for medical services. The latter are covered by a fee-for-service system, the former by a prospective budget based on per diem and patient day quotas. Hospitals get a share of the fees earned by the resident doctors. Hospitals receive most of their money from the federal level, but are managed by the communities. This can lead to tensions, as when the communities award higher salary increases than the federal authorities have allowed for.

3.3   HOSPITAL POLICIES, 1965–2005

We will begin with a brief chronology for each country.

Basic Timeline: English Hospitals Policy, 1965–2005

One central thread in the story of English hospitals throughout the period is the drive to rationalize. At its inception in 1948 the NHS inherited an unplanned patchwork of hospitals of all shapes and sizes. For the first 15 years there was very little new building, but from the mid-1960s onwards there were a series of attempts to close down small, old or inconveniently placed hospitals and replace them with a more planned, efficient system. Later, as medical techniques advanced, average lengths of stay began to fall, and conditions which had once required inpatient treatment could now be handled by primary care doctors or on an outpatient basis. Together with an ongoing (and periodically intense) government pressure for economies, this led to a marked fall in the total number of beds in the system (see Table 3.1).

The number of separate sites offering hospital services also declined – from 2063 in 1978 to 1624 in 1990/91 (surprisingly, figures for sites are not available since then, because the statistics are collected by trust, and many trusts have more than one site – Hensher and Edwards, 1999). However, the falling numbers of both sites and beds have been matched by falls in the average lengths of stay that patients make. These fell continuously over our period (from 49.3 days at the start of the NHS in 1949 to 19.8 days in 1979, and much more again since then). Yet activity has increased:

Alongside the growth in day cases, one of the critical mechanisms by which throughput has been increased and total inpatient activity expanded has been the fact that the length of stay has consistently fallen at a faster rate than the number of beds. (Hensher and Edwards, 1999, p. 912)

With this background, we can turn to the specifics of the chronology.

Table 3.1   Beds in English hospitals, 1987–2006

Year	All specialities	General & acute
1987/88	297 364	180 889
1992/93	232 201	153 208
1997/98	193 625	138 047
2002/03	183 826	136 679
2005/06	175 646	133 033

Note: These figures represent the average daily number of available beds.

Source: Department of Health form KH03, see www.performance.doh.gov.uk/
hospitalactivity/data_requests/beds_open_overnigh, accessed 1 September 2007.

1962

Central government published its *Hospital Plan for England and Wales* (Ministry of Health, 1962). This marked the first major programme of new hospital building since the setting up of the NHS in 1948. It also ushered in a model of the District General Hospital (DGH) which was to have 600–800 beds and would offer a comprehensive service, including outpatients and diagnostics (Allen, 1979). At this time the NHS as a whole was still organized on the 'tripartite' basis which had been adopted at its foundation. Hospitals were the third of the three legs, the other two being general practitioners and local governments (who provided public health and prevention, child welfare and various other services). The hospitals had their own hierarchy, based on 20 hospital regions, each with a medical school and each guided by an appointed, part-time Regional Hospital Board (Harrison, 1988, pp. 9–12).

1967

A joint committee of the Ministry of Health and the medical profession published the first of a series of reports on hospital management (known as the first 'Cogwheel Report'). It recommended the setting-up of speciality-based divisions within hospitals. Each speciality would send a representative to a medical executive committee, the chair of which would be the chief spokesman for the profession within the hospital. This model was widely, though far from universally, adopted (Harrison, 1988, p. 14).

1974

The first major restructuring of the NHS since its creation in 1948. Henceforth there were to be 14 Regional Health Authorities and 90

Area Health Authorities (all non-elected). There was also a subordinate tier of districts. Individual hospitals were subordinate to their District Management Teams. The recommended mode of decision-making was consensus, within multidisciplinary teams in which the medical profession was heavily represented (Harrison, 1988, pp. 16–20). Administrators were generally 'on tap not on top'. There was an elaborate cascade of plans from districts up to the national level. Harrison and McDonald characterize these reforms as the highpoint of the 'blueprint' era of health care policymaking – a time when policies emerged from an elaborate set of consultations with the main stakeholders and when there was an underlying faith in the steady and relatively unproblematic progress of science and technology (Harrison and McDonald, 2008, pp. 142–7).

1976
Fiscal crisis. The NHS suffered from the harsh expenditure cuts introduced by the Treasury for the whole of the public sector.

1978
Introduction of a new system for resource allocation between health authorities, based on standardized mortality rates rather than on historic costs (the result of the 1976 report from the Resource Allocation Working Party – RAWP). This led to significant redistribution between geographical areas (for example towards poorer areas in northern England and away from wealthier, healthier areas in the south). Given that the redistribution took place during a period of severe fiscal restraint this meant that some health authorities actually had to lose money. But this was still very much part of the era of policymaking-as-planning.

1979
Report from the Royal Commission on the National Health Service (the 'Merrison Report'): no striking changes, but a large number of piecemeal recommendations. The government was able to pick and choose what it implemented.

1980s
During the 1980s there was only one year (1987/88) when there was a substantial increase in real resources for the NHS, despite evidence that demographic and technological change required an increase of perhaps 2 per cent per annum simply to maintain the status quo in service levels (Harrison et al., Chapter 2). Thus the background during the 1980s was that of an almost constant resource squeeze.

1982

In January the Secretary of State (Norman Fowler) announced measures to 'improve accountability', the main ones being a review process and a set of performance indicators. Each year ministers were to review the performance of each Regional Health Authority (RHA), and each District Health Authority (DHA) was to be reviewed by its RHA. Performance indicators would be developed to assist in these review processes. The 1974 structure was changed.

1983

January: the Secretary of State introduced central control of NHS manpower.

September: publication of the first national set of NHS performance indicators (Pollitt, 1985). In the same month compulsory competitive tendering was introduced for NHS laundry, domestic and catering services.

October: the NHS Management Inquiry (the 'Griffiths Report') strongly criticized NHS management and proposed the creation of general managers for every NHS unit, district and area. At the national level an NHS Management Board was to be created, supervised by a Health Services Supervisory Board chaired by the Secretary of State. The inquiry had been launched by ministers and its personnel consisted of four businessmen, led by a supermarket executive, Roy Griffiths. Its recommendations were rapidly accepted by ministers and promulgated as government policy. A flavour of the report can be gained from the following:

> it appears to us that consensus management [the previous doctrine in health authorities] can lead to lowest common denominator decisions and to long delays in the management process. (National Health Service Management Inquiry, 1983, p. 17)

> there is no driving force seeking and accepting direct and personal responsibility for developing management plans, securing their implementation and monitoring actual achievement. (p. 12)

Harrison and McDonald regard the early 1980s as a watershed, when the style of policymaking changed from 'planning' to 'bright idea'. Increasingly, the Conservative government opted for 'the conscious adoption of policy based on "bright ideas" to be fleshed out in the implementation process' (2008, p. 142). Sometimes these bright ideas came out of relatively small groups of policy entrepreneurs, and were then implemented through a process of 'manipulated emergence', in which hospitals or general practitioners were encouraged to volunteer to try the new policy, in return for rewards of money or autonomy or status. The era of elaborate planning, and time-consuming detailed consultation with all the main stakeholders, was largely over.

1989

The White Paper *Working for Patients* (Department of Health et al., 1989) introduced wholesale restructuring of the NHS, along the lines of an 'internal market', with hospitals as providers and health authorities as purchasers of services on behalf of defined resident populations. At the heart of this was the creation of NHS trust status, which hospitals could apply for and which brought them corporate legal status and enhanced management autonomy. This huge and quite radical change was very much a 'bright idea' developed in secret within a very small group of politicians and political advisers. It also involved changes in notions of representativeness, with trusts being run by relatively small corporate boards which lacked the local authority and trade union members that had characterized their predecessors.

Early and mid-1990s

As the internal market developed it became clear that ministers were not, in practice, willing to risk the closures and takeovers that the existence of a competitive market would usually imply. Neither did the medical profession favour cut-throat competition:

> Research suggests that relationships were more usually based on collaboration than competition . . . Thus ministers were reluctant to leave the market to run its course and the fierce commitment to the market which accompanied the launch of the white paper became progressively diluted. (Harrison and McDonald, 2008, pp. 92, 93)

1998

Hospital trust chief executives (who for the most part had no clinical training) were for the first time given responsibility for the clinical as well as the financial performance of their organizations. Trusts were given a statutory duty to deliver high-quality care.

1999

The government set up the National Institute for Clinical Excellence (NICE), a powerful regulatory body which had the authority to approve particular treatments as cost-effective, promulgate clinical guidelines and approve models of clinical audit. This therefore represented a major incursion into the territory of 'clinical freedom'.

In the same year another major regulator was created, the Commission for Health Improvement (CHI). The CHI was to carry out regular reviews of the management of individual hospitals. In 2004 the CHI and other regulatory agencies were merged into a new Healthcare Commission. In 2005 it was announced that this commission was itself to merge with the Commission for Social Care Inspection (which dealt with social workers and care homes).

2001

The eight NHS Regional Offices were restructured into four Regional Directorates of Health and Social Care. In 2003 these were themselves replaced by 28 Strategic Health Authorities. Thus the organizational level 'above' the hospitals seemed to be in a state of constant flux (see Pollitt, 2007). Meanwhile, for individual hospital trusts, the government introduced what became known as the 'star system'. Each hospital was awarded three, two one or zero stars according to its composite score against a range of performance indicators. These were much publicized. At the same time, and connected with these league tables, the rate at which NHS chief executives were moved (or fired) accelerated to a high level (see Table 3.2). The changing number of trusts (due mainly to mergers and new creations) should also be noticed.

2002

The government announced that it would move towards a system by which hospital services would be commissioned by Primary Care Trusts from a wider range of NHS and private hospitals, including envisaged 'independent treatment centres'. This was, therefore, a return to competition as a major selection mechanism, and one explicitly aimed at creating a 'mixed market'. The government also announced a new type of NHS hospital, the Foundation Trust (FT). FTs would be given greater financial

Table 3.2   Rate of CEO turnover, NHS trusts, 1998–2005

Year	Number of trusts	Rate of CEO turnover (%)
1998	89	13.48
1999	171	12.86
2000	166	16.26
2001	179	23.46
2002	183	25.68
2003	169	21.89
2004	168	21.42
2005	143	20.27

Source: Derived from Ballantine et al. (2008), p. 395.

and managerial autonomy and would be free to undertake joint ventures with the private sector. By mid-2006 48 FTs existed, but the government's stated intention was that all NHS hospitals would eventually become FTs.

Patterns in the English story?

The above story of policymaking for the English hospital system does exhibit some distinct trends. Just as with the police, we see increasing monitoring, standard-setting and intervention by central government and its various agencies. We see the development of similar batteries of performance indicators and published national league tables of local units. In terms of Table 1.1 from Chapter 1 this looks like a Stalactite type of change, in that a whole series of policy changes over quite a long time eventually produced a very different NHS – one which was far more tightly controlled from the centre. The attempt to shift the balance between central and local influences in favour of the former is common to recent governments of both main political parties, but reached a kind of crescendo with New Labour from the late 1990s on. We also see a significant, if intermittent, attempt to introduce competitive elements into the hospital system, both under the Conservatives from 1989 on and then again under Labour from 2002. The 1989 White Paper was so radical that it was seen at the time as an Earthquake, although it could also be argued that the subsequent retreat from competition means it became more of a Boomerang.

We now move to the Belgian story.

Basic Timeline: Belgian Hospitals Policy, 1965–2005

1945

The main characteristics of the Belgian health care system date from decisions taken after the Second World War, when a compulsory public health insurance system was set up, based on the principles of:

- Independent medical practice.
- Free choice of health care provider by the patient (and therefore an element of competition that was absent from the NHS until Mrs Thatcher's 1989 reforms).
- Fee-for-service payment of providers, with reimbursement (European Observatory on Health Care Systems, 2000).

1963

August: 'Leburton's Law' created the National Institute for Sickness and Invalidity Insurance (INAMI/RIZIV). This separated the insurance system for the health care system from that for the invalidity (incapacity to work) system. INAMI/RIZIV oversees the general organization of compulsory health insurance but the actual provision of this insurance falls to statutory sickness funds, the mutualities, which are private non-profit organizations. As mentioned earlier, they are distinguished by religious or political affiliations (for example the National Union of Socialist Mutualities, the National Alliance of Christian Mutualities).

1963

Hospital Act, December: (the 'Cluster Law'). The first law explicitly directed at hospitals, which no longer linked hospitals to the compulsory health and invalidity insurance system. Hospitals were obliged to guarantee hygiene, safety, comfort and quality of care. Cluster's Law had four objectives:

- Free hospital care for all insured citizens.
- Improve quality of care.
- Ensure financial viability of public and private hospitals.
- Introduce planning.

1966

The first hospital plan was formulated, with target figures for each region.

1960s

During the 1960s health care insurance was progressively extended to wider social categories.

1973

Hospital Act (6 July): this introduced a model of imperative planning. No new investment or subsidy or approval would be forthcoming unless it fitted with the federal hospital plan. It was aimed at structural rationalization and cost reduction by restricting the supply side (Peers, 1994b, p. 20; see Table 3.3)

1980

Many elements of health care were delegated to the two communities, and the ministries of Public Health and Environment were merged.

1982

The Royal Decree of 22 July imposed a Moratorium on the opening of new hospital beds. Beds had increased by 30 per cent between 1971 and

Table 3.3   Beds in Belgian hospitals

Year	Total beds	Average per hospital	Beds per 1000 inhabitants
1977	36366	155	6.63
1980	37564	152	6.67
1985	37313	179	6.57
1990	32596	192	5.65

Source: Adapted from Table 2, Peers (1994b), p. 22.

1982. According to the planning criteria there was a 20 per cent surplus (11 200 beds)

1986

April: Royal Decree No. 407 introduced a process-led policy: input criteria (bed approvals) were replaced by process criteria (for example numbers of babies delivered in a maternity hospital).

Explicit in this law was a new understanding of what a hospital was:

> De belangrijkste kenmerken van het nieuwe ziekenhuisconcept worden . . . het specialistisch karakter van de medische zorgverlening, het pluridisciplinaire aspect van het therapeutische team en de permanente beschikbaarheid binnen een geïntegreerd organisatorisch kader. [The most important characteristics of the new hospital concept become the specialist character of the medical care, the multidisciplinary aspect of the therapeutic team and its permanent availability within an integrated organizational framework.] (Peers, 1994b, p. 22, author's translation)

December: the Hospital Act established that hospitals had to have a minimum of 150 beds. A compulsory and detailed 'enquiry procedure' was also established, whereby cooperative interdependence was envisaged between the hospital boards (with administrative responsibilities) and medical councils (with professional responsibilities). However, 'more than 15 years later, not all hospitals have achieved this intended harmonious result' (Eeckloo et al., 2004, p. 11).

1989

Royal Decree on regrouping and merging hospitals.

Late 1980s/early 1990s

A priority objective for the government was to minimize hospital admissions. During this time the evolution of medical technology was an important influence. Several new forms of less invasive diagnostic technique (for example endoscopy) meant that patients did not have to spend so long in hospital. A greater range of care could be given on an ambulatory basis. However, this carried a number of other consequences, including the need for hospitals to work more closely with primary care doctors and community-based care service, and the fact that the patients that were admitted to hospital now tended to be sicker and to need more intensive forms of care (Peers, 1994b, pp. 22–3).

1990

Legislation strengthened state intervention in the process of forming contracts and agreements. If budgetary limits for each care sector are exceeded fee levels can be reduced. If committees fail to implement the correction mechanisms the Minister of Social Affairs can intervene to impose them.

1990

November: a Ministerial Decree coupled hospital budgets paid by INAMI/RIZIV to aspects of hospital structure and activity profile. Target lengths-of-stay were introduced.

The establishment of Crossroads Bank for Social Security. This 'bank' aims 'to be the motor of e-government in the social sector' (www.ksz.fgov.be/En/CBSS.htm, accessed 11 December 2008). It connects up information flows between more than 2000 separate institutions, including health care providers and insurers, greatly reducing the number of different forms that have to be filled in and the time taken for transactions. In 2006 it won a United Nations Public Service award.

1993

1 October: a Royal Decree increased co-payments and co-insurances for visits to generalist and specialist doctors (for specialists from 25 per cent to 40 per cent of the agreed fee). On 1 January 1994 co-payments and co-insurances for clinical tests and medical imaging were also increased. The aim was to reduce system costs by promoting more 'responsibility' among patients. But Belgians can take out private insurance to cover these co-payments. By 1999 about 30 per cent of Belgians had such insurance.

13 December: national accreditation of doctors was introduced by a national agreement between the mutualities and the physicians. Fees-for-service were increased for accredited doctors.

1994

Legislation merged the financial management of all social security sectors, with the aim of making the social security system independent of state intervention. This was part of the effort to control the public expenditure deficit. The background to this and other moves was Belgium's need to meet the Maastricht criteria for entry to the European Single Currency.

A Royal Decree of 12 August 'responsibilized' the mutualities' health-care expenditure. From 1995 the mutualities would receive a prospective budget to finance the health care costs of their members but they would be responsible for financing any discrepancy between this prospective and the actual spending. Initially only 10 per cent of their funds were allocated prospectively, but by 2000/2001 it was 30 per cent.

1995

The Ministry of Public Health and Environment (see 1980) was merged with the Ministry of Social Provision, to become the Ministry of Social Affairs, Public Health and Environment. Yet the responsibility for health care remains divided at federal level because the separate Ministry of Social Affairs is still responsible for the National Office of Social Security (which collects social security contributions) and the National Institute for Sickness and Invalidity Insurance (which manages compulsory health insurance).

There were 191 private (mainly non-profit) and 97 public hospitals.

1996

Federal government introduced a Diagnostic-Related Group (DRG) system for hospital pharmaceutical expenditure (which had been rising rapidly).

1997

The percentage of total healthcare spending going to inpatient care reached 39.4 per cent, having risen fairly consistently from its 1970 share of 25.7 per cent (1980 = 33.1 per cent).

First moves were made to set quotas for the numbers of doctors who could be accredited, aimed at curbing oversupply.

1998

Hospitals were not meeting basic infrastructural standards by 1 October 1997 were to be closed.

2000

At the turn of the century Belgium had the lowest rate of private health care expenditure in the Organisation for Economic Co-operation and Development (OECD) (12 per cent). Total health spending at constant prices had risen 1970–90, but declined from 1994. As a percentage of gross domestic product (GDP) health care spending was 7.6 per cent in 1998, close to the OECD average of 7.9 per cent and considerably lower than the share in Germany or France.

Patterns in the Belgian story?

This mini-history does not seem to contain any obvious Earthquakes, but rather exhibits examples of more incremental kinds of change. The long-term struggle of the federal authorities to get hospital spending under better control could be thought of as a Stalactite change – quite a big shift over 40 years but achieved by a series of particular, generally unspectacular policies which tended in the same direction and eventually produced a substantially new situation. We can also see some more Tortoise-like policies in respect of control of the medical profession: various moves, but neither sufficiently big nor so clearly unidirectional as to alter fundamentally the 'bargain' between the state and the medical profession.

3.4 THE ENGLISH AND BELGIAN TRAJECTORIES COMPARED

Whilst both the British and the Belgian governments have, perforce, needed to take action to control the seemingly incessant growth in the costs of their hospital systems, their means for doing this have differed considerably. In the Belgian system, where hospitals are mainly autonomous actors rather than state organizations, the government has necessarily acted 'at a distance' by attempting to control reimbursement rates and planning permissions. Only recently, cautiously, and to a limited degree has government tried to reach inside hospitals to influence what doctors – the group that, de facto, actually commits a large part of the expenditure – actually do (for example through doctor quotas from 1997, or threatening to close establishments which do not meet basic physical standards). By contrast we can see a major shift in the strategic approach of British governments from the middle of the 1980s. Whereas in 1988 Harrison could write that: 'In the period from 1948 to about 1982, governments have had little real interest in control of doctors by NHS managers' (Harrison, 1988, p. 22), this statement could not be applied to the period since then. Since the mid-1980s we have seen governments of both major parties launching a series of policies which have been intended to strengthen the grip of professional managers over what happens in hospitals. And – particularly since the creation of NICE in 1999 – government has attempted directly to prescribe the content of clinical practice: what protocols should be followed for particular diagnoses, what drugs should prescribed, and so on.

This Whitehall incursion into the heart of the clinical arena has not been instead of, but in addition to, strong financial controls. The centralized, state-owned, tax-based nature of the English hospital system means that the Treasury is able to control the overall size of the NHS capital and revenue budgets far more directly than would be possible for the Belgian federal government. Overall, then, we find that the English hospital system is far more centralized and more tightly government-controlled than its Belgian counterpart.

But while battles over money and doctors' autonomy may have claimed the political headlines, other equally important changes have been running without so much media attention. Hospitals have become, on average, bigger and more productive – and this has been supported by government, in both countries. 'The current trend in many countries is towards larger hospitals because average costs are believed to decline with size and because patient outcomes are believed to be better in hospitals in which clinicians have the experience of a larger volume of cases' (Eeckloo et al., 2004, p. 2). This has been a Stalactite-type process, by which the average hospital of 2005 was much bigger than its average 1965 counterpart. Patients come and go more quickly and, on average, the inpatients have become sicker (because lesser conditions can now be effectively dealt with in community-based facilities or on an outpatient basis). And the technology inside the hospital's doors has been transformed, with all sorts of consequences for staffing and training and financial outlays. In both countries governments have felt obliged to try to control the spread of the most expensive items of new medical technologies, both to limit expenditure and to try to ensure a balanced geographical spread.

Thus we see both strong contrasts between the two systems and also some very similar underlying trends. One might say that although the governments operated with very different political constraints and somewhat different policy toolkits, they were nevertheless obliged to address some rather similar-looking problems.

4. National reforms: police

4.1 KEY INSTITUTIONS IN POLICE POLICY

In both countries the key institutions evolved over the period of study, and some new ones emerged. The most obvious pattern in England was the creation (or enhancement) of a series of national-level bodies to deal with the perceived gap left by the famous absence of a national police force. These included bodies devoted to scrutiny or improvement, such as a strengthened and more inquisitive HM Inspectorate of Constabulary, the Audit Commission (which has carried out a number of influential performance audits of different aspects of policing – see, for example, Audit Commission, 1990, 1996) and, more recently, the National Policing Improvement Agency. Alongside these have appeared a number of new executive and operational units, including the National DNA Database, the National Criminal Intelligence Service, the Home Office Police Standards Unit and the Serious Organised Crime Agency. Perhaps most important of all has been the development of the Association of Chief Police Officers (ACPO):

> The Home Office has . . . encouraged (ACPO) to develop a much higher profile and expand its role, as a means of enhancing the standardization and centralization of policing. (Reiner, 2000, p. 192; see also Jones, 2008, pp. 7–8)

By 2004 the ACPO appears repeatedly on the face of government planning documents, cited as a partner and guarantor of the professionalism of the proposed measures (for example Home Office, 2004).

In Belgium our period begins with three main groups of police, each rather different from each other. First there was the national police (Rijkswacht/Gendamerie) then the local police (in each municipality, reporting to the Mayor) then the specialized police (for example the Judicial Police). Reforms were driven partly by the wider reform of local government (for the Municipal Police) and partly by manifest failures which attracted public attention and generated political pressure for change (Maesschalck, 2002). Apart from the relevant ministers (Interior, Justice, Defence) and the police themselves, there have been a number of other important policy actors. The mayors have been of great importance, because of their direct control of the Municipal Police. As in England, the police themselves have been represented by strong trade unions (four were recognized by the Royal Decree of 13 February 2007). And from 1991 Parliament set up 'Committee P', a board consisting of judges and seconded police officers which monitored all aspects of police behaviour on behalf of the legislature. Finally, since the late 1980s management consultancy companies have played an increasingly important role providing evaluations and models for the Belgian police (for example Team Consult, 1988, 1995; see also Tange, 2004).

At the national level the scandals and disasters of the 1980s and 1990s (see timeline, below, for details) eventually led to the basic structural reform of 1998. This established a federal force reporting to the Minister of the Interior and local forces which report to mayors – with cooperation but no hierarchical relationship between these two levels.

4.2 POLICE POLICIES, 1965–2005

We begin with brief chronologies of major policy developments in each country.

Basic Timeline: British Police Policy, 1965–2005

The first ten years or so after the Second World War had been a kind of 'golden age' for the police, in the sense that they had been widely regarded as resourceful, incorruptible and a core part of British society, exemplifying what many liked to believe were its defining qualities of quiet, pragmatic good sense. They were 'one of us' (McLaughlin, 2007, Chapter 1). However:

> From a position of almost complete invisibility as a political issue, after 1959 policing became a babble of scandalous revelation, controversy and competing agendas for reform. The tacit contract between the police and the public, so delicately drawn between the 1850s and the 1950s, began to fray glaringly. (Reiner, 2000, p. 59)

During the mid-1970s the fraying of trust was accelerated by a series of corruption scandals in the Metropolitan Police. Robert Mark was brought in as an 'outsider' Commissioner to clean up the force (Reiner, 2000, pp. 62–4).

1964
The Police Act merged smaller forces to create 49 larger police forces.

1967
'Unit beat policing' (UBP) was introduced, leading to more car patrolling and fewer foot patrols.

1969
The Police National Computer was set up.

1972
The National Reporting Centre was set up.

1976
The Police Act set up the Police Complaints Board.

1977
The Fisher Report found that police had repeatedly violated the rights of three teenage boys charged with murder. This was one of a number of incidents that eventually led to the 1984 Police and Criminal Evidence Act (see below).

1978
The Edmund-Davies report recommended large increases in police pay and an inflation-proof formula. This was immediately implemented when the Conservative government came to office the following year and (at a time of high unemployment) helped make the police an attractive career. The percentage of graduates applying for police work climbed rapidly, with later consequences for the generation of individuals who became chief constables in the late 1990s and 2000s.

1980
The Parliamentary Select Committee for Home Affairs reported that there had been a growing number of deaths in police custody (from 8 in 1970 to 48 in 1978). This seemed to be yet another area in which the police were not following appropriate rules and procedures.

1981
After a sweeping Labour victory in the Greater London Council (GLC) elections the GLC established a Police Committee with a support unit to monitor police policy. A number of London boroughs also established 'monitoring groups'. This was generally depicted as 'politicization', and at first there were many tensions between chief constables and these committees. This is often seen as the beginning of a new, 'bottom-up' policy in which democratically elected local authorities (or at least some of them)

attempted to gain greater scrutiny and control over the police forces in their areas. (The municipal Belgian police were already under detailed political control – there was little of the British tradition of 'operational independence' for chief constables.)

The Scarman Report (Scarman, 1981) followed major riots against the police in a deprived, extensively black area of south London. The subsequent Scarman Report 'dominated police reform throughout the 1980s' (Reiner, 2000, p. 204; see also McLaughlin, 2007, pp. 66–67, 144–7). It made many recommendations aimed at improving police–community relations, and reducing racism within the police.

1982

Sir Kenneth Newman became Commissioner for the Metropolitan Police and introduced a Scarman-derived strategy that became the model for many other forces. He based his measures on what he termed a 'notional social contract'.

1983

Home Office Circular 114 introduced an emphasis on value for money (VFM) and required the police to set objectives and priorities. This marked the beginning of a growing concern with measured efficiency.

1984

The Police and Criminal Evidence Act (PACE) attempted a codification of the powers of police to investigate crime, and of the safeguards over the exercise of these powers. It also enabled the establishment of police–community consultative groups. The powers given by the Act were framed by the accompanying five Codes of Practice, which 'provided detailed procedures regulating stop and search; search and seizure; detention and questioning of suspects; identification parades; and tape-recording of interviews' (Reiner, 2000, p. 177). Failure to comply with the codes was a disciplinary offence, and a breach could be admitted in evidence in criminal proceedings. PACE is generally seen as a watershed in making the police more accountable and professional.

1984–85

The Miners' Strike. Very large-scale police operations were used during this highly political strike. The police could not avoid being drawn into controversy, and they became a target for growing left-wing criticism of heavy-handed tactics and breaches of civil liberties. For example, in 1984 the (Labour-led) South Yorkshire Police Authority attempted to instruct its Chief Constable to disband certain units, ostensibly on financial grounds. But the Home Secretary warned them that they might be in contravention of the Police Act 1964, and the Police Authority soon backed down.

1985
The Prosecution of Offences Act created a separate Crown Prosecution Service (CPS), removing this responsibility from the police.

Highly publicized urban disorder occurred in Handsworth, Brixton and Broadwater Farm (all areas with a large ethnic minority populations)

1987
Her Majesty's Inspectorate of Constabulary (HMIC) produced a first Matrix of Police Performance Indicators.

1988
The British Crime Survey recorded an apparent decline of public confidence in the police. From 1988 to 1993 there was a very substantial rise year on year in recorded crime.

1988/89
During this time there were a series of successful, high-profile appeals against convictions for terrorist activities. These helped to throw the probity and competence of the police into doubt (the 'Guildford Four', the 'Maguire Seven' and the 'Birmingham Six').

1990
ACPO published *Setting the Standards for Policing: Meeting Community Expectations* (Association of Chief Police Officers, 1990). Intensified the focus on performance and quality. It subsequently served as a cornerstone for the Quality of Service (QOS) intitiative. These developments took place against the backdrop of the Conservative government's loss of confidence in the police, as injections of additional resource did not seem to bring greater public satisfaction. The ACPO was attempting to put its own house in order, but the Conservative government eventually took its own steps (see 1993, below).

1992
The Europol Organization was set up by the Maastricht Treaty. Europol is based in the Netherlands and is responsible to the European Council of Ministers. Its task is to facilitate police co-operation across the EU, and since its foundation its mandate has been broadened several times.

1993

'In 1993 the Home Secretary, Kenneth Clarke, launched a re-structuring of police organization and accountability intended to make policing more "businesslike" according to standards set by central government and its local appointees' (Reiner, 2000, p. 209).

Group 4 (a private firm) won the contract for prisoner transportation.

Publication of the Report of the Inquiry into Police Responsibilities and Rewards (Sheehy, 1993). This called for performance-related pay (PRP), short-term contracts and the abolition of certain management grades. Strong resistance from police unions considerably diluted these proposals.

First set of national police performance indicators (Home Office Circular 17/93).

Stephen Lawrence was murdered. The police handling of this racially motivated crime drew huge criticism for its inefficiency and insensitivity.

The Audit Commission report *Helping with Enquiries: Tackling Crime Effectively*, calculated that only 40 per cent of police resources go into crime.

1994

The *Police and Magistrates Courts Act* changed the relationship between the Home Office, local authorities and the police authorities. The Home Secretary became responsible for determining 'national key objectives'. Police authorities became more independent of local authorities, but their funding became subject to central cash limits. The composition of the authorities was nine local councillors, three magistrates and five appointed members. Police authorities were to act as though they were the purchasers of police services, using monitoring against performance indicators. In general this legislation was seen as a further weakening of the local authority role in policing and a strengthening of the role of the Home Secretary (Loveday, 2000; Reiner, 2000).

Promulgation of the first set of national police objectives (SI No. 2678/1994). The national priorities were altered in 1998, 1999 and 2000 (Collier, 2006).

1996

'The Police Act 1966 contains the seeds of conflict in so far as the Act, in a strict sense, gives the police authority a responsibility to set priorities, when it is the chief constable who controls resources to pursue those priorities' (Butler, 2000, p. 307).

1997

The Police Act 1997 set up the National Criminal Intelligence Service and the National Crime Squad – important steps in the growth of a range of specialist police units at national level, not attached to particular forces. These developments were linked to arguments that European integration (and, beyond that, the growth of international crime) required enhanced capacities at the national level.

Election of a 'New Labour' government: 'Above all, Labour has launched a new approach to crime reduction overall which, while not downplaying the role of the police, places it in a broader context of policing, in partnership with local government and other agencies' (Reiner, 2000, p. 210).

1998

'*Ministerial priorities*' document published. It announced that Best Value (BV) regime would be introduced from April 2000. Under BV police authorities had a statutory duty to consult the public in determining police priorities:

> Probably the most significant development in respect of performance management was the introduction of the annual policing plan. The potential tension between centrally imposed national objectives and local priorities has been managed to date without too much difficulty. However, that potential still exists. (Butler, 2000, p. 307)

The Crime and Disorder Act introduced Anti-Social Behaviour Orders (ASBOs).

The National Crime Squad was created.

1999

Report of the Macpherson Inquiry into the murder of Stephen Lawrence argued that the police had been 'institutionally racist'.

2001

Home Secretary Blunkett created a Home Office Police Standards Unit which had an operational remit to increase police effectiveness and identify issues that might require new legislation.

2002

The *Police Reform Act* required the Secretary of State to produce a National Policing Plan (NPP) each year, which would include strategic priorities, objectives and performance indicators for police forces over the next three years. During the first three NPPs there were quite important changes in priorities, for example the introduction, in the 2005–08 plan, of an objective to 'reduce people's concerns about crime, and anti-social behaviour and disorder'. The Act also ushered in a new category of staff,

Police Community Support Officers (PCSOs – sometimes unkindly termed 'plastic police'). They were uniformed, but less expensive and less well trained than the 'real' police, and they lacked any power of arrest.

2004

The new set of Statutory Performance Indicators (SPIs) signalled a shift from a majority of process indicators to a larger share of output (for example detections) and outcomes (for example surveys of public satisfaction) indicators (Collier, 2006).

2005

Of the set of national performance indicators for 2005–08 Collier (2006) commented:

> The national targets for these priorities, particularly those derived from Public Service Agreements (PSAs) have been politically generated rather than evidence-based. The national policing plans, which began with targets for specific volume crimes have shifted emphasis to a 15% across the board target.

Patterns in the English story?

To conclude this timeline we had originally intended to show two tables: the first giving figures for changes in total crime and the second for changes in the size of the police force (and later in the chapter we were hoping to do the same for the Belgium). This, we thought, might show how the size of the police forces and the size of their tasks varied over our 40-year period. This, an innocent might suppose, was pretty basic background. In fact it turns out to be a very difficult, and possibly unwise endeavour. We should have guessed, perhaps, that the absence of any such data from most of the most respected academic texts on the police was an ominous sign (take, for example, the monumental standard Belgian text, Van Outrive, 2005, where 662 pages pass by with hardly any statistics). When we sought expert help from criminologists and police experts (on both sides of the North Sea) the dominant response was: 'Don't do it, but if you must, then make it clear that there are all sorts of problems both with comparisons over time and even more with comparisons between different countries.' Next, we discovered that there were whole reports devoted to discussing the difficulties of these numbers (for example Bruggeman, 1986; Home Office, 2001) and that those few reports which did contain comparative data cautiously spent almost as much space in warning readers what they could not deduce from the figures as they spent presenting the figures themselves (for example *European Sourcebook of Crime and Criminal Justice Statistics – 2006*). Among these warnings are the following:

- Figures for 'total crime' are a kind of vast aggregate, including brutal murders and minor misdemeanours: it is often important to know what is happening to particular parts of the picture, and modest changes in the grand total may be fairly meaningless. (For example, while total crime falls, and, within that, total violent crime also falls, gun and knife crime may nevertheless go up quite sharply, leading to conflicting headlines and political claims and counter-claims.)
- Categories of crime change over time (new crimes are defined and legislated; sometimes old ones disappear – for example homosexuality between consenting adults in many Western countries).
- Categories of crime differ considerably from one country and legal system to another (even, for example, 'homicide' is classified differently).
- The rules for counting crimes change over time (for example there were substantial changes in England and Wales in 1998 and again in 2002 – see Hough, 2008).
- Even different police forces or units within a single country may have different practices for recording crimes.
- Many or most crimes recorded by the police are reported by the public. But the rate at which the public report particular types of crime are known to vary from time to time and place to place depending on a host of sociological and economic factors (for example domestic violence is notoriously under-reported; theft where an insurance claim depends on the loss being reported to the police is likely to be well reported, at least among those social groups who have insurance). Therefore recorded crime is unlikely to be a very good indicator of 'real' or underlying crime.
- Instead of relying on crimes recorded by the police one can look at data reported by the public – such as that in the British Crime Survey. This should have the advantage that it includes crimes experienced by citizens which are not reported to, or recorded by, the police. Even here, however, some will choose not to take part in the survey, or to take part but conceal certain things that have happened to them (Hough, 2008).
- A good deal of crime in any case follows economic cycles and changing lifestyles, and these trends cannot usually be smoothed out by any police action. For example, economic hard times tend to generate more thefts; a society awash with small, portable phones is also likely to suffer a range of phone-related crimes.
- In the case of police numbers, one may again find different counting rules in different forces (Home Office, 2001).
- 'The count of police numbers is already skewed by the changing use

of civilians, increasing investment in IT and outsourcing of work' (Home Office, 2001, p. 1).

Having made all these caveats, we will nevertheless present some figures – both in this chapter and later in the book. Readers are therefore asked to regard them with all the caution that the above warnings suggest. In practical terms we cannot spell out every limitation to every figure, even in these relatively limited and selective tables – both because we cannot know them all ourselves, and because if we did, half our book would disappear under technical detail, which is not what we are trying to achieve.

Table 4.1   Police numbers in England and Wales

Year	Police officers	Other police staff
1965	83 940	13 416
1970	92 446	26 061
1975	102 738	34 945
1980	114 543	37 965
1985	120 600	39 200
1990	126 777	44 525
1995	127 222	54 709
2000	124 170	53 227
2005	141 230	70 869

Notes: There are minor differences between the years concerning the exact date at which these figures were collected. Also, since the 2002 Police Reform Act certain civilian police staff can be made 'Designated Officers' and allocated duties such as investigation and detention, but they are not included in the above table.
It is also interesting that when the Serious Organised Crime Agency (SOCA) was created in 2006 the police officers who joined it had to resign as police officers (and thereby disappeared from police strength numbers). They became agents of SOCA, along with ex-Customs and immigration officers and others who joined the new agency.

Source: Personal communication, Home Office Direct Communications Unit, 9 February 2009.

Both tables appear to show increases, Table 4.1 in the numbers of police officers and Table 4.2 a far bigger increase in recorded crime. But both tables – especially Table 4.2 – are subject to the kinds of interpretive cautions mentioned earlier. The figures on recorded crime have long been the object of criticism and interpretation from criminologists and sociologists (Reiner, 2000, pp. 199–202). Hough makes the basic point that:

While they are often used as an index of crime, they are better thought of as a measure of police workload – the crimes that are brought to police attention.

Table 4.2   Recorded crime, England and Wales 1965–2002

Year	Total recorded crime	Homicides[1]	Total violence against the person	Burglaries
1965	1 134M	325	25 548	251 306
1975	2 106M	515	71 002	515 429
1985	3 612M	616	121 731	866 697
1995	5 100M	745	212 588	1 239 484
2001/02[2]	5 525M	891	650 330	878 509

Notes:
1. Homicides include murders, manslaughters and infanticides.
2. The statistical series ends in 2001/02 and is then replaced by a different series.

Source: Compiled from www.homeoffice.gov.uk/rds/pdfs07/recorded-crime-1898–2002xls accessed 9 January 2009.

> They can mislead as an index of crime because the proportion of crime reported to the police, and recorded by them, can change over place and time. (Hough, 2008, p. 65)

Yet despite these important caveats, the trends are so broad that the general message of Tables 4.1 and 4.2 may still be plausible: that during the period which we cover in this book there was a huge increase in recorded crime, and that increase dwarfed any increase in police numbers.

Certain longer-term themes are clearly apparent in the foregoing English police timeline. One is the trend to greater central government regulation and standardization of the police, through adjustments to the constitutions of police authorities, through increasingly elaborate planning systems, through sharper and sharper sets of targets and performance indicators, and through the work of the Inspectorate of Constabulary. This trend appears to shift fairly sharply upwards from the early 1990s – what had previously perhaps been a Tortoise becomes something rather faster. A second is the recurrent prominence of demands for the police to connect more closely with the concerns of local communities. This almost seems to go in cycles, peaking every time there are serious episodes of public disorder in specific localities. A third is the increasing professionalization and specialization of the police. This was manifested in a myriad ways, not least the improvements in handling suspects following PACE, but also locally (as we shall see in Chapter 4) by the creation of special units and teams for different types of crime (gun crime, computer crime, domestic violence, rape and so on) and for much more proactive community relations. Taken together these innovations could be seen as a Stalactite-like process of change.

Now we turn to Belgium. As will be immediately apparent, the chronology for Belgium is somewhat shorter than that for Britain. In part, no doubt, this relative brevity derives from the fact that Belgium is a smaller country and that the community of Belgian police scholars is smaller and they are much less prolific in their publications than their British counterparts. However, there also is a deeper reason. It does seem that there was simply less policymaking in Belgium – in the sense that the Belgian politico-administrative machine produced far fewer distinct policy initiatives than appeared in the UK. We will revisit this issue in the final section of the chapter.

Basic Timeline: Police Policy in Belgium, 1965–2005

Since the end of the First World War there had been three main police forces in Belgium: the Rijkswacht/Gendarmerie (national, hierarchical, somewhat militaristic), the Judicial Police (attached to public prosecution offices and organized in judicial districts) and the Municipal Police (under local mayors, and with a somewhat 'softer' image than the Rijkswacht). In addition there were various specialized police forces – for airports, harbours, railways and so on – but these will not feature in our analysis. In 1957 an Act redefined the Rijkswacht/Gendarmerie, emphasizing their military character and replacing the 160-year-old legislation which had stood since the period before Belgian independence. The Rijkswacht was responsible to three ministers: Defence, Justice and Interior.

1960s
The Rijkswacht expanded and developed a Central Bureau for Investigation (CBO – Centraal Bureau voor Opsporing) and a Surveillance and Detection Branch (BOB – Bewakings-en-Opsporingsbrigades). Technological changes got under way, including a first radio network, the first computers and dogs trained to seek out drugs.

1970s
Expansion and specialization. 'More authority, more logistics, more policemen, the establishment of specialized units, automation, centralisation' (Bergmans, 2005, p. 1). Considerable investment was made in the SIE/DYANE (Special Intervention Squad) which was designed to deal with hostage-taking and other serious, organized crime. The emphasis was on the policeman as a 'crimefighter'. In parallel, however, a 'turf war' for criminal information and the 'best' cases was going on between the Rijkswacht and the Judicial Police. There were also extensive amalgamations of Municipal Police forces, pursuant to local government

restructuring. Mayors wanted to keep control of these local forces but were often unable or unwilling to invest heavily in modernization and professionalization. The result was a growing gap between the national and local forces. At the local level, restructuring meant that the 2359 municipalities of 1975 became only 589 in 1976 (308 in Flanders, 262 in Wallonia and 19 in Brussels). Then in 2001 new legislation gave local police forces a separate legal personality from their municipal authorities. At the time of writing (2009) there are 196 police zones, 50 of which correspond to single municipalities and 146 to combinations of municipalities.

1982

There was a strike by the Municipal Police. This caused a certain resentment on the part of the Rijkswacht (who were prohibited by law from striking). It therefore did not help the attempts to bring the Rijkswacht and the local police closer together.

1982–85

The Brabant killers (the Nivelles Gang): robbers carried out 22 armed attacks on restaurants, stores and so on, resulting in 28 deaths and 20 injured. The gang leaders were never identified. The degree of precision in the organization of the attacks led some commentators to claim that disaffected members of the Gendarmerie/Rijkswacht were involved.

1984–85

The affair of the Cellules Communistes Combattantes (CCC): 14 bombings took place, targeted at 'enemies of communism'. Two firemen were killed and 28 people were injured. There was public anger when it emerged that the terrorists had warned the authorities but the messages had not been passed on quickly enough to the firemen. Furthermore the popular speculation was that the terrorists must be receiving help from the national security organization. The latter had infiltrated the cells but it failed to take preventative action. Carette, one of the leaders of the CCC, was convicted for murder in 1986.

1985

Football hooligans fought in the Heysel Stadium, Brussels, during the European Cup Final between Liverpool and Juventus. A wall collapsed, resulting in 39 deaths and 600 injured. There was widespread international criticism of the Belgian authorities, both for the condition of the Heysel Stadium and for the ineffective policing of the crowd. The events of the Nivelles Gang, the CCC and the Heysel disaster generated a good deal of popular and political discontent with the police, and a desire for change.

May 1986 (and again in April 1987): violent suppression of striking miners by the Gendarmerie/Rijkswacht.

1987
The December general election returned the socialists to the governing coalition. Louis Tobback, an entrepreneurial policymaker who wanted change, became Minister of the Interior, and De Witte joined his cabinet from a think tank. These two were going to be very significant players in the future development of police policy. In opposition the Socialists had prepared a policy perspective on the police (see Tobback, 1989).

1988
On 24 May a Parliamentary Committee of Inquiry into the Nivelles Gang was finally set up (known as the Banditism Commission). In the same year a major audit of the police service for the Minister of the Interior was published (Team Consult, 1988).

1990
June: the Banditism Commission came forward with the Pinksterplan (in English, Pentecost Plan), proposing a new emphasis on 'community policing' and the demilitarization of the Rijkswacht/Gendamerie. The plan was 'clearly not a coherent master plan, but rather a somewhat unfocused collection of intentions' (Maesschalck, 2002, p. 180; Van Outrive et al., 1992, pp. 320–21). Much of it was not implemented, but it helped set the agenda for the later reforms (see 1998, below).

1991
July: a new law created 'Committee P', a standing committee of judges and persons with police experience with an overall responsibility for monitoring Belgium's police forces and intelligence services. Ever since then Committee P has issued detailed reports covering many aspects of policing (see www.comitep.be). General elections saw the rapid rise of far right parties. The first law relating to police reorganization was proclaimed, coming into effect in 1992.

1992
Second 'Pinksterplan': Municipal Police forces were to be required to cooperate with each other in 'interpolice zones'. Instead of 589 Municipal Police forces there would be fewer than 200 such zones. Also introduced was a new crime prevention policy based on 'local security contracts'.

1992 Implementation of the Police Function Act, which re-defined the respective functions of the municipal police, the Rijkswacht and the judicial police. This was intended, *inter alia*, to promote greater integration between the municipal police and the Rijkswacht.

1995

The first (voluntary) initiatives with respect to 'interpolice zones' – attempts to improve coordination between forces at the local level. The provincial level played an active role in stimulating local collaboration. De Witte (see above) became Governor of Flemish Brabant, and was an influential figure in the police policy process.

1996–97

The Dutroux Affair hits the headlines. Marc Dutroux was a paedophile who sexually abused six girls, killing four of them. The case showed gross inefficiency and a lack of coordination – indeed, sometimes active hostility – between the judiciary and the three police forces and among the police forces themselves. There were also suspicions of police corruption and complicity. The Dutroux Affair triggered the 'White March', the largest public demonstration in Belgium since the Second World War, when 250 000 to 300 000 people marched through Brussels to express discontent with the handling of the affair by the police and the courts. This came as a major shock to the public authorities, and finally led to substantive change. A Dutroux Parliamentary Committee of Inquiry was set up almost immediately, and proved to be the final catalyst for real police reform.

In April 1997 new legislation gave mayors a say in local branches of the (national) Rijkswacht/Gendamerie.

1998

In April Dutroux briefly escaped from custody. The Ministers of Justice and of the Interior immediately resigned. Prime Minister Dehaene invited the four opposition parties to join the four government parties to discuss reforms in the criminal justice and police system. These eight-party talks led to the 'Octopus Agreement' of 24 May. This proposed an integrated police force on both national and local levels.

1998

The Police Reform Act (which resulted directly from the 'Octopus Agreement') grouped together three previous polices forces (Municipal, Judicial and Gendamerie). The Judicial Police had not originally been part of the main story, but: 'There was a conflict between the BOB [special investigation branch of the Rijkswacht] and the judicial police. Tobback and Michiels agreed that something had to happen also with the judicial police' (interview 32 – Michiels was a senior and influential police officer).

Now there were to be two autonomous levels, federal (from 1 January 2001) and local (196 zones starting 1 January 2002). They were to have national and local security plans with goals. This was considerably more 'managerial' than anything that had been seen in Belgium previously.

1999
General elections saw the arrival in power of a 'rainbow coalition' of liberals, socialists and environmentalists.

2000
May: Federal Security Plan and Prison Policy.

December: two ex-Gendarmes/Rijkswacht appointed, as General Superintendent of the Federal Police, and General Inspector of the Federal and Local Police.

Euro 2000 Football finals were held in Belgium and NL amidst international security concerns. Coincidentally, these fears strengthened the hands of the police unions, who threatened to strike during the championships and eventually secured generous pay deals for the new police structure.

2001
Beginning of implementation of 1998 Police Reform Act. Also a royal decree organizing police training establishments. '[T]here is today an unambiguous move towards organizing the police along "managerial" lines' (Tange, 2004, p. 233).

2002
Establishment of 196 local zones for the police (see entry for the 1970s, above).

2004
A ministerial circular announced the introduction of organizational development and quality management programmes for the police. The introduction of an integrated security framework also meant that, for the first time, combating crime was seen as a task involving other partners beyond the police and the criminal justice system.

2005
The Vesalius Acts sought further to integrate existing police personnel into the new structure of local and national forces. These harmonization measures turned out to be rather expensive. At this point there were roughly 13 000 federal police and rather more than 30 000 local police. In addition

(as in England) there was a growing private security industry – employing perhaps 1000 investigators plus another 10 000 general security staff.

Patterns in the Belgian story?

Looking back over the Belgian trajectory, certain broad themes emerge. A principal one was a concern for achieving larger-scale local forces. This thread ran from the municipal mergers of the 1970s through the interpolice zones of the 1990s to the implementation of 196 police areas in 2002. The latter could be regarded as an Earthquake – certainly it was the biggest shake-up of the Belgian police organization during our 40-year period. Yet at the same time the 1998 reform was part of that much longer story, a process described by the leading Belgian police scholar as 'Le déroulement sinueux de la réforme' ('The sinuous unfolding of the reform') – (Van Outrive, 2005, p. 127).

A second theme (connected to the first) was a Stalactite-like trend towards a more managerial and a more professional approach. The 'Vlerick generation' of the 1980–1990s were a group of senior officers who had taken management training in the Vlerick Business School, and who became increasingly influential. A widely used training textbook was based on work undertaken at this school (Delarue, 2001). This thinking also included a more developed notion of police accountability than had obtained in the past:

> there was a different debate between Flanders and Wallonia. However, there was not a problem with the *Gendarmerie*, which was dominated by Flemish generals (Berckmans, De Ridder, Franssen) which received management training at the Vlerick School. (interview 32)

Indeed, managerialism spread rapidly through the Belgian police system, sometimes taking forms that were directly borrowed from the business world (Van Outrive, 2005, Chapter 7)

A third trend was the gradual emergence of a more integrated approach to crime, with the national police dealing with serious crime and the municipal police addressing local crime. Competition should be replaced by collaboration. Community policing and 'more blue on the streets' became an important component in local policing. This could be seen as a Tortoise-like process, quite slow-moving and gradual. Here as elsewhere, however, it can sometimes be difficult to separate the rhetoric of reports from the practice on the ground.

The 1990 Pinksterplan and the related setting up of Committee P marked something of a watershed. They signified a wish – by some at least – to plan the police force as a whole, something which had not really happened before. The Pentagon platforms (coordinating committees composed of representatives from different parts of the police system) represented a move against fragmentation and non-communication between different police cadres, and between local governments, magistrates and ministries. 'The Pentagon platform (*vijfhoeksoverleg*) remedied this lack of communication between the administration of justice, national-local, justice and interior' (interview 32). But implementation required a lot of persuasion: 'the round of provinces and mayors was made to convince them. Also, there were consultations with the federations of *commissaries* and *commissaries adjoints*, not with the association of municipalities' (interview 32). It seems that Pentagon platforms worked much better in some places than in others.

Overall, a distinct direction of movement can be discerned. One of our most experienced interviewees put it like this: 'It was a combination of personalities, a long term vision which was not changing, and political opportunities' (interview 32).

As for background statistics on crime and force strengths, the Belgian position seems to be even more opaque than that for England and Wales. The figures do not go as far back as those in Table 4.1, and Belgian experts assured us that even over this limited time range they are 'difficult to compare, because of inconsistencies in the operationalisation and measurement' (personal communication, 16 January 2009). All we can offer is Table 4.3 and 4.4.

Table 4.3 does not appear to show any dramatic increase in recorded crime during the decade from 1996, indeed, there is some slight fall at the end of this period. (To repeat an earlier warning, these figures do not

Table 4.3   Total number of registered criminal acts, Belgium, 1996–2005

Year	Total number of registered criminal acts
1996	741 534
1997	818 660
1998	858 245
1999	857 445
2000	1 015 011
2001	988 246
2002	1 042 086
2003	1 026 452
2004	1 017 324
2005	989 153

Source: http://statbel.fgov.be/figures/d352_nl.asp, accessed 19 January 2009.

Table 4.4   Numbers of police officers per 100 000 population, 2003

	Number of police officers per 100 000 population, 2003
Belgium	352
England and Wales	264

Source: European Sourcebook of Crime and Criminal Justice Statistics (2006), p. 74.

measure the actual amount of underlying or 'real' crime. Furthermore, their breakdown into categories – which we decided not to show here – represent all sorts of peculiarities and specificities of Belgian law, for example a distinction between 'autotheft' and 'motortheft'.) Meanwhile total Belgian police numbers (adding up all the various different types of force) do not seem to be altered too dramatically – from about 37 000 at the end of the 1980s to about 35 000 in 2003. If we look at these levels in relation to the size of the population, and compare with England and Wales, we get Table 4.4

4.3   COMPARING THE BELGIAN AND ENGLISH STORIES

Even if the English story is more hectic, more crowded with new policies and initiatives, there are some commonalities between the two countries. In both, failures to solve headline crimes (or failures to solve them fast enough) brought demands for reorganization. In both there were instances not just of incompetence but also of corruption, or presumed corruption, which took their toll on public attitudes towards the police. In both there were periods of difficulty when the police were brought in to deal with large-scale public order problems (miners' strikes, and so on) which took on an overtly political character. In both there was a steady tendency towards larger geographical units for police operations, although, as explained earlier, the main English forces are much bigger than the municipal forces in Belgium, but lack the national reach of the Belgian Rijkswacht/Gendarmerie. The interest in having bigger units was propelled by several common motives, including a belief in economies of scale, better geographical coordination, and improved management and technical services. This essentially structural approach was probably a more prominent part of the Belgian reform process than the English. Indeed, as we shall see in our local study (Chapter 7) an enormous amount of effort went into renegotiating local Belgian police boundaries and coordination

– often on what was, by English standards, a rather small scale. In both countries also there was a periodic, popular demand for greater attention to be given to local issues and neighbourhood approaches (in Belgium, *een bevolkingsgerichte politie* – see the Foreword to Politie PZ Leuven, 2005). And finally, in both countries there was a concern that the police needed to become more 'professional', which entailed better and more intensive training. This had both a 'social' and a 'technological' component to it. Police had to be trained how to 'get closer to the community', which meant dealing with socially and culturally diverse groups in a sensitive manner. They also had to learn to use new technologies, some of which had significant implications for operational practice. For example, during the later stages of the writing of this book the UK government announced that it was arming all English and Welsh police forces with 10000 new 'taser' guns. These 50000-volt electric stun guns were to be used in the fight against violent crime, and were presented politically as a way of avoiding having to extend the arming of police with conventional firearms (Leppard, 2008).

Meanwhile, a less commented-upon trend that was common to both countries was the expansion and diversification of the 'police family', that is, members of staff of various types who were not full police officers (either in terms of training or legal powers) but played some kind of ancilliary role. There have been various, often rather obvious, reasons for this diversification. One is that of economy – fully trained police officers are expensive, and if some parts of their task can be done by somewhat cheaper types of staff, that is obviously attractive to budget-holders. In England and Wales the Police Community Support Officers are a prime example – they offer the police the opportunity to put more uniformed people on the street at lower cost (especially where they are initially paid for by central government). Another is the growing army of civilians – some of them highly skilled – doing police-related work, often but not always inside police stations. That brings us to the second main reason – to provide specialist skills which ordinary police cannot easily acquire. Hence police 'profilers', computer experts, DNA testers and many others. This trend can also be seen in Belgium, though there the process of civilianization does not seem to have gone nearly so far, and there is as yet no direct equivalent of the English PCSO. There are, however, *Hulpagenten*, who wear uniforms, but, like PCSOs, have no power of arrest. In Belgium, however, they are classified as the lowest rank of police officer. Also uniformed and on the streets are the *Stadswachten* (town watch) who are town hall staff rather than police staff, and who walk around the streets helping visitors and reporting broken street lamps and other minor infrastructural problems. They are not part of the 'police family' but they do wear a kind of coloured jacket with their role labelled on it. There are, therefore, some (rough) parallels between England and Belgium, even if the details and degree of differentiation within law-and-order work are substantially different in the two countries.

Nevertheless the sheer pace of change in England, especially since the late 1980s, demands attention. The managerialist apparatus of plans, standards, targets and performance-linked budgets – although present to some extent in Belgium – arrived sooner and has been developed much further in England. The application of high-tech, specialized techniques of information management, force deployment, crime scene analysis and neighbourhood policing all appear to have flourished in England beyond anything we encountered in Belgium. On the other hand, it could be argued that much of this managerial apparatus was designed at least partly to improve the ability of UK ministers to see and control what the police were doing, while in Belgium political control was already present, though in a quite different form. Certainly the influence of local mayors over Municipal Police forces has no parallel in England. In the latter, it is true that local councillors sit on police authorities, but this is a far cry from the kind of detailed, single-minded influence that can be achieved by a determined Belgian Mayor.

5. National reforms: intersectoral comparison

5.1 SIMILARITIES AND DIFFERENCES IN BRITISH AND BELGIAN POLICYMAKING

To some extent, but only to some extent, the opening stereotypes (Chapter 2) do appear to have survived closer scrutiny. Thus there has indeed been a significant contrast in policymaking styles and intensity between the two countries – in respect of both police policy and hospitals policy. Given that the two countries faced many similar problems, this degree of difference stands as a remarkable tribute to the divergent influences of the respective cultural and political frameworks. England has been the site of relentless activism, with one reform following another. Belgium has been much slower-moving, with big reforms emerging only occasionally, usually after long periods of public indignation and political pressure. Graphically, one might portray the different frequencies and amplitudes as the kind of 'cardiogram' beloved of TV hospital dramas – see Figure 5.1

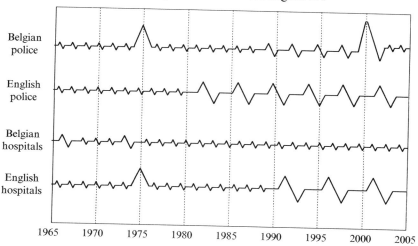

Figure 5.1   'Cardiogram' of frequency and intensity of reforms in Belgium and England

What kind of changes have these been? Here we may first return to the three-level scheme of Hall introduced in Chapter 1, section 1.5. The first (most detailed) level was changes in the levels set for specific policy instruments. Here there have been many changes in both countries – in fact these have been far too numerous to reiterate them all here. For the English police the 1979 pay increase was significant, and the more recent annual adjustments of performance targets also falls into this category. Meanwhile in Belgium there was the gradual demilitarization of the federal police and the equally gradual professionalization of the local police (more training, more specialization). In English hospitals the period since 1997 has undoubtedly witnessed a large, policy-driven reduction in average waiting times for elective inpatient treatment. In Belgian hospitals the 1982 moratorium on opening new hospitals beds or the 1993 increase in patient co-payments for visits to doctors represented changes in the level at which policy instruments were set. Overall, the greater activism in England has meant more specific changes of this kind, but neither country has been at all static.

On the second level Hall (1993) was concerned with shifts in the type of policy instrument used. This is a bigger type of change and therefore it is not surprising to find fewer shifts of this kind. For the English police we could cite the multiplication of specialist bodies at national level, including the 1997 National Criminal Intelligence Service and the 2004 Policing Improvement Agency. For the Belgian police there was the introduction of local security contracts from the early 1990s. In the English hospital service the increased use of market-type mechanisms has been a notable innovation – first following the Conservative government's reforms of 1989 (the 'provider market') and then more recently under the banner of the New Labour government's commitment to 'choice'. Among the Belgian hospitals – where 'choice' had always been part of the system – one could say that the idea that the whole population of hospitals constituted a system which required federal-level planning was a change which gradually grew during the 1970s and 1980s, and required the federal government to fashion new regulatory instruments. On this level the contrast between England and Belgium appears rather clear. The second-level changes in England were more marked and more numerous than those in Belgium.

Hall's third level denotes paradigmatic change – a new concept of the policy and/or its objects. Such changes are not common – at least not with established services such as the police and hospitals. They may occur incrementally over time (Stalactite-type changes in Table 1.1) or as an Earthquake (punctuation). It is hard to see such changes in Belgium at all. Perhaps one candidate would be the role of management itself: in the Belgian hospital sector hospitals gradually became entities which were regarded as something that should be managed. As one experienced doctor-manager told us, at the beginning of the 1970s the Belgian hospital sector 'really was a non-organized world. The hospital as a unity did not exist' (interview 5). Over the next two decades it became widely accepted that hospitals needed internal professional management, and the growth of 'management' still continues, Stalactite-fashion. (This is not to imply that there was no discipline within Belgian hospitals. Some hospitals were undoubtedly strictly run, for example by religious orders, but that traditional approach was gradually replaced by modern ideas of management.) The police, by contrast, always had a strong organizational tradition, albeit largely hierarchical and militaristic. However, it might be argued that there has been a paradigm shift towards seeing the police as a community-based organization with a prime mission to maintain public order, increase public safety and reduce the average citizen's fear of crime. There have been no shortage of policy statements stressing this dimension, which therefore can look like an Earthquake or, at least, a Stalactite. Yet we are doubtful about this, on several grounds. First, high-profile crime fighting has lost none of its political and media pre-eminence – indeed, with the growth of international crime and fears of terrorism, that side of policing can arguably be said to have been given increased emphasis. Second, whilst there have undoubtedly been a variety of community-oriented initiatives – some of them relatively successful – we have found no evidence to indicate a massive shift of resources into this area. Within the police forces, cultural change that will give community relations a higher profile may well have begun, but again there seems little evidence that it has suffused Belgian police organizations, which generally retain a more 'separate' and traditional, authoritarian style than their English counterparts. A better candidate for an Earthquake would be the 1998 restructuring of the Belgian police, although even that was preceded by almost a decade of political debates and manoeuverings.

Paradigm shifts were not common in England either, but a plausible case could perhaps be made for at least two shifts of a fairly fundamental kind. First, there has been a growing realization among policymakers that the police are not the only or even always the principal instrument in the fight against crime. The police are one player in a complex network, including local authorities, the burgeoning private security industry, the courts, prisons and probation services – and local communities themselves (McLaughlin, 2007, pp. 88–104). This would therefore be a Stalactite change. Whilst the considerations which prompt this realization are certainly known in Belgium we do not see that this shift to thinking about public order as something that goes far beyond the public authorities themselves has yet penetrated far into the consciousness of either the public or the policymaking elite. Second, in the English health care arena, there has arguably been a fundamental shift away from 'doctor power', almost to the point where the medical profession is seen as the problem holding back the development of a more efficient and effective health service. The demands for better management and more clinical transparency have been endless, and although the medical profession has been a powerful defender of its autonomies, since around 1990 it has been obliged to cede a great deal of ground. Like a Stalactite, management has just gone on growing. Again, while some of the arguments can also be found in Belgium, we see no equivalent shift – the talk has not yet become the practice or the policy.

We must be careful, however, not to read strong normative lessons into these contrasting histories. We should not assume that English hospitals are therefore better than their Belgian counterparts, or that the English public are happier with their hospital system. Neither should we assume that crime is better tackled in England, or that the public fear of crime is lower there, or even that the many English community policing initiatives and programmes, however enthusiastically pursued, have ensured higher levels of public order and public trust in the police. Indeed, we will now look at some measures which seem to show a rather more complicated picture.

Before we come to the figures themselves we need to acknowledge their limitations, which are many. Sometimes the relevant figures are available only for the UK, or for England and Wales, rather than for England alone. Sometimes the figures are available only for one year – when a particular study was undertaken – or are available for only a small subset of our 40-year timespan from 1965 to 2005. Often categories do not fit both countries in quite the same way (for example with respect to questions about the affordability of healthcare, where the payment systems in the two countries have been so very different). Frequently, also, when surveys tap public perceptions, the responses may be conditioned by cultural expectations and norms specific to that country. For all these reasons, therefore, we must be careful not to put too much weight on comparative statistics. On the other hand, it would seem foolish to ignore them. So we have chosen what seemed to us the most relevant and interesting comparisons, and treated them as much as a source of further questions as a set of definitive answers.

First, then, let us look at certain aspects of healthcare and hospitals (see Table 5.1).

The Belgians, it seems, spend rather more on their health care system. It appears to be a more generous, less efficient system (in the sense of having more nurses, doctors and hospital beds per capita) than that in the

Table 5.1   Selected Anglo-Belgian health care comparisons

Aspect	Belgium	UK
Total expenditure on health as a % of GDP, 2002	9.1	7.7
Total public expenditure on health as a % of GDP	6.5	6.4
Total private expenditure on health as a % of GDP	2.6	1.3
Acute hospital beds per 100 000 population	583	390
Average length of stay (days) 1996[1]	7.5	4.8
Nurses per 100 000 population	1075	497
Physicians per 100 000 population	448	390
Life expectancy	78.4	78.2
Infant deaths and neo-natal deaths per 1000 live births	9.2	8.7
% of people who perceive their own health as good or very good	78.2	74.0

Note: 1. From European Observatory on Health Care Systems (2000), p. 46.

Source: World Health Organization Europe (2006), pp. 10, 11, 31, 33, 47.

UK. It is true that long English hospital waiting lists, which used to be characteristic of the UK (but not of Belgium) have been much reduced by the intense reforms (and large expenditure increases) of the New Labour government after 1999. A Eurobarometer survey in 2007 found that 87 per cent of Belgians found access to their hospitals 'very easy' or 'fairly easy' but that the UK was not that far behind, with 80 per cent. Against that there is the financial aspect. NHS hospitals are free at the point of access (financed principally from general taxation), whereas in Belgium insurance is normally required. The same survey found that 31 per cent of Belgians thought healthcare was 'not very affordable', or 'not at all affordable', while only 6 per cent of UK citizens fell into this category (Special Eurobarometer, 2007, pp. 28–32).

Health status outcomes are not strikingly different between the two countries, but Belgians do feel a bit healthier than the average UK citizen. On the other hand we need to treat life expectancy statistics with the knowledge that probably only about one-quarter of the health of people in developed countries can be attributed to the doings of their health-care systems. The rest can be traced to the physical, economic and social environments (which influence lifestyle choices), genetic inheritance and human biology (Canadian Institute for Advanced Research, 1997).

Now we turn to the police. In Tables 5.2 and 5.3 we see further evidence that policy activism does not automatically translate into better outcomes. In Table 5.2 we see that there are many more Belgian police per capita than English and Welsh police per capita. It also appears that 'civilianization'

Table 5.2   Selected police statistics

Measure	Belgium	England and Wales
Police officers per 100 000 population[1]	337	241
Civilian police employees per 100 000 population	40	106

Note/Source:
1.   Average per year, 1999–2001. The EU average was 337. Source: Barclay and Tavares (2003).

Table 5.3   Selected aspects of crime: rank order among 18 EU countries

Measure	Belgium	UK
Victimization rate for 10 common crimes in 2004	6	2
Car theft in 2004	12	1
Burglary victimization rate	7	1
Assault and threat victimization rate	4	1
Contact with drug problems in area of residence	9	6
Feeling unsafe on the street after dark	12	8
Victims satisfied with police after reporting crimes (lower number means more dissatisfaction)	11	9

Note: The rank of 1 = highest crime in the EU-18 and a rank of 18 = the lowest. Thus, for example, the UK has the highest reported rate of car theft among the 18 EU countries surveyed.

Source: Drawn from EUICS Consortium (2005).

has gone much further in England and Wales, where in 1995 there were 106 civilians working for the police per 100 000 population, compared with only 40 in Belgium. The EUICS Consortium report *The Burden of Crime in the EU* (2005) shows that, in general, crime rates have been falling throughout most of the EU since the end of the 1980s. Belgium is unusual as the only country where crime has actually slightly increased during that period. However, before any assumption is made that this means that the serially reformed UK police are doing much better than in Belgium, look more closely at Table 5.3. Both Belgium and the UK are fairly high-crime countries by overall EU standards – they are both in the top halves of most of the tables in the report. But within that unfortunate category, Belgium comes out better on all four of the common crime rates shown in the table than the UK. Furthermore, the people surveyed in the UK had more contact with drug problems where they lived, and greater fear when out in

Table 5.4   *Percentage of crime victims who have received specialized support from the police, 2005*

Country	% Crime victims supported
England and Wales	17
Belgium	12
Sweden	9
Germany	2

Source: EUICS Consortium (2005), pp. 76–7.

the street after dark. They were, however, more satisfied than the Belgians with what happened when they reported crimes to the police. That may in part be because, when victims of crime, they received somewhat more support – see Table 5.4. However, all these crime figures should be read with all the caveats already discussed in Chapter 4.

When we come to the issue of general public trust in the police (Table 5.5), we find a large contrast. Despite the various scandals and problems alluded to above, the majority of the British public evidently trust their police. In Belgium, however, confidence in the police was for some years at one of the lowest levels in Western Europe, although it has recovered somewhat, and by 2005 was only slightly below the EU average (whereas in the UK confidence in the police is five percentage points above the EU average). In both countries confidence in the police is considerably higher than confidence in the legal system.

In short, it would be a gross oversimplification to assume that greater policy activism usually leads to either better policy outcomes or more public satisfaction. There are far too many other factors that may influence these outcomes, including, obviously, how sound the policies are, how well they are implemented, what else is happening in the social and political environment at the time, and what the relevant public expectations and social norms may be. (For example, the exceedingly low confidence score of the Belgian police in 1997 – see Table 5.5 – was almost certainly influenced by the fact that the Dutroux affair was headlines at that time.) Crime is influenced by many factors largely beyond police control (such as the economic cycle and lifestyle changes) and health outcomes by many influences beyond the control of hospitals (culturally influenced patterns of diet and exercise, levels of pollution). Furthermore, each country starts from a different place – a different current norm. Thus crime may have fallen faster in England and Wales than in Belgium during the period 1988–2004, but that still left absolute crime levels higher in England and Wales, even after a decade and a half.

Table 5.5   Trust in the police

Country/institution	1997 %	2005 %	EU average 2005 %
Belgium – police	30	64	65
UK – police	69	70	65
Belgium – legal system	14	40	47
UK – legal system	48	35	47
Belgium – trade unions	36	41	38
UK – trade unions	36	42	38

Note: The percentages in the table are those who said they tended to have confidence in the police and the legal system.

Source: Eurobarometers 48 (Autumn 1997) and 57 (Autumn 2005).

A more plausible, limited, argument is perhaps that the greater English policy activism – permitted by its more centralized and hierarchical institutions and the plasticity of its constitution – has produced more efficient police and hospital systems. There is some evidence for that, and the idea fits in well with the stereotypes we started out with. On the other hand there are many points that could be made against a simple claim that 'England is better because it is more efficient'. To begin with, let us use Figure 5.2 to help define a few terms.

The figure makes it quite clear that efficiency (the ratio of inputs to outputs) is only one policy value. Effectiveness is another, sustainability a third. Furthermore there are other important policy values which are not represented in the figure at all, including equity and responsiveness to diversity. It is possible, therefore, that higher efficiency may be gained at the price of less of some other policy value. Thus, for example, we have seen from Table 5.1 that the effectiveness of the Belgian health care system in terms of some important outcomes (life expectancy, public self-perceptions of good health) would seem to have been at least marginally superior to the effectiveness of the UK system, even if its efficiency may have been less.

Against this, those who believe in the predominant importance of efficiency can argue that resources saved through greater efficiency are then freed to be applied to other good public purposes. This gives an ethical edge to arguments for raising efficiency – the resources poured into all those extra Belgian doctors and hospital beds could be used for public transport or higher pensions or even longer holidays (Goodin and Wilenski, 1984). But the argument does not stop here. There are at

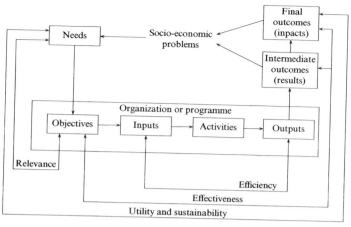

Source: Pollitt and Bouckaert (2004), p.106.

Figure 5.2 The policy input–output model

least two counters to such an argument. First, it could be that the more 'relaxed', better-resourced nature of the Belgian hospital system reflects, however imperfectly, a collective Belgian preference that this should be so. That Belgians do not want their hospitals to be straining for the lowest possible length of stay, sending patients home as soon as is possible so that beds can be used with maximum efficiency. That they want the choice that comes from a looser system (where they do not necessarily even have to go through a primary care doctor to get to hospital). Perhaps they are prepared to pay for more slack in the system, and/or they are prepared to vote for politicians who will act to preserve that higher level of provision. (Or, at least, to vote against anyone who seems to want to cut back on hospital spending.) Second, there is, of course, no guarantee that resources released from efficiency gains in the hospital sector will be used for noble public purposes. They might equally be used to grant additional tax breaks that wealthy people seize upon to buy bigger motor cars and drink more champagne, or indeed to finance public sector programmes which voters may not approve of, such as lavish office blocks for civil servants or motorways through environmentally sensitive localities.

These are fairly high-level arguments (although none the less important for that). In addition, there are practical complications. Looking at the big picture (Table 5.1) it may appear that UK hospitals must be more efficient than their Belgian counterparts. But how and why? Unless one has much more specific information, it will be very difficult to fashion pro-efficiency reforms. Is the Belgian 'bed surplus' concentrated in particular places or medical specialties, or is it general? Similarly, are the shorter NHS average lengths of stay equally distributed across all hospitals and specialties, or are they achieved in some places but not in others? Are the shorter lengths of stay clinically neutral, or is there evidence that they produce higher rates of complications and returning patients who need additional attention? Does the availability of more doctors in the Belgian system lead to shorter waits and/or more time spent taking patient histories and, if so, do these factors have clinical impacts? (They very probably at least have psychological impacts, in terms of patient anxiety and convenience, but these things have not usually been included in policy equations.) In real life, policymakers would (ideally) need to know all these things (and more) before intervening in such complex and internally interconnected organizations as acute hospitals. And, if and when such things were known, judgements would have to be made about how important they were, relative to each other (values again). It is no good saying, as politicians tend to do, 'all these things are important', because they cannot all be given equal weight. Implictly or explicitly, hard choices have to be made.

Such complexities should not be too surprising or, indeed, disappointing. If it were possible to make a straightforward efficiency calculation that would adequately sum up all the important features of a whole policy sector, then we would no longer need politics, politicians and public debate – we could leave it to the economic experts to work out what was undeniably the best policy. Few observers would be content with that (probably not even most economists). Theoretically and practically, policies are often far more complicated than any such formula could capture. Not only are multiple and conflicting values involved, but these values and their supporting groups are themselves shifting and regrouping over time. The complexity of the situation will become even more obvious as, over the next two chapters, we move to the local level. How have the national shifts in policies and priorities which we have outlined above worked out in specific localities?

6. What happened locally? Hospitals

6.1 INTRODUCTION

In the previous chapter we experienced a first encounter with some of the (many) broad quantitative indicators of policy inputs, processes, outputs and outcomes. In doing so we were obliged to face up to the complexities and ambiguities of linkages between what policymakers say, what they do, and what eventually happens, 'out there', 'in the field'. In this chapter (and the next) we move closer to that 'field'. We look at what happens when national polices 'hit the ground' locally. Are they enthusiastically embraced, reluctantly accepted and implemented, creatively interpreted, astutely deflected, diluted, delayed, resisted or even ignored? And how far do national policies dominate the local agenda anyway? Are there also significant locally generated polices, particular to the place (as one would expect in a genuinely multilevel system)? How do local and national agendas interact?

To create this local perspective, we conducted research in two cities: Brighton and Hove (southern England) and Leuven (just east of Brussels, in the Vlaams Brabant – Flemish Brabant – region). As we said in Chapter 1, we chose these as two reasonably prosperous, reasonably cosmopolitan, middle-sized cities which were not burdened with any major handicaps such as the collapse of local industries, geographical remoteness or high levels of ethnic tension and division. (For details of the research, see Appendix).

Brighton was, with neighbouring Hove, jointly designated a 'city' (rather than just a town) in 2000. Together they have a population of roughly 250 000. On the south coast, and backed by areas of beautiful chalk downland, Brighton is quite a fashionable venue, hosting many national and international conferences as well as its traditional holiday trade. It supports two universities and a wide variety of cultural and sporting facilities. Visually, it is famous for its handsome seafront Regency terraces and its pier(s) – there have been two since Victorian times but one has suffered serious fires and, at the time of writing, is no more than a burned and distorted skeleton.

Leuven is somewhat smaller – the central city has a population of around 50 000, but the surrounding necklace of villages add almost as many again. Along with Brugge, Gent and Mechelen it is one of Belgium's ancient Flemish cities, full of beautiful old buildings, including a spectacular fifteenth-century Gothic town hall. It is also a university town, housing Katholieke Universiteit Leuven (KUL), founded in 1425 and the oldest university in the low countries. The 35 000 students give a youthful air to the town, and a cosmopolitan one too, since more than 12 per cent of them currently come from outside Belgium. Leuven is also influenced by being only a 20-minute drive (17 kilometres) to the capital, Brussels.

In this chapter we will tell the stories of 40 years of development in the Brighton and Leuven hospital systems. These stories will be compared, one with the other, and particular attention will be paid to how far developments in these two localities can be 'read off' from the national policies discussed in Chapters 2 and 3, and how far they seem to have had a more distinctively local character.

6.2   HOSPITALS: TWO CONTRASTING STORIES

For most of the period since the mid-1960s Brighton has had two medium-sized general hospitals, the Royal Sussex County Hospital (hereafter RSCH) and the Brighton General. Both are nineteenth-century foundations, both have rather untidy campuses. Neither has ever been fully modernized. Since the mid-1960s the relevant authorities have made two or three attempts to get a new hospital built on a new site, but each attempt has failed. As the Chair of the Brighton Health Authority put it in her 1985 New Year message to staff, local acute health care was constrained by 'the enormous obstacles presented by our obsolete buildings. A new hospital is essential' (Cumberlege, 1985). Six years later Brighton's medical consultant staff wrote a joint letter to the then Conservative Secretary of State for Health saying:

> To our dismay we . . . hear that any money set aside . . . for Hospital Building programmes in Brighton has now disappeared. New building worth £51 million had been approved in principle five years ago. Our three remaining acute hospitals:
>
> Royal Sussex County Hospital, largely built in 1828
> Brighton General Hospital, built in 1865
> Hove General Hospital built in 1888
> are falling apart with a £23 million maintenance backlog. (Hartley, Fletcher and Strachan, 1990, p. 3)

But the new hospital did not come. Instead, a number of small hospitals have been closed and acute services have been incrementally concentrated on the increasingly crowded RSCH site. Since the late 1990s a good deal of new investment has been put into that site, but it was still the case that, at the end of 2006, 209 beds were in buildings constructed before 1850, compared with only 277 in those built since 1960. Meanwhile acute services at the Brighton General have been run down, and no advanced surgery has been conducted there since the early 2000s.

This has been, therefore, a local history of slow, Tortoise-like incremental change, false starts and disappointments, but a definite underlying trend towards concentrating 'hot' services at the RSCH. In 2005 the RSCH suffered the ignominy of simultaneously failing to gain any stars at all in the government's hospital performance league tables (*The Argus* 2005, p. 1), developing one of the largest budgetary overspends of any hospital in the country (Brighton and Sussex University Hospitals NHS Trust, 2005), and being the subject of an 'undercover' BBC TV documentary showing nurses ill-treating elderly patients on one of its wards (BBC News, 2005). Significant bed closures followed as management attempted to right the financial position. Thus, by the end of our period of study (1965–2005) Brighton's hospital services could hardly be termed a 'flagship' for the NHS.

We now turn to Leuven. A major turning point here came right at the beginning of our period – the events of 1968, known in Flemish as *de splitsing* – the splitting-up. What was splitting was the university (Katholieke Universiteit Leuven, or KUL), as the Francophone academics and students were virtually expelled, and left to set up an alternative, Francophone (Walloon) university 50 kilometres away at Louvain-la-Neuve. The Flemings remained *in situ*, and that applied as much to the Leuven hospitals and the medical school as to the rest of the university. The whole drama was part of the larger conflict between the two major language groups in Belgium – the Flemings and the Walloons.

Shortly after *de splitsing* Piet De Somer, the then Rector of KUL, appointed an enterprising young doctor, Jan Peers, as Director of Medicine and General Director of the St Rafaël Clinic. Building on previous planning and extensive investigations of alternative hospitals systems by his predecessor, Jan Blanplain, Peers soon became the formative influence in pushing for a new, single-site hospital on a low hill just outside the old city, at Gasthuisberg. Within a decade a huge new hospital, designed on a low-rise, key pattern was beginning to manifest itself on the site. This was a startling new development, a real Earthquake. Formally inaugurated on 26 January 1985, the new UZ Leuven (University Hospital Leuven) is now the biggest hospital in Belgium (1800 beds by 2003) and in a recent survey of primary care doctors' opinions scored as the best teaching hospital in Belgium in 12 out of 13 medical specialties (Test Gezondheid,

2005). It has swallowed most of the smaller, pre-existing facilities and is in many respects the trendsetter for the whole country, and certainly for the Flemish part of it.

The two stories thus appear to be startlingly different. Brighton tries and fails (several times) to get a new hospital, and ends up with most of its acute services concentrated at an apparently 'failing' hospital. Leuven emerges from a major political crisis (*de splitsing*) with a plan for a single-site new development, which it manages to push through rather rapidly, and then goes on to develop a flagship national teaching hospital.

6.3 A FOCUS ON NEW BUILDINGS AND ORGANIZATIONS

It should be noted that this history is being given a very particular focus – one concerned with the development and decay of physical and technological facilities, and of organizational forms. New hospital buildings, technological advances, changes in organizational structures and financial constraints are the prime concerns. These are, of course, far from being the only aspects of hospital life. A great deal depends on the skills and management of staff, the availability of finance, changes in the patterns of disease and hospital usage, and so on. These factors will not be ignored, but they will be treated mainly in relation to the prime focus.

However, a firm caveat needs to be entered to the effect that good medicine and nursing can be (and frequently are) practised in old buildings, and even with poor local management. Equally, local managers may be doing their remarkable best yet be undone by ill-considered national reforms which are forced upon them, or by low-quality clinical practice within their institutions (which managers can seldom, if ever, closely control). The latter may never be discovered, or (increasingly likely these days) it may bring both political and media criticism down upon their hospitals. Nothing written here should be interpreted as a judgement of particular individuals.

6.4 SOURCES AND METHODS

Sources are a crucial feature of any historical account. In this case we had generous access to both persons and papers, although the nature of the documentation differed somewhat on either side of the Channel.

One reason for choosing the period since the 1960s was that a good proportion of the key decision-makers were still alive and potentially available for interview. In the event, we were able to interview all the hospital chief executives for both the Brighton and Leuven hospitals for virtually the whole period, plus a good number of other senior figures, including some with broader political responsibilities. In all we conducted 17 interviews with the key players and observers, using a standard schedule of questions but departing from that if the respondent wanted to lead us onto new or different issues. Records of these interviews were usually sent to the respondents so that they could correct any mistakes and add further thoughts if they so wished. We also examined a large number of documents. In Leuven we were able to see speeches and policy papers, consultancy reports, an example of a strategic plan and a number of retrospective accounts produced for the 75th anniversary of the foundation of the university hospital in 2004. In Brighton the documentation was more extensive. Hospital Board minutes and planning documents were available back to 1993. A full set of the monthly local *Health Bulletin* was analysed back to that journal's foundation in 1967. The Brighton newspaper, *The Argus*, has an archive which enabled us to track down reports on the hospital going back to 1985. The far greater public documentation for the Brighton case probably reflects the fact that it is a unit within a publicly accountable National Health Service, whereas Leuven University Hospital is a non-profit foundation, subject to government regulation but not a direct part of the state apparatus, even if it treats and relies upon public patients largely paid for through the Belgian national health insurance system. But it also reflects a more general difference in political cultures: as one of our Leuven interviewees put it to us in mid-2006: 'the debate on public disclosure is only just starting in this country' (interview 9).

The research was carried out from 2006 to 2008.

6.5 THE BRIGHTON HOSPITAL STORY, 1965–2005

Now it is necessary to fill in somewhat more detail concerning the two stories. Unsurprisingly, this produces a more complicated picture, in which Brighton's 'failure' and Leuven's 'success' become more shaded and nuanced. It is important to understand national and local political contexts, issues of geography and place, the management strategies, the climate of thought and a number of other factors.

Table 6.1 summarizes the main turning points of the development of the Brighton hospital system.

Despite the apparent neatness of Table 6.1, the evolution of hospitals in Brighton cannot be read exclusively, or even primarily, as just a local story. For the first 15 years of the existence of the National Health Service

Table 6.1   The Brighton story

Period	Main events
1960s	Brighton and Lewes have two major hospitals (the RSCH and the Brighton General) and 11 smaller hospitals. Major redevelopment of the RSCH is planned and the first part of a large three-part tower block is built at the end of the decade.
1970s	Second and third parts of the tower block are cancelled. Instead a new greenfield site hospital is proposed at the Falmer site, near to the new University of Sussex. Because of the mid-1970s fiscal crisis central government refuses to provide the necessary capital investment to finance this project.
1980s	Piecemeal developments at the Royal Sussex and the Brighton General. The smaller hospitals begin to close down and merge with the two larger units. In the late 1980s the health authorities put forward a proposal for a major new hospital at Holmes Avenue, Hove. This would coexist with the RSCH, giving two 'hot' sites for the town.
1990s	Holmes Avenue proposal is rejected by the government (although a polyclinic is sited there instead). Brighton General declines (still consisting mainly of mid-19th century workhouse buildings) and begins to lose acute services but the Royal Sussex gains a major new building on site. More small hospitals close.
2000s	The Royal Sussex scores very badly in the national government quality league tables, and at the same time becomes one of the hospitals with the largest budget overspends in the country (2005). Central government sends in a team of accountants. On the other hand, a total of almost €100 million worth of new investment is put into the RSCH site, creating new buildings and refurbishing old. Also, after negotiations with the two local universities a medical school is set up.

(NHS) virtually no new hospitals were built anywhere in England. Then the 1962 Hospital Plan unlocked the situation at national level, so starting our story in the 1960s makes sense. More specifically, throughout the period under scrutiny the main Brighton hospitals have been constituent parts of the UK National Health Service and, more specifically, of a varying sequence of superordinate area, district, regional, strategic and NHS trust authorities. The first major restructuring of this organizational superstructure took place in 1974, and further important upheavals followed in 1982, 1985, 1993, 2001 and 2006 (Pollitt, 2007). The periodic proposals for major new hospital construction in Brighton tended to founder at one or more of these higher levels – at region, or in the ministry itself, or at HM Treasury. One of the main reasons for this was that one thing new hospitals inescapably require is capital – and lots of it – and in the NHS system capital could only be obtained from above. However, the authorities 'above' had far more to worry about than Brighton's wishes and needs. They had to look at which were the most urgent needs across the whole region. The ministry had to look at what were the national policy priorities. The Treasury had to look at the state of the economy and of public finances, and to take consequential decisions about what should be the overall level of public investment. Multilevel, networked governance is nothing new to the NHS.

So why didn't the 'higher levels' furnish the capital Brighton so clearly needed and demanded? It appears that there is at least a three-part answer to this. First, Brighton may have been needy, but it was not the neediest place in the area or region. Two other south coast towns – Eastbourne and Hastings – had hospital facilities that were judged to be in even worse condition, and they received priority capital to fund major new developments (interview 3). Second, Brighton was singularly unfortunate (or tactically clumsy) with the timing of its bids for new hospital development. The mid-1970s bid for a new hospital on the Falmer site (out of town, next to the university campus) coincided with the biggest public expenditure crisis since the Second World War. (Figure 6.1 shows the locations of the principal sites in this narrative.) Humiliatingly, the Labour government of the day had to go to the International Monetary Fund for a loan, and part of the price of that was a particularly savage series of public expenditure cuts. New public sector investment virtually disappeared for a while, the Falmer hospital included (interviews 3, 21). The second bid, in the late 1980s, combined a major redevelopment at the RSCH with a brand new medium-sized hospital at Holmes Avenue in Hove (the site was never going to be big enough to have a full-scale general hospital there). The bidding process dragged on for years, and in the end it too ran into a period of strict national capital rationing by the Treasury (accompanying the severe economic downturn at the end of the 1980s). The third reason was that the local elites never spoke with one voice – there was constant internal controversy. As one ex-Chief Executive said, despite a careful analysis of many possible sites, 'the harsh reality was that nobody could agree' (interview 18). To put it crudely (the actual dispositions were somewhat more subtle) local Brighton politicians were nervous about the closure of the old Brighton General while a new hospital was built in the rival town of Hove. Meanwhile the Hove politicians were keen on the Hove (Holmes Avenue) development, although many of the doctors were publicly critical of the impracticality of having two 'hot' sites (at RSCH and Holmes Avenue) because of the staffing and time implications of

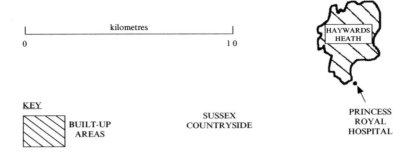

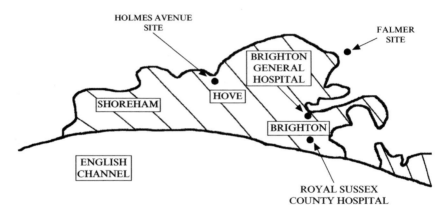

*Figure 6.1   The RSCH, Brighton General, Princess Royal, Holmes
Avenue and Falmer sites*

inter-site travel. One interviewee described the Holmes Avenue project as
'a preferred option for the local political elite, but absolutely not for the
local medical elite' (interview 22).This led to a public wrangle between
the doctors' leaders and the influential Conservative MP for Hove, Tim
Sainsbury (*Bulletin*, April 1991, p. 2 and May 1991, p. 7; *Evening Argus*,
1991). So this did not look to the region or the ministry like a unified bid
with all the key players behind it.

Eventually the Holmes Avenue proposal was downgraded to a poly-
clinic, and government approval was finally secured for almost £50 million
of new investment on the RSCH site. For the second or third time since
the mid-1960s, the substantial lobby that favoured a new, greenfield site
hospital lost out. They failed to get their project inserted in the national

programme. Redevelopment of the existing RSCH site finally became the central infrastructural policy for the Brighton and Hove area and its hinterland. This continues, 'despite the fact that it was not a very suitable site' (interview 21) and is 'relatively inaccessible' (interview 22).

Turning from capital to revenue expenditure, there were again 'higher reasons' why Brighton suffered a rough ride, manifesting itself in drearily regular 'crises' and round of cuts, dutifully reported in the *Brighton Health Bulletin* and the local paper, the *Brighton Argus* (see, for example, *Brighton Health Bulletin*, 1980, p. 2). Being part of a national service, it was not only capital that was rationed on a regional or national basis but also current spending. From 1976 onwards these area and regional budgetary comparisons took a very particular form. In that year the government received and adopted the report of the Resource Allocation Working Party (RAWP). This recommended a new method for allocating NHS revenue funds. Instead of looking at last year's expenditure and adjusting it for inflation and new developments (that is, an incremental approach), the RAWP proposed to allocate funds where they were most needed, with need being measured by standardized mortality and morbidity statistics (Pollitt, 1987). In plain words this meant that revenue monies went to areas that had sicker populations – which, by and large, meant a shift of resources out of southern England (wealthy, healthy) to northern England (poorer, sicker). Clearly this was not good news for the South East Region, or, within that, for Brighton. Throughout the 1980s it led to persistent complaints by doctors and managers in Brighton that they were 'underfunded' (interview 3). Yet the accuracy of these claims were contested by others, and contemporary studies of the effects of the RAWP formula, conducted at regional and departmental level, apparently did not show Brighton as a particularly hard-hit case (interview 18).

The constraining influence of 'higher levels' on the wishes of top managers and medical staff in Brighton appears to have become more, rather than less, sharp as the years have gone by. The focus of control moved beyond broad issues of capital and revenue, and concentrated more and more on specific aspects of performance. According to one long-standing Brighton manager the Regional Health Authority during the 1980s had constantly probed and questioned (and sometimes said 'no') but had basically maintained a civilized and constructive dialogue (interviews 3, 7). From the late 1980s, however, there was a shift. Much of the top-down direction was now originating in Whitehall itself rather than at area or regional level. As early as 1993 – the year the new trust came into existence – one finds the board minutes dominated by national, not local initiatives: waiting list targets, financial targets, market testing of services, the 'New Deal' for junior doctors and so on. Under the New Labour administration from 1997 Whitehall's grip intensified. In the late 1990s and early twenty-first century there was 'much more interference and even bullying' (interview 3). One experienced ex-Chief Executive acknowledged that nowadays 'there was an obsession with top-down performance management', and that under Alan Milburn's period as Secretary of State (1999–2003) central 'performance management went into orbit' (interview 18). 'We are now performance managed to the nth degree' (interview 18). Nationally (as we saw in Chapter 3, Table 3.2) many chief executives had lost their jobs for perceived performance failures, and fear and disillusionment had become widespread. There grew up 'a culture of bullying' by the ministry and their regional offices: 'it is *so* counterproductive' (interview 22).

One brighter note in the history of the Brighton hospital system was the setting up, in 2001 of a medical school, linking the hospital to the two Brighton universities. Again this was connected to central government, in the sense that the latter had decided to encourage a limited number of new medical schools, and Brighton's bid was (eventually) one of the successful ones. The first attempt to bid failed because parts of the University of Sussex (seen by the government as an essential partner) were 'as cold as custard' towards the idea (interview 15). Eventually, however, the academic politics of it was sorted out, and a successful application, binding the hospital trust and the universities of Sussex and of Brighton, was made. The existence of a medical school not only gave an academic flavour to medical life, it also boosted research, brought in extra money, offered new possibilities for clinicians who wanted to develop beyond their day-to-day clinical practice and was 'really, really good for morale' (interview 22).

However, by 2005, as indicated earlier, the trust was in crisis, hit by a large overspend, a score of zero stars in the government's performance league tables, and a deeply embarrassing undercover TV documentary showing indefensible nursing practices on a geriatric ward. How had this come about? One persuasive story is that the trust had entered a period of instability, during which management had 'taken its eye off the ball' (interview 25). Previously, there had been only three chief administrators and managers since the NHS was created back in 1948. Then the incumbent Chief Executive (CE) had fallen ill and there had suddenly been a succession of three acting or temporary CEs in the space of 12 months. Moreover, during this time there had been a number of major new developments which had distracted attention from the basic business of controlling finance and monitoring the quality of the hospital's services. First, there was a merger of Brighton with Mid-Sussex, bringing the Princess Royal – quite a modern hospital at nearby Haywards Heath – into the same organization as the RSCH. Second, there had been the arrival of a Medical School, as described in the previous paragraph. Initially, this had been a statutorily separate organization. Third, there were problems with the development of a private hospital on the Haywards Heath site, where, in the initial stages, there were quality issues plus a modicum of tension between some of the doctors most involved and the trust management. In addition to all this, there had been a kind of 'cultural drift', during which a previously slightly autocratic style of management had become diluted and some of the clinical directors (top doctors) had begun to operate as barons bidding for their own territory instead of taking collective responsibility for finding solutions.

The instability was arrested by the arrival of a new Chief Executive, Peter Coles, in 2004. To clarify and fix internal accountability he reorganized the nine existing Clinical Directorates into three Clinical Divisions, and discouraged details being passed up the line to the top. The eventual impact of these reforms were still unclear at the time our account ends in 2005. As explained in Chapter 2, a significant consequence of the nature of the national political system is that single-party governments have been able to reach out and apply their current organizational doctrines within the NHS rapidly and without much direct constraint. The unending parade of reforms and new initiatives since the early 1980s is testimony to central government's unfettered powers both to meddle and to mend. The following is no more than a selection of the major restructurings that impacted directly on the Brighton hospitals:

- 1974: NHS reorganization. Introduction of system of 'consensus management teams', in line with national policy. Relations between the Brighton District Health Authority and the East Sussex Area Health Authority were difficult throughout the remainder of the 1970s (interview 3).
- 1982: Brighton becomes a District Health Authority as part of the national reorganization into districts, areas and regions.
- 1985: Introduction of general managers at each level, replacing the previous system of 'consensus management'.
- 1989–92: The 1989 *Working for Patients* White Paper (see Chapter 2) ushered in the era of hospital trusts competing as 'providers' in an internal market. Brighton applied to the government to become a 'first wave' trust, on the understanding that a capital spending programme of about €25 million would be part of the new status. When it became clear that less than €1 million would actually be on the table, the authority withdrew its application. 'There was a unanimous view that we had been misled' (interview 3).
- 1993: Under a new Chief Executive the RSCH finally became part of Brighton Health Care Trust – an independent public corporation in the NHS internal market.

- 2001: The system of eight Regional Offices was abolished and replaced by four Regional Directorates of Health and Social Care.
- 2003: The four Regional Directorates were themselves abolished and replaced by 28 Strategic Health Authorities.

It would be wrong, however, to suggest that local politics had no influence at all on the Brighton hospital system. Although after the 1989 White Paper local authorities lost their direct representation on the boards and authorities that were supposed to oversee hospitals, they still possessed other, more direct means of constraint. Most significantly, they were the guardians of land-use planning, and they wielded these powers to considerable effect (interviews 18, 20, 22). In the case of the 1990s redevelopment of the RSCH site Brighton Council drove a very hard bargain over car parking. There had been 'considerable difficulties with the local Council' (interview 24). Ironically, in the early 1960s the RSCH site had been somewhat bigger, but the hospital had been obliged by then prevailing government policies to sell part of their land to the Council. Decades later, when they tried to ease their congestion problems by buying extra land in precisely that area, the Council rejected their attempts.

6.6   THE LEUVEN HOSPITAL STORY, 1965–2005

Again, the main events are summarized in tabular form (Table 6.2).

A federal-level hospital policy began to emerge in Belgium during the mid-1960s – just prior to the launching of the idea for a new, greenfield site KUL Hospital. The first Hospital Act came at the end of 1963, and introduced the idea of planning the hospital system as a whole. The first national plan itself appeared in 1966 (European Observatory on Health Care Systems, 2000).

The early years of the project for a new KUL hospital were remarkable in many ways. *De splitsing* was a national political crisis, and one where the most dramatic manifestations were centred on KUL. The Flemish politicians and academic leaders were, as they saw it, decisively ending more than a century of dominance of their half of the country by a patronising Francophone elite. This provided the immediate backdrop for the emergence of the new hospital, envisioned from the outset as an international-class Flemish teaching hospital. 'We can do it as well as the French universities' (interview 5).

As usual, political opportunity favoured the prepared. During the 1960s the Director of St Rafaël had carried out a study of 55 university hospitals, looking for the most suitable solution for future development (Blanplain,

Table 6.2   The Leuven story

Period	Main events
1960s	1968: KUL splits between Francophones and Flemish speakers. The KUL Rector appoints a young doctor to lead the project for a new university hospital (extensive research into different hospital designs already having been undertaken).
1970s	Support coalesces around a major new development on the Gasthuisberg site at the edge of the city. Rival plans for redeveloping city centre hospitals gradually fade. The Medical Director secures a new salary arrangement for medical staff that binds them closely to the collective success of the new hospital. Construction gets under way. In 1973 the new hospital and the two principal existing hospitals (St Räfael and St Pieter) were brought under a single, coordinated management.
1980s	1985: inauguration of new UZ buildings on Gasthuisberg site. Rapid growth of beds and income.
1990s	UZ suffers a major financial crisis in 1997/98. Management consultants are called in and the top management arrangements are changed. The hospital is more closely bound in to the university's governance structures.
2000s	UZ returns to a positive financial balance, and is placed top of almost all categories in a national quality survey of primary care doctors. It appears to be the largest and best hospital in the country.

2004, p. 9). (St Rafaël was one of two university hospitals within the old city of Leuven, and attached to KUL – St Rafaël was the Flemish one and St Pieter was the Francophone one. Geographically they are virtually back-to-back. This twinning symbolized the divisions between the two language communities in Belgium.) So at the time of *de splitsing* the senior medical establishment at KUL already had ideas for the way ahead. Furthermore, *de splitsing* led to the need for the Francophones ejected from Leuven to redevelop their medical facilities, which they did by building a new university at Louvain-la-Neuve and a new medical school at Wouluwe St Pierre, an eastern suburb of Brussels. These new projects involved considerable federal government finance and so, by the unwritten rules of the Belgian political game, the Flemings were also entitled to ask for something comparable (interview 9). And at that moment there were no serious Flemish rivals – no other Flemish university was proposing a major new tertiary hospital. KUL was, in fact, in a strong position. Not only had it been so centrally involved in *de splitsing*, but it had also been responsible for training more than two-thirds of Flemish doctors.

So the politics of the situation were crucial. Once the federal government gave its permission for the building of a new hospital, everything else followed. The federal government provided a 60 per cent subsidy itself and the remainder was borrowed from banks, but these loans were reimbursed over a 30-year period through an element in the running cost payments which the hospital received – also from central government. Getting government permission was eased by the coherence and relatively small size of the Flemish elite. In the allocation of ministerial portfolios at the federal level the Ministry of Health usually went to a Christian Democrat (at least until the late 1980s) and the new UZ at Leuven was every inch (or we should say every millimetre) a Christian Democrat (CD) project (though not only a CD project) (interviews 6, 10). KUL and the medical school were closely connected not only to the political party but also to the Roman Catholic hierarchy (the university's Chancellor is, ex officio, the Cardinal Archbishop of Mechelen-Brussel). All these fractions of the Flemish elite could be expected to welcome the idea of a major new hospital run by a Christian institution rather than by the state. It was possible, at least temporarily, to achieve a unity – or near unity – that would have been far more difficult in a much bigger, more diverse country like the UK.

However, not everything was plain sailing. There was one rival – an internal one – for the scheme to build a brand new hospital outside the city at the St Gasthuisberg site. This was a proposal to rebuild and merge the two inner city hospitals, St Rafaël and St. Pieter's. It was supported by a group of Flemish medical staff led by the then Dean of the Medical faculty. The contest was settled in a way unthinkable within the hierarchical British NHS – by allowing both projects to proceed until one of them became an obvious winner and the other an obvious loser. That is why, in 2006, it was still possible to walk around an empty, decaying 1970s tower block which was to have been part of the new inner city hospital, had it not become clear that: (1) there would not be enough money to finish both projects; and (2) the Gasthuisberg project embodied more modern and progressive concepts of care, and commanded a stronger network of support, including the Minister and the Rector of KUL (interview 9).

From the mid-1970s to the late 1980s the new hospital grew and grew, and its finances remained tolerably healthy. There were fluctuations, with downswings into losses in the early 1980s and early 1990s, but this pattern was understood to be largely the outcome of a system in which university hospitals developed new treatments and technologies and were only fully reimbursed for these some years later, when the federal payment authorities had adjusted their payment categories to accommodate the novelties. This decade was, therefore, something of a golden age. At the formal inauguration in January 1985 the KUL Rector referred to the ambitious new hospital as the result of nearly 20 years of planning, and thanked the government for supporting the investment without insisting on too much detailed control (De Somer, 1985). The UZ Director, Professor Peers, then spoke, emphasizing the special characteristics of a university hospital. He noted the need to integrate a highly diverse range of specialist services, the high turnover of patients (many being quickly returned to their local hospitals or primary care doctors), the need for a large size (to support 24/7 availability of the full range of services and the large hinterland, stretching well beyond the region; Peers, 1985). No doubt with the presence in his audience of the Prime Minister and Minister of Health in mind, he then devoted a substantial part of his speech to the need for the government fully to recognize the higher costs per bed day of university hospitals in its reimbursement system. He noted, inter alia, that, if one compared university hospitals in Leuven, West Berlin, Leiden, London and San Francisco, the budget per bed was lowest in London, then next-to-lowest in Leuven.

Thereafter UZ Leuven became, de facto, steadily more independent of the central KUL authorities – why would the latter interfere when everything seemed to be going well (interviews 6, 9, 19)? In the end, however, the growth-and-independence formula seemed to come unstuck. From the late 1980s the Belgian federal authorities had been tightening reimbursement formulae and rules, trying to get a grip on soaring hospital care expenditures and 'surplus' beds. Between 1980 and 1990 the number of hospital beds per 1000 Belgian inhabitants fell from 6.67 to 5.65. UZ Leuven seems to have been slow to anticipate this, with the result that by 1996/97 a large deficit had developed and the rate of growth of activity had slowed. Many new staff were appointed during a financial upswing and the full impact of their additional salaries was felt as the financial cycle turned down (interview 19). Different parties to this crisis still disagree about the seriousness of the underlying position (interviews 5, 6, 9, 10). 'I don't think there was a financial crisis at the time', says one well-placed interviewee. Another opined that: 'It's delicate. It was not a real crisis, in fact.' A third, equally well placed, was firmly of the opinion that the hospital's financial losses were huge and 'we had to act quickly', and a fourth confirmed that the financial situation had been out of control. But, whatever ultimate truths might lie beneath the accountancy, it is also clear that more was involved in the upheavals than just a negative bank balance. There were also issues of management styles and systems. A feeling had grown in some quarters that the university, although still the final guarantor of the UZ's finances, had lost control over its strategy. There were also concerns about the degree of internal control: were the mechanisms in place to steer this large and expensive organization in a rapidly changing financial and political environment?

At any event, in October 1997 the Management Committee decided that a major structural reform of the hospital was essential. The management consultancy McKinsey's was brought in to make a report, and this diagnosed a serious lack of necessary information for top management, a lack of transparency and a failure to develop detailed processes for budgeting and strategic decision-making (McKinsey's, 1998). Significant changes swiftly followed. Professor Peers stepped down as Director, and a new governance regime was instituted which strengthened KUL's control of the UZ and made the Vice-Rector for Biomedical Sciences the Chair of the hospital's supervisory board. In effect these changes marked the passing of the pioneering generation of leaders who, from the late 1960s, had created the new UZ Leuven and presided over its rapid growth (interview 19).

It is therefore worth noting that, in terms of organizational form and management continuity, UZ Leuven has, by the standards of the British NHS, been very stable indeed. The organizational form – a Christian-based university hospital, financed mainly by the state but not of the state – remains unchanged, although there have been a number of major adjustments to the reimbursement formulae which have necessitated management action. In more than 30 years the hospital has had just two directors. The major structural change was the tightening of KUL supervision represented by the 1998 insertion of a Vice-Rector as ex officio Chair of the supervisory board – a significant indicator in Flemish terms, but hardly an upheaval by the standards of NHS restructuring.

In the early years of the twenty-first century UZ Leuven enjoyed a financial upswing that seemed to confirm the correctness of the actions taken during the 1997–98 crisis. By 2006, however, there were some clouds on the horizon. Politically, Leuven had long ago lost the pre-eminent position it had held during the 1960s and 1970s. Since the late 1980s the relevant Minister was no longer from the Christian Democrat Party. The tightly knit first generation of the independent Flemish elite had reached the ends of their careers, and their successors were facing a more complicated world. Other university hospitals had sprung up in Flanders, obliging UZ Leuven to begin building a formal network among other Flemish hospitals to give it a better bargaining position than it would have had if it had tried to stand alone (UZ Leuven, 2000). Acquisition of new medical technologies also allowed some non-university hospitals to provide competitive services (interview 9). One loyal UZ Leuven manager expressed the anxiety thus: 'Leuven is nothing: a small town' (interview 19). The federal government redoubled its efforts to control hospital spending and reduce perceived over-bedding, producing financial crises at a number of institutions (Joye, 2003). Nevertheless, the story closes in 2005 with UZ Leuven as the biggest, best-regarded teaching hospital in the country, an undeniable achievement, both professionally and politically.

6.7   CONCLUDING REMARKS

The first impression taken from the comparison of the two hospital stories is of marked differences – the very different political contexts, the closeness of the Flemish elite, the speed of the construction of the new UZ Leuven, as contrasted with the relentless, incremental, bureaucratic politics of the NHS and the repeated disappointments of those Brighton managers and medical staff who believed that a new hospital was the best solution to the area's problems of acute provision. Brighton had its ups and downs – and among the former the new investments on the RSCH site from the mid-1990s onwards have been weighty and significant. Yet it never experienced the cathartic moment – a historical Earthquake if ever there was one – which *de splitsing* represented for Leuven. If Leuven managed a 'great leap forward' in 1969 then the best that can be said of Brighton is that it shuffled forward for most of our 40 years, breaking into a brisk stride only for a few years at the beginning of the twenty-first century (a period of unusual general largesse from central government as far as the NHS was concerned). And this was not just a matter of bricks and mortar (although that has certainly been one of our central foci) because the new UZ Leuven also represented a philosophy of integrated care and a new way of binding in the loyalty of medical staff to the institution.

It is worth dwelling for a moment on the difference between the political processes in the two countries. Our interviews with key actors gave a very strong impression of the nature of that difference – and of the different realities of 'multilevel governance' in Belgium and England. In Belgium multilevel governance in health care is simultaneously more integrated and yet more fragmented. It is more integrated in the sense that contacts between the local players and the national players are closer, more informal and more frequent. A hospital boss can talk directly to the Minister, and at the same time be personally known and accepted as a fellow medic by the doctors heading the main service departments in the hospital. Politicians hold roles at local, regional and national levels, moving from being Mayor of this to Minister of that, and sometimes back again. The scale of the whole network is obviously considerably smaller than in England, which helps everyone to know everyone else. In the Brighton case, however, local managers are many steps away from the Minister. They may see him or her very occasionally, on brief visits or at rare meetings, but these are formal and infrequent occasions. Most of the time the manager has to handle hierarchical bureau-politics – working detailed proposals up through several layers of hierarchy, with formal scrutiny and veto points at each level. 'Multilevel governance' in this context is very one-sided: it is about what 'they' at the top of the centralized, national hierarchy will or will not do to or for 'us' down here in Brighton. It is about competing with other towns or other regions in planning games whose rules are devised at the centre. It is multilevel, certainly, but the local level is almost always the supplicant rather than the collaborator or the partner. As one of our Brighton interviewees said in 2007: 'Local autonomy has more or less gone now' (interview 24).

Yet we certainly should not idealize the Belgian system. Whilst it appears more informal, more comprehensible, more 'political' and less centralized, it is also handicapped in a number of ways. It is fragmented between many political parties, divided between the three main geographical regions and their two languages, and therefore often slow-moving or even totally bogged down. The implementation of national policies can often be weak, and there is no sense of a strong central executive that will drive through programmes in the way that central government can in England. One reason why the space for local initiatives may seem greater in Belgium than England is the relative weakness of the federal ministries in dealing with hospitals, municipalities and other subnational authorities.

A further Anglo-Belgian contrast, from the mid- or late 1980s, was huge stress on better management as a principal solution for the NHS's problems. This does have an echo in Belgium, but only a relatively muted one. In Belgium, although the principle of non-medical management has been accepted, the fact is that UZ Leuven has always been managed at the top by individuals trained as doctors (even if they have subsequently also been trained as managers).

Yet alongside these real differences it is possible to detect some significant parallel trends. We are struck by three in particular:

1. The constant struggle by governments to limit the growth of public spending on health care, and the impacts this has on hospital management.
2. The growing attention to hospital management itself, as a new 'science' or set of solutions.
3. The impacts of social and technological change on the role and distribution of hospital services.

Every Western government – not only in Belgium and the UK – has been obliged, from the late 1970s onwards, to attempt to restrain the growth of public spending on health care. It is an international problem, endlessly discussed internationally as well as nationally. As we observed in Chapter 1, this huge fiscal pressure is fuelled by a number of virtually universal trends. People live longer and the rapidly developing medical technologies can do more and more for them. As several of our interviewees confirmed, the expectations of hospital patients have also risen. They expect prompt and respectful attention, minimal pain, pleasant surroundings and effective care – all to higher degrees than in the past. Even partially meeting these expectations costs money. Yet it is extremely hard for politicians to push most of this cost back onto the sufferers, whether the third-party payments come directly from the government (as in the UK) or indirectly through a system of subsidized social insurance (as in Belgium) (Harrison and McDonald, 2008, Chapter 1). Direct cuts to health care entitlements are some of the most unpopular things politicians can advocate, and very few are prepared to volunteer to become targets for public outrage. What happens instead, therefore, is a whole series of measures to clip the edges of growth: marginally to increase 'co-payments' by patients; to limit the number of hospital beds; to constrain what hospitals charge; to promote more cost-effective forms of intervention and treatment; and so on. Both England and Belgium have experienced many policy initiatives of these kinds, and they certainly play a part in our two local stories. Just two examples will have to suffice. The 1997/98 financial crisis and management changes at UZ Leuven were at least partly connected to new policies of cost restraint being practised by the federal government. Meanwhile policies aimed at restraining the growth of NHS spending were at the bottom of several of Brighton's disappointments: from the government investment freeze of the mid-1970s that killed off any hope for a new hospital on the Falmer site to the withdrawal of Brighton's first application for trust status under the post-1989 internal market reforms when the board discovered that trust status would not bring with it anything like the large new capital injection which had been anticipated.

Although we argued earlier that more attention had been given to 'management' in the Brighton case than the Leuven case, that is not to say that Leuven has given it no attention at all. That would be far from the truth. That Belgian hospitals in general – and Leuven in particular – needed a strong dose of 'modern professional management' was a theme in a number of our interviews (5, 6, 10, 19). At the beginning of the UZ Leuven story the Belgian hospital sector 'really was a non-organized world' (interview 5). By the end it was not. The 1997/98 crisis had included a key analysis by external management consultants, a new system of hospital governance and the beginning of detailed strategic planning (see, for example, UZ Leuven, 2000). 'Management' as a phenomenon had not grown to the huge proportions that it had in the NHS and, in particular, Belgium had avoided the rapid turnover of non-medical managers at the tops of hospitals. (One English ex-Chief Executive observed to us that his 13-year period in office represented six times the then national average appointment span of an NHS hospital Chief Executive – interview 18.) Nevertheless, hospitals were definitely now seen as entities that needed professional management, management conducted on recognized principles, using generic management techniques and concepts.

Finally, we come to the impact of social and technological change on the management of hospitals. As was suggested above, hospital patients seem to have become more demanding, and to have done so during the same period in which the development of medical technologies appear to hold out more and more things that can be 'done' for more and more conditions. Our interviews were spattered with references to different manifestations of this. One administrator with half a century of NHS experience commented that the scandal of nurses maltreating geriatric patients in the RSCH could have happened at any time in the last 70 years, but it had achieved national prominence in 2005 because the media were more aggressively investigatory and their public was far less tolerant of such neglect (interview 21). Another experienced manager commented that patients were less willing to put up with pain and discomfort than had been the case a generation earlier (interview 20). And a senior clinician who had carried major management responsibilities remarked that security management had become a major topic at the RSCH because the number of assaults on staff had risen considerably over the past decade (interview 24). In the case of UZ Leuven one of the pioneers told us that although the hospital had managed to create a patient-friendly atmosphere it was now time to move beyond that in order to give patients a much larger and more active role in their own care process (interview 5).

Meanwhile technological change poses a constant challenge to the form, and sometimes to the very existence of hospitals. Improved technologies allow complex treatments to be delivered safely in a variety of settings – day centres, smaller hospitals, the offices of primary care physicians, and so on. Advice can be delivered electronically instead of by face-to-face appointments. Big tertiary hospitals like UZ Leuven and the RSCH have to try to keep up with these changes, and to retain their status as research centres as well as nodes in the network of treatment. Although such developments in medical technology have not been the central focus of our research, we have seen plenty of evidence that they are common to the two countries and hospitals, and that they do impact not only on infrastructures ('Where can we fit this new machine into the existing hospital buildings?') but also on management itself ('Where can we find the capital for a must-have €5 million MRI scanner and what new staff and new training is needed so that we can operate it?'). If 'management' is centrally concerned with making the best use of scarce resources, then a world where new drugs and equipment are constantly coming onto the market is bound to be one where the question of prioritization is ever-present and usually uncomfortable.

7. What happened locally? Police

7.1 INTRODUCTION

Having set out national police policies in Chapter 4 we will now turn to two local police jurisdictions, to see what policy change (or policy stasis) looked like closer to the ground. As in Chapter 6, we will look at Brighton and Leuven, although here we immediately encounter one important difference between the two countries. Whereas Leuven has had its own police force since 1796, Brighton is only a division within a much larger police area – the Sussex force. This is typical of the more general national patterns – police areas in England are much bigger than in Belgium. As we will see, this immediately makes for substantial differences in terms of the size of forces, the levels of internal specialization, and the range of technologies and problems with which the 'local' police deal. This size difference is partly a reflection of the fact that, whereas the local Belgian forces had always operated with the umbrella of a national police force (the Rijkswacht), England has never had a national force. (However, as we saw in Chapter 4, it has developed more and more specialist units at the national level, such as the Serious Organised Crime Agency created in 2006 or the National Policing Improvement Agency established under the 2006 Police and Justice Act. But these are not police forces, they are special units.)

7.2 SOURCES AND METHODS

We should first say that we are extremely grateful for the generous cooperation we received from the Sussex Police and the Leuven Police (De Leuvense Politie). They made available documents and records and also afforded us 20 lengthy, semi-structured interviews with senior officers and political leaders, both past and present (12 of these were in Sussex, eight in Leuven – for further details see the Appendix).

As with hospitals, one immediately noticeable difference between the two organizations was the amount of detail and the number of documents in the public domain. English police forces publish more reports and more detailed reports than do their Belgian counterparts, and many of these are more obviously 'glossy' documents intended for public consumption. Nevertheless, the Leuven Police furnished us with a number of key documents and, for example, their current local security plan (Politie PZ Leuven, 2005) is a 200-page document packed with staffing, financial and operational information.

In addition to such official sources we have looked at local newspaper coverage of the police. In the case of the Sussex Police we have also had the unusual benefit of being able to read three recent crime novels by Peter James, all set in Brighton and Hove (James, 2006a, 2006b, 2007). In writing these novels James enjoyed close cooperation with the Sussex Police (including some of the officers we interviewed) and the operational details and local colour in the books provided us with a highly enjoyable, if unconventional, additional source. The most famous Belgian detective, Hercule Poirot, was a private operator and conducted most of his cases in England. Thus we did not find his exploits, interesting though they may have been, quite so relevant as a source for the Belgian reforms of 1965–2005.

7.3   THE SUSSEX POLICE: BACKGROUND

The Sussex Police area is full of contrasts. It has two urban centres with pockets of poverty and relatively high crime rates – Brighton and Hastings (see Figure 7.1). Brighton has the second-largest police station in England, and the post of Divisional Commander there is coveted as a career stepping stone to the Assistant Chief Constable level. Most of Sussex, however, is quiet and rural – and fairly rich. But in the north lies Gatwick – London's second airport. This is policed under a contract between the Sussex force and the airport authority. It supports a special police unit – heavily armed and, nowadays, trained in counter-terrorism techniques. The internal contrasts of Sussex were illustrated by several of our interviewees, who mentioned that car speeding was a real problem in the sleepy rural lanes of Sussex, but hardly in the traffic jams of Brighton.

7.4   THE SUSSEX POLICE: TIMELINE

1968
Sussex Police formed from a merger of five previous forces. In the 1960s the force had been autocratic and hierarchical, 'very military' (Interview 35 – ex-senior police officer). 'We policed the community the way we thought best. *We* were doing it to *them*'. As far as planning was concerned, 'We had no objectives' (interview 35).

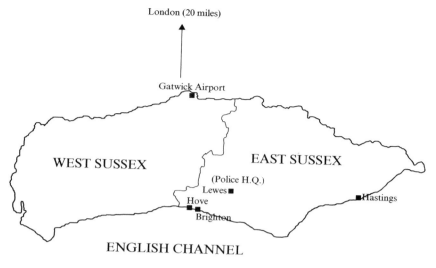

Figure 7.1   Map of Sussex

1975

Sex Discrimination Act. 'It was a truly unpleasant time', said one senior woman police officer: 'It had taken a long time for the fuss that started in 1975 to die down.' Previously woman police officers had only been allowed to work in units commanded by other women, and they could only work between 0900 and 2200. The changes triggered all sorts of cultural resistance, including nasty letters to the local Brighton paper, which had been pinned up in the (interviewee's) police station. 'We barely tolerated women' (interview 35 – ex-senior police officer; confirmed by several other interviewees).

1980

Chief Constable George Terry complained that: 'In this day and age, although it is understandable, almost everything is being measured in money! I am, however, somewhat at a loss to understand how one measures peace of mind in terms of cash . . .' (Sussex Police, 1980, p. i). He also mentioned as worrying: (1) the increase in the number of burglaries; (2) drink driving; and (3) the increase in the work of the Operations Room, especially the rapid rise in emergency calls (p. ii). Force strength was 2823 on 31 December 1980.

1981

The Chief Constable in his annual report referred to his continuing efforts to direct more of his officers to foot patrol: 'The result was the redeployment from a number of specialist roles, including a high proportion of sergeants, of a total of 146 officers' (p. 4). Is also reducing the vehicle fleet by 86. Offences up by 7.2 per cent, with percentage detected down from 50.2 per cent to 47.1 per cent. (It is interesting to note that the police were responding to demands to 'put bobbies back on the beat' even as early as the late 1970s.)

1982

The Chief Constable (CC) pointed out that in 1982, 62 025 crimes were reported compared with 29 124 in 1968 (a rise of 113 per cent). Over the same period manpower had risen from 2385 to 2822 (20 per cent).

The CC remarked that: 'The keynote for the future must indeed be the prevention of crime and to this end the help of the public as a whole is absolutely essential along with the inter-relationship of all law-enforcement agencies.' But he went on to say: 'The relationship between the police and the public should not be confused or directed solely towards the extreme development of what are being called consultative committees, otherwise our vociferous elements will wish to spend their time talking incessantly and hindering the preventative role of the police' (Sussex Police, 1982, p. 4). (As we saw in Chapter 2, this was the time when left-wing elements on the Greater London Council were attempting to set up Council committees that would monitor the police. This was regarded with great suspicion by many police, although by the end of our period it had become quite routine.)

> After three years of 'nil' growth all areas of the budget have been reviewed, pared and constantly monitored until on reaching the present stage there is no room left for manoeuvre. Since 77% of the total budget figure relates to salaries, it is difficult to see how it will be possible in the immediate future for the service to further develop with improved techniques, in order adequately to support the most important part of the service, the uniformed patrol officer. (p. 15).

1983

Roger Birch took over as Chief Constable, and opened his annual report by stating that: 'It is a well established fact that the style of policing unique to this country depends for its efficacy almost entirely on its acceptance and consent by the local community' (Sussex Police, 1983, p. 3). He suggested that changes recommended by the Scarman Report (see Chapter 4) were not necessary in Sussex, and gave his opinion that: 'there is no evidence to suggest a need for a major change in the area of consultation and . . . to introduce change for change's sake can be counter-productive' (p. 4).

1984

The *Sussex Police Annual Report 1984* referred to both 'the substantial and protracted role played by the Sussex Police in providing their share of aid to hard-pressed Chief Constables in the mining areas' (p. 3) and 'the trauma of the terrorist attack on the Grand Hotel, Brighton, which became instant world news and which tested the professional skills and morale of the Force as never before'.

The bomb attack (carried out by the IRA against government leaders in Brighton for the Conservative Party Conference) took place at 0245 on 12 October. Senior politicians were killed and injured, and Mrs Thatcher herself only just escaped. The Grand Hotel bombing became a leading news item worldwide. In the search for evidence 3790 dustbins and 36 skips of debris were recovered and removed, in poor weather, and 40 000 vehicles daily were diverted while the site was secured and investigated.

The annual report also mentioned that the Police and Criminal Evidence Act would require extensive training for every officer, and the extension of the fixed penalty system would also require more training – as well as adding an administrative burden.

The report refers to Home Office Circular 114/83, *Manpower, effectiveness and efficiency in the police service.* The annual report says 'Perhaps more than any other of recent times, this circular has concentrated the minds of senior and middle management levels in the service' (p. 50). Emphasizes the importance of timely and accurate management information.

Offences up 9.1 per cent to 63 971. Detection down 1.2 per cent to 38.3 per cent.

1985

The Chief Constable opened by mentioning the importance of community links, and singled out 'the growing enthusiasm of the public for Neighbourhood Watch' (Sussex Police, 1985, p. 2)

He also mentioned that an investigation carried out into the adequacy of the policing arrangements for the Conservative Party Conference exonerated the Sussex force from all blame, adding that: 'The implications for the future in terms of manpower and equipment are enormous but there can be no stepping back from the terrorist threat, which will not go away' (p. 2). (It is interesting to find statements like this a decade and a half before the 9/11 attacks.)

Later sections of the annual report show how other demands can undermine the intention to emphasize traditional, 'beat' policing:

Indeed, in June when police uncovered an alleged IRA bombing campaign planned for seaside towns, it was necessary to form a team to carry out enquiries and searches for a period of some three weeks. During that time there were 223 suspect packages and hoax bomb calls in the Division, all of which were investigated by members of that group. To help form such a team it was necessary temporarily to withdraw most of the Resident Constables in Brighton. Such was the measure of public feeling that many residents in the town wrote to the Chief Constable expressing their concern over that move.

The management services section recorded the large training requirements arising from PACE. It also mentioned the Transport Act, the Data Protection Act and the Prosecution of Offences Act. The comment was: 'The implementation of one major Act presents more than enough problems, but four statutes which radically affect policing systems and procedures simultaneously, are bound to impose additional pressures on an already overstretched Force.'

1986

The annual report mentioned that one aspect in which Sussex was 'ahead of the field' was:

the recently formed full-time, highly-trained Special Operations Unit with a responsibility for all security and protection duties, as well as for providing armed protection for VIPs or an armed response in case of potentially serious incidents involving firearms. (Sussex Police, 1986, p. 3)

(This is, of course, exactly the kind of development which takes officers away from traditional policing.)

Offences were up by 0.07 per cent and detections down by 15.8 per cent. Government grant constituted 42.5 per cent of income, and constituent authorities 41.5 per cent.

1987

The CC's foreword to the 1987 annual report began:

In writing this foreword I have concentrated at the expense of all else on a single subject which has far reaching consequences for the future well being of East and West Sussex, namely police manpower.

It is a stark fact that since 1979 the authorized establishment of the Sussex Police will have been increased by a mere 12 officers, if the special needs of Gatwick Airport are set aside' (Sussex Police, 1987, p. 2).

It went on to ask for 'a totally new approach to the way in which police establishments are determined and a willingness on the part of local and central government to grasp the nettle of financial implications' (p. 2).

For the first time this report contained short sections written by officers and civilian staff. The first, by Inspector George Divall, said: 'On starting at Shoreham I realized how uniform policing and policemen had changed. The job itself had become violent.'

3700 Neighbourhood Watch (resident participation) schemes were now operating in Sussex: 'The continued growth of schemes has inevitably created a problem in providing effective support from limited police resources' (p. 31). So Neighbourhood Watch assistants had been introduced on an experimental basis.

1987 was also the year in which the local authority in Brighton created a special committee for monitoring the police. A new advisor came from London who had had experience with the Greater London Council (GLC) system (see Chapter 4.2). Although this was politically a sensitive development, relations between the Sussex Police and this new committee never became as hostile as they had in the GLC (several interviews).

1988

The annual report opened with: 'Chief Constables cannot hope for additional police manpower unless they are able to demonstrate that they have gone as far down the road of civilianization as possible' (Sussex Police, 1988, p. 2).

The 1988 report included a 'Force Statement of Purpose', which said that:

> The aim of the Sussex Police is to contribute, in co-operation with other agencies in the community, to the development of the quality of life in Sussex by preserving a peaceful society, assisting those in need, protecting life and property and preventing and detecting offences. Sussex Police exists to provide a caring service to the public.

The total establishment numbered 2923, and 56 per cent of the Force budget went on police salaries, 12 per cent on pensions, 9 per cent on civilian salaries, 5 per cent on National Insurance.

1989

Chief Constable began his report by noting that: 'Sadly, many of the headlines have reflected alleged police impropriety or apparent inefficiency rather than success' (Sussex Police 1989, p. 2). But he went on to say: 'I happen to believe that we are equal to, if not better than, a large part of the private sector when it comes to the management of resources and that we are streets ahead of the majority in the business of managing people' (p. 2).

Commenting on the relations between the police, local authorities and central government, the CC said:

There are already signs that the balance of the tripartite arrangement is tilting towards the centre, the latest illustration of this being a move to the central control of capital expenditure which could well damage the initiatives of forward thinking and progressive Police Authorities such as Sussex. (Sussex Police, 1989, p. 3)

The 1989 report included an elaborate multi-page 'Force statement of purpose, goals and objectives'. It also included a section by the Organizational Monitoring Unit, which said:

The increasing use of performance indicators to assess police effectiveness and efficiency is becoming more and more prevalent for both the Audit Commission and the Home Office (through Her Majesty's Inspectorate of Constabularies Matrix of Indicators) have focused attention on the Police Service . . . the main derivations involve examinations of variables (crime, accidents, incidents etc) either per established officer or per 1,000 of population which enables some direct comparisons to be made between Forces. It is clear that the Home Office intends Police Forces to make use of this sort of data. (Sussex Police, 1989, p. 13)

1990

In the annual report the CC described the research project *Policing in Sussex*. A team from the University of Sheffield had designed a survey of public opinion; 646 people were interviewed, 341 of whom were randomly selected and the other 305 had been in contact with the police during the previous year. When asked about problems in their areas 57 per cent cited at least one, including traffic, noise, dogs, congregating youths and vandalism. Crime was rarely mentioned spontaneously, but burglary, vandalism and theft were seen as worrying. Only 27 per cent admitted a strong fear of crime, and this appeared to be affected by whether there was a community beat officer for the area and whether police were seen patrolling. 'There was overwhelming support, more than 85% for the concept of local officers, who were more clearly visible in the rural areas than in the towns' (Sussex Police, 1990, p. 11).

On 30 July Ian Gow, Conservative MP for Eastbourne, was killed by an IRA bomb which had been placed under his car at his home near Eastbourne.

1992

The last annual report of CC Sir Roger Birch. He used it to reflect on the changes after 39 years in the police:

The pace of life has quickened, moral standards have changed radically and the family bond has loosened. Society is restless and changing, at an accelerating pace but in an uncertain direction. Crime has escalated and knows no boundaries, national or international. The cancer of drugs is spreading and publicity given to mindless violence induces fear in even the most peaceful community. The phenomenal increase in traffic has added enormously to the police task. (Sussex Police, 1992, p. 3)

He continued: 'at a time when the financial outlook is bleak, it is more important than ever to establish our main priorities, recognizing that the police cannot do everything' (p. 4).

Actual crime was up 6.5 per cent (from 25 077 in 1991 to 26 935). The detection rate was marginally up from 22.5 per cent to 22.6 per cent.

1993
The first annual report with Paul Whitehouse as CC. He wrote that:

As the changes facing the police service nationally take effect Sussex Police, like every other Force, will increasingly be judged on its performance. There is thus a danger that our activities will concentrate too much on achievement in the short term. We need to devise long term plans to balance this effect. (Sussex Police, 1993, p. 2)

The report recorded that, after a major consultative exercise with the Police Authority and community groups, the *Sussex Police Standard* had been published. This 'landmark document' 'spelt out to the public the standard of service they properly expect from Sussex Police in each of those areas' (the areas were: response to calls, crime, public order and reassurance, traffic and community assistance).

1994/95
(From now on the annual reports followed the financial year rather than the calendar year.)

The CC reported that: 'The adoption during 1994 of our Force Crime Strategy enabled us to capitalize on the lessons learned during our anti-burglary initiative, Operation Bumblebee, launched the previous October. This was based on intelligence and actively targeting active criminals' (Sussex Police, 1995, p. 2). He also mentioned animal rights demonstrations at the port of Shoreham, where livestock exporters were operating. A major police operation had been required. The first Local Policing Plan for Sussex was now ready.

The CC also remarked that: 'I have made it clear that we will not allow our integrity to be compromised by the pressure to improve our position in national league tables' (p. 3).

The main body of the report gave details of the Force restructuring:

The aim was to identify police resources more clearly with the community so that policing can become more truly accountable. For this reason parishes were grouped into natural policing sectors. These sectors are to be the key units for the delivery of police services. (p. 6)

The Sussex Police Standard, published in 1993, set out the minimum levels of service the Sussex public is entitled to expect in five core areas of policing – crime, response to calls, public order and reassurance, traffic and community assistance. The Force Service Plan, and subsequently the Policing Plan for Sussex, set out targets against which to measure our performance. These targets have been set by the Chief Constable in consultation with the Sussex Police Authority and in response to the Key Policing Objectives set nationally by the Home Secretary. (p. 7)

13 August 1994: An IRA bomb exploded in Bognor Regis. Later the same day a larger bomb was found, unexploded, on the seafront in Brighton.

1995 saw a huge police operation at the port of Shoreham, just west of Brighton and Hove. Animal rights protesters attempted to prevent trucks carrying live animals for export from reaching the waiting ship. At first the police were surprised – 100 officers failed to control the situation. Subsequently up to 1300 officers were involved, with reinforcement being drawn from neighbouring police forces. The bill for police action soon exceeded €4 million. Eventually the police decided to limit their policing effort, which led to a partial ban on the controversial exports, and to court actions against the police.

At the same time (April) the CC found himself defending the low place Sussex had achieved in a national league table on crime detection. Paul Whitehouse argued that the league tables were calculated in a misleading way (*The Argus*, 1995, p. 1).

Also in 1995, the method of fixing the central government grant to police authorities changed. 'In practice the new system gave the Department of the Environment [local government ministry] a more influential role over police finances' (interview 4 – ex-senior police officer). In the same year police authorities were restructured (see Chapter 4.2 – 1994 Police and Magistrates' courts Act).

1997

The government agreed to pay €750 000 towards the cost of policing the Labour Party Conference in Brighton. Both major parties frequently held their annual conferences in Brighton and the cost of the extra security had hitherto fallen on Sussex taxpayers.

1998

In January armed police in Hastings shot dead James Ashley, while carrying out a drugs raid. It subsequently transpired that Ashley had been unarmed, and had not been one of the persons the police had been looking for. The incident, which became known as the 'Hastings Shooting' was immediately referred to the Police Complaints Authority and also became the subject of an independent investigation by senior police officers from outside the Sussex force. The Hastings Shooting became a major and ongoing media story. As it unravelled over the next three years six officers were suspended (including a Deputy Chief Constable) and eventually, in 2001, Chief Constable Paul Whitehouse took retirement. The aftermath of the shooting 'tore the superintending ranks apart. Everyone took sides . . . At that point we *began* to be a failing organization' (interview 13 – senior police officer). 'Massive ramifications' (interview 29 – senior police officer). It was 'a real watershed – we learned that if it wasn't written down it hadn't happened' (interview 14 – senior police officer)

2001
In July the merger of the Brighton and Hove police districts into a single division was approved. This followed the award of city status to Brighton and Hove combined.

After unprecedented pressure on the Sussex Police Authority from the Home Secretary (David Blunkett) over the Hastings Shooting, Chief Constable Paul Whitehouse gave notice 'with some sadness' of his intention to retire: 'my priority now is to protect the good name of the Sussex Police' (*Patrol*, August 2001, p. 3). 'We lost a lot when he left – he had encouraged a more open environment, more consultation, a more analytic, questioning approach' (interview 16 – ex-senior police officer, and other interviews). Deputy Chief Constable Maria Wallis took over temporary operational command of the Sussex force, until Ken Jones was appointed Chief Constable in 2002.

2002
Ken Jones – the new CC – pushed for visible up-front accountability and immediately launched a full-scale operational review. 'League tables have become much more important', performance indicators were vigorously applied to Basic Command Units (BCUs) and the Chief Constable would hold regular meetings interrogating his officers about their results (interviews 14 and 11). 'We've got to be a 24 hour service *and* achieve results. Performance has become almost your *raison d'etre*' (interview 11).

2002–03
The *Joint Annual Report of the Sussex Police Authority and the Chief Constable of Sussex Police* explained that, following a 15-month operational review, 42 Inspector-led neighbourhood police teams had now been

set up covering every part of Sussex. (Above that there were 12 Districts, each matching local authority areas and commanded by a Chief Inspector. Brighton and Hove consisted of three Districts.) It also mentioned 62 new Police Community Support Officers (PCSOs) who would be patrolling the streets. Crime fell again – 600 fewer recorded crimes than two years previously (3.1 per cent). The number of crimes detected increased by 5 per cent. The report showed detailed achievements in different aspects of crime against targets (for example, 'We aimed to reduce the number of domestic burglaries by 2% and increase the burglary detection rate to 18% . . . There was a 7.8% increase in burglaries and a detection rate of 12%' (p. 6).

> Police authorities in the south are seeing a reduction in central government funding for local policing as resources are switched to metropolitan police authorities and the north. This means that a greater contribution of the cost of the policing must be met locally. (p. 2)

48 per cent of funding came from Home Office grants, 10 per cent from Revenue Support Grants, 28 per cent from local Council Tax and 17 per cent from non-domestic rates.

2003–04

That there were two public consultation exercises each year, and the two top priorities for the public were: (1) more policing on the streets; and (2) better call-handling arrangements (Sussex Police Authority, 2004a, p. 2).

The report said that key crime indicators, including vehicle crime, were moving downwards, but anti-social behaviour had increased and was 'a key issue for policing in Sussex' (p. 4). More than 200 Police Community Support Officers were now deployed to help tackle this, 'helping to keep a lid on low level incidents – loutish behaviour, vandalism and the like' (p. 4).

The Annual Report included a section on an independent assessment of Sussex Police by Her Majesty's Inspectorate of Constabulary (HMIC). It said Sussex was rated as excellent in 3 areas, good in 7, fair in 5 and poor in only one – call handling.

2004–05

The annual report congratulated itself on having had Neighbourhood Policing Teams in place since 2003 (the government had just announced that it wanted them throughout the country by 2008) (Sussex Police Authority, 2005, p. 1).

The detection rate was up from 24.2 per cent to 25.4 per cent. Burglary (–13.5 per cent), robbery (–13.5 per cent), car crime (–19.1 per cent) and major violent crime (homicide, attempted murder and serious woundings) were all down. But overall recorded crime was up 4.3 per cent because of large increases in recorded total violent crime and criminal damage.

The report also had user satisfaction figures, which were mainly high (for example domestic burglary: 91.6 per cent of victims were satisfied overall)

The Sussex police website reported on the HMIC Report *Closing the Gap* on the structure of policing. The HMIC had put forward three options: merger of the Sussex, Surrey and Kent forces, merger of Sussex, Surrey and Hampshire, or merger of Sussex and Surrey. At a Police Authority meeting on 15 December 2005 all three were rejected. An alternative proposal was for much closer collaborative working, especially with Surrey (http://www.sussex.police.uk/about_us/annualreport_2005/index.asp).

7.5   THE SUSSEX POLICE: ANALYSIS

The above timeline should have given a flavour of the issues confronting the Sussex police over the four decades from 1965 to 2005. In this analytical section we will draw out some of the more prominent themes.

First, the impacts of central government initiatives were considerable throughout the period, but the frequency and detail of these initiatives seems to have grown since the late 1980s or early 1990s. 'What is happening now is that central government is coming up with something new every week or so, and we are going round the change cycle much more quickly' (interview 13 – senior police officer). PACE was a watershed in 1984, but the process accelerated further from the early 1990s. Interviewee 29 saw the 1993 Sheehy Report (*Inquiry into Police Responsibilities and Rewards*) as a milestone (Sheehy, 1993).

Interviewee 28 argued that the balance of power between the police, the Police Authority and the Home Office 'has shifted hugely' – in favour of the Home Office. 'Now they have a huge hand on local policy – it is almost delivered to a formula' (interview 16 – ex-senior police officer). 'The interference is more. The ability of Chief Constables and the BCU commanders to deliver a locally-tuned service is better than before [but] you'll never get away from a targeted, performance-driven culture' (interview 14 – senior police officer). 'There has been an increasing emphasis on central targets' (interview 2). Some, while acknowledging the growth of central controls, argued for a more nuanced picture: overall 'the Chief Constable still has a lot of room for maneouvre' (interview 4 – ex-senior police officer). In Sussex, for example, they resisted the national trend to use CS gas (preferring pepper sprays) and they went against the national norm by employing unmarked cars for armed response. Nevertheless, over the period as a whole, central influence on the local force has grown. The categories of Table 1.1 do not seem to fit this process very neatly. It has had elements of Stalactite, certainly, but there have also been sudden spurts – such as the target-setting requirements of the 2002 Police Reform Act – although none quite big enough by itself to qualify as an Earthquake. In terms of images one might think of a Stalactite that dripped steadily over long periods but speeded up during particular storms.

Second, the tension between two rival images of the police – on the one hand the high-tech crime fighters and on the other the friendly local constable who 'knows their patch' – runs throughout the whole period. One could argue that, with increasing police specialization, the contrast has become more institutionalized. 'Over the years I have seen an increase in the number of specialized units and teams' (interview 11 – senior police officer). On the one hand, one has the Serious Organised Crime Agency, the National Police DNA Database and local drives against drugs or 'muggings' or knife crime, or whatever is the latest form of crime to attract media and political attention. On the other we have Neighbourhood Watch, the growing army of Community Support Officers, neighbour- hood police teams, Local Criminal Justice Boards, the Safer and Stronger Communities Fund and a host of other initiatives aimed at maintaining public order locally, at reassuring people that their streets are safe, and at working with other local agencies to reduce anti-social behaviour and low-level crimes. This difference between 'real policing' and 'the soft stuff' is also a fault line running within the police culture itself, as ethnographic work in a force immediately adjacent to Sussex recently illustrated (Davies and Thomas, 2008). Scrutiny of the annual police reports and the local newspaper show endless stories of popular demands for more police offic- ers on the street, and almost equally frequent announcements by the police that they were responding to this. One interviewee cited as a major change in the police task 'massive partnership membership' (interview 35) and other senior officers also mentioned the growth in the time commitment to various forms of community liaison. The 1998 Crime and Disorder Act had been important because it 'had enshrined partnership working in law' (interview 2 – local authority officer). But as many of our interviewees stressed (and as the police regularly explained in their public statements) the possible calls on the police are without limit, and therefore prioritiza- tion is unavoidable. 'At what point should the balance be set?' (interview 35 – ex-senior police officer); 'Work got done in the areas the government thought were important and didn't get done in the other areas' (interview 4 – senior ex-police officer); 'So the background is a huge increase in the demands on the police' (interview 14 – senior police officer). 'We simply cannot do all that people would like us to do, all the time. When I, or any of my colleagues, have to choose between competing demands for our service, the priorities contained within the Performance Plan are our guide' (CC Paul Whitehouse, 2001, p. 5). This is an interesting issue in terms of change because it leads to many small, short-term changes (Tortoise-like) but in the longer term looks more like an alternation between two desirable but mutually exclusive poles.

Third, it is absolutely clear that, as was the case with hospitals (Chapter 3) the salience of management, of a managerial way of thinking and organizing, has grown enormously over the period since 1975. Most of our police interviewees picked this out in one way or another. Interviewee 29 said that notions of good management had become very prominent in police training from the late 1980s. Interviewee 35 referred to the Home Office Circular 114 of 1983, which focused on efficiency and effectiveness: 'previously we hadn't *managed* resources at all'. Many interviewees commented on the growing impact of performance indicators and targets, beginning in the mid-1990s but reaching a new peak in Sussex after Ken Jones became Chief Constable in 2002. One of the interesting differences between the police story and the hospital story, however, is that, by and large, the police have remained as their own managers. In the National Health Service (NHS), as we saw in Chapter 3, there has been a large growth in professional managers who have no clinical background, but nevertheless take responsibility for running hospitals (including, since 1997, responsibility for the clinical performance of hospitals – that is, what doctors and nurses do). The police, however, have not placed themselves under a new cadre of secular, non-police managers. They have trained themselves to be modern-style, performance-oriented professionals and leaders. Of course they always did have a clear management style of their own – highly disciplined and hierarchical – in a way that the clinical professions arguably did not, and it seems that they have been able to build upon and adapt this. This assumption of a far more managerial approach has been felt throughout, but has impacted differently on different ranks. Several of our interviewees, when asked what they thought had not changed so much, mentioned that the work of a constable on the beat had considerable elements of continuity to it – the situations they were confronted with, the values, the camaraderie, and so on. Even more fundamentally, 'they are still a disciplined, hierarchical force' (interview 2). However, our interviewees immediately went on to say that for the superintending ranks the job had changed enormously, principally because of the range of management responsibilities and considerations which now defined the lives of those more senior officers. This seems a reasonably clear case of a Stalactite.

Fourth, social changes have unmistakable effects both on and within the police. A number of our interviewees indicated that policing had been made harder by the loss of respect for and trust in the police by some parts of the population. 'The respect for authority – be it police or schools or elsewhere – has definitely diminished' (interview 11, senior police officer). Assaults on the police have increased. Brighton has become very prosperous – which influences leisure styles, drugs and other opportunities for crime – but alongside this there are still pockets of deprivation and poverty. And at the same time these and other social changes have affected the police force themselves: partly through the increasing civilianization but even more through programmes for gender and ethnic equality within the force. Brighton, with a large gay community, has made something of a reputation for itself both in recognizing gay and lesbian officers within the force (they have their own association) and in developing carefully negotiated ways of policing places and events of special interest to that community (such as the Gay Pride parade). More broadly, the Sussex Police has been one of the more active forces in promoting close community liaison and neighbourhood-based policing – activities which themselves, in a sense, require a different type of police officer if they are to be effective. Again, these environmental shifts can be seen as Stalactite-type changes, and policy-prompting rather than policy-driven.

7.6   LEUVEN POLICE: BACKGROUND

Leuven is the administrative capital of the province of Flemish Brabant, with a Governor. It is also a judicial centre of the arrondissement, supporting a Royal Public Prosecutor (Procureur des Konings/Procureur du Roi). Within its 57 km² or 5.663 ha (Figure 7.2) Leuven has about 92 000 inhabitants, plus – during term time – around 35 000 students.

The 1976 merger of Leuven was a complex reshuffling of municipal borders, driven by economic and political criteria. From 1 January 1977, Leuven consisted of the ancient city of Leuven, plus the surrounding suburban and adjacent villages of Heverlee, Kessel-Lo and Wilsele, the centre of Wijgmaal, and parts of Herent, Korbeek-Lo and Haasrode (Table 7.1).

Leuven is a wealthy city of which Heverlee is the most residential and rich part. In 2007 it had an unemployment rate of 6.6 per cent and an average income of €16 345 per capita (2005). The population includes 19.59 per cent who are younger than 20 years old, and 16.95 per cent over 65 (2006); 11.74 per cent are foreigners (2008). The city is run by a

Figure 7.2   Map of the City of Leuven (after 1977, with the km² of the districts)

Table 7.1   Leuven area and population (2008)

Community part	Surface (km²)	Population (31/12/2007)	Density (Pop./ km²)
Leuven	5.52	30283	5486
Heverlee	21.60	21721	1006
Kessel-Lo	16.06	27755	1728
Wijgmaal	4.59	3519	767
Wilsele	8.86	9454	1067

Source: Jaarverslag bevolking Stad Leuven.

coalition of Socialists and Christian Democrats. Mayor Louis Tobback is a nationally prominent socialist who has previously been Party President and a Minister. In 2009 he was still Minister of State and a Member of parliament – an example of the accumulation of offices at different levels which is common in Belgium but unknown in England.

The history of the Leuven Police follows the general trends of the Belgian Municipal Police. Until the end of 1976 there were 2359 municipalities with their Municipal Police for cities and main villages, and 'Veldwachters/Champêtres' for the smallest and most rural villages (Figure

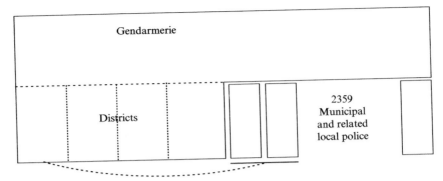

Note: The figure should not be read as implying that the municipal police were
hierarchically subordinate to the Gendarmerie. Also, this figure does not show either the
judicial police or the specialized transport forces.

Figure 7.3   Belgian police organization until 1977

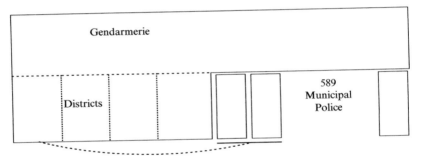

Figure 7.4   Belgian police organization (1977–2001)

7.3). Meanwhile the (national) Rijkswacht/Gendamerie had their own set
of districts, which were usually considerably bigger than the municipal
police zones.

In the Leuven case there had been separate police organizations for
Leuven, Heverlee, Kessel-Lo and Wilsele. From 1 January 1977 nationally there was a reduction from 2359 to 589 local government areas, with a
parallel amalgamation of the local police organizations (Figure 7.4)

In the Leuven case this resulted in the 1976 merger of the police organizations of Leuven, Heverlee, Kessel-Lo and Wilsele.

In 2001 the Leuven municipal police merged with parts of the
Gendarmerie district staff. This resulted in the Leuven Police Zone which
consists of only one city, instead of a large number of multi-city/village

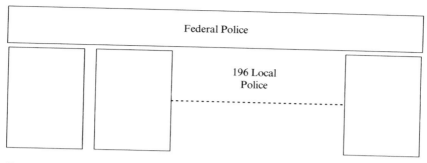

Figure 7.5   Belgian police organization since 2001

police zones. This was the local outcome of the fundamental national reorganization described in Chapter 4. The Leuven Rijkswacht District covered a considerably larger area – about 500 000 people, with 13 brigades and 50 BOB agents (total about 400 people – BOB (Bijzondere Opsporings Brigade) is the Rijkswacht's guard and investigation brigade – a kind of Criminal Investigation Department, CID in English terms). However, within Leuven city, the Rijkswacht was complementary to and non-competitive with the municipal force. Most of the Rijkswacht support was for smaller villages to guarantee a 24/7 service. Community policing became one of the guiding principles for local police. In order to improve the collaboration between Rijkswacht and Municipal Police services, Interpolice Zones had been established from 1995 onwards (see PZ Leuven, 2006). This was beneficial for Municipal Police stations since they could transfer night shifts to the local Rijkswacht. The 1997 Act allowed mayors to have a say in the local districts of the Rijkswacht. It was hoped that police activities would therefore become better matched to local needs.

The Royal Decree of 7 September 2001 established the local police basic functions within the spirit of community-oriented policing. However, the structure of a local police organization is not fixed by statute. The six basic functions were district operations, reception, intervention, caring for victims, local investigations, and maintaining law and order. In addition to these six basic functions, local police could also be assigned tasks from the federal level. District operations imply that police are visible, approachable and responsive, given local circumstances and density. Reception implies that citizens always should have the opportunity to contact police services, intervention implies a proportional response to a call. Caring for victims should result in adequate reception, information and support provided to victims (although, in general Belgium has a lower level of such support than does the UK – see Chapter 5, Table 5.4). For investigation assignments between 7 and 10 per cent of the total resources are supposed to be made available. Maintaining law and order refers to re-establishing public rest and security, and public health. This does not only imply organizing security for major events – such as demonstrations, football games, local festivities – but also dealing with environmental issues and traffic.

The head of the local police zone is the Commissioner who is under the authority of the Mayor (for single police zones) or a college of mayors (for multi-police zones).

Each local police zone has its security council which consists of the Mayor, the Royal Prosecutor, the 'Chef de Corps' of the local police, the Administrative Director/coordinator, plus experts by invitation.

7.7   LEUVEN POLICE: TIMELINE

The origin of the Leuven police was related to the fire service, which had first been set up in 1807. With the foundation of Belgium in 1830 the municipal government confirmed the complete integration of the municipal police and the fire service. In 1841 the city established a municipal neighborhood watch, initially volunteer-based but very soon professional. The city consisted of 60 geographical sections. Public criticism of the organization of the police function and its equipment continued. In 1879 the fire service was replaced by a new police organization consisting of a Commissaire, eight Adjoints, and 30 policemen for six districts of the city. One of their responsibilities continued to be the fire service. Social and student riots in 1901 and 1902 resulted in further criticism of the police. During the First World War, initially the Germans abolished the police, but then re-established it. In 1924 white helmets were made mandatory in order to make policemen more visible for cars. In 1935 a preventive air attack watch service was established. This eventually led to the separation of the police and fire services. 1942 marked a key turning point for the municipal police since recruitment and structured training was organized for the whole country. Also the strength of the force was determined per municipality. For Leuven this was 87 officers, for Kessel-Lo the number was 17. The German occupiers were very critical of the police and accused them of political crimes and acts against the occupying authorities. Leuven was liberated on 1 September 1944. Police Commissaire François Chevalier, who was in office from 1935 till 1969, was accused of collaboration with the Germans, but he was subsequently recognized as being part of the armed resistance.

The schools for officers (Tervuren) and other ranks (Bokrijk) which had been established during the war were abolished. They were re-established by the provincial council of Braibant in 1948. This bilingual school for officers was split in 1966. For ordinary police men the re-establishment of the police school with compulsory training did not take place until 1986. However, the Leuven Police were obliged to take classes and training from 1971, in the Brussels police school, on the initiative of the new Commissaire who was originally from the Brussels Police. Until 1975, Leuven Police, when hired, had to prove that they were able to provide information in French (even though this was now an illegal requirement according to the language laws).

1968

The basis of an entente between Rijkswacht and the Leuven Police grew from the 'Leuven Vlaams' crisis (*de splitsing* – discussed in the previous chapter). The Rijkswacht guaranteed good public order. In fact, from 1968 until 1975 the Rijkswacht rather than the municipal force dominated the city.

1971

Mayor Smets (Christian Democrat) was often absent and was replaced by his First Alderman, Louis Tobback (Socialist). Ray Ieven became the new head of the Leuven Police and succeeded François Chevalier who had been chief of the Leuven Police from 1935 till 1969. Ieven remained head of police until his retirement in 1995.

There was a shooting incident in which a student was killed. Ieven was pressured to resign in the press and by students. He organized shooting training, which had not previously existed.

1975

At this time there was a tradition, mainly among Francophone students, to have regular Thursday riots in the centre of the city:

> It became part of the folklore. The *Gendarmerie* had an agreement with the students on this issue. Slowly this folklore disappeared: the culture of students changed, the political polarisation disappeared (between left and right), and 'de splitsing' pushed out the francophones. (interview 31)

'Ieven's policy was to reduce the dominance of the *Gendarmerie* [Rijkswacht] in the city centre. He managed to reduce the riots, and to define his position in the city centre' (interview 30). The Leuven branch of the Rijkswacht accepted that the Leuven Municipal Police would become more important in the city centre. Ieven's policy was to increase their capacity, quantitatively and qualitatively.

1972
Decision to modernize the car fleet and to create civilian assistants for the uniformed police officers.

1976–77
Merger of the Municipal Police forces of Leuven, Heverlee, Kessel-Lo and Wilsele. Ievens developed a comprehensive and technical document for the reorganization of these four entities (Ieven, 1976). Within the merged organization new specializations were established. Alongside the regular administrative services and surveillance with district services, traffic, judicial and social services were established. Later on a dog section and motor cycle section were established.

Mayor Smets reached the end of his term of office. He had been Mayor for the period 1947–52, and then for another three terms from 1958 until 1976. Alfred Van Sina, up to 1976 the Mayor of the previously separate village of Kessel-Lo, became Mayor of Leuven, where he remained for 18 years, until the elections in 1994.

The mergers of the municipal administrations in general, and of the four police organizations in particular, were not easy. Four to five years later 'the 1976 merger was still not processed by the organisation' (interview 26).

After the merger, the situation remained political and parochial:

> If you have a party membership and a uniform you are a police man. All constituent parts of the police (previous municipalities) were autonomous: Van Sina (mayor of Kessel-Lo) protected 'his' previous police men. There was also serious understaffing. About 185 people were available but 220 were needed. (interview 27)

1980
The first female police officer was appointed.

1982
Mayor Van Sina was re-elected and started his second term of six years.

1988
Mayor Van Sina was re-elected and started his third term of six years.

1989
Louis Tobback became Minister of the Interior (until 1994). One of the members of his cabinet was Lode De Witte, who later became Tobback's Chef de Cabinet (Chief of Staff). Later, in 1995, De Witte became Governor of the Province of Flemish-Braibant, with extensive police responsibilities.

1992

Implementation of the 1992 Police Function Act describing the respective competencies of the Municipal Police, the coordination of tasks and assignments of the three existing police forces (Rijkswacht, Judicial and Municipal) through the 'Pentagon' platform.

Several initiatives were taken to encourage integration. This integration policy was a combination of top-down policy and bottom-up voluntarism. In the Leuven case there were special circumstances. Leuven was one of the first pilots for all these initiatives. The Leuven IPZ (Inter Police Zone) was guided by the Ministry of the Interior. Municipalities got financial incentives to collaborate on a voluntary basis with other municipalities (in these zones). For the Rijkswacht, also guided by the Ministry, it was compulsory to collaborate and support these voluntary initiatives. The major objective was to move from an IPZ status to become an integrated Police Zone (PZ).

1994

Louis Tobback was elected Mayor of Leuven. He took over after Van Sina's 18 years in office.

The management consultancy, Team Consult, was contracted to undertake a local evaluation.

Louis Tobback became President of the Flemish Socialists (until 1998).

1995

Team Consult reported. They recommended better development of decentralized district teams and a 'holistic approach'; 76 of the 138 officers were to be assigned to districts (*wijkteams*) and 62 to more centralized intervention functions. The district teams were to be the principal 'homes' of officers, with periodic assignments to the intervention units.

Ray Ieven: retired after having headed the Leuven police for 24 years.

Hugo Michiels was Ieven's successor and he started a reorganization ('fundamental contribution to the general security of the city of Leuven'). He remained in office for nine years.

Lode De Witte, the former Chef de Cabinet of Tobback at the Ministry of the Interior, became Governor of Flemish-Braibant with a special emphasis on police and security policy.

As of September 1996 there were 215 police plus 25 civilians.

1996

Four district bureaus were established: Leuven Centre, Heverlee, Kessel-Lo, Wilsele-Wijgmaal. An agreement on cooperation was reached with the local district of the Rijkswacht (PZ Leuven, 2006).

1997
Leuven City Security Charter (Veiligheidscharter). This was the operational consequence of the 1992 law. It identified certain priorites (*kracht-lijnen*) for Leuven: burglaries and robberies, transport safety, car crime and drugs (IPZ Leuven, 1997).

1998
Louis Tobback became Vice-Prime Minister and Minister of the Interior.

2000
Leuven became a Pilot Police Zone PPZ.
 Mayor Tobback was re-elected for a second term of six years.

2001
Leuven Police Zone was created. The merger of the local branch of the Rijkswacht with the Municipal Police meant that two-thirds of the Leuven Rijkswacht staff went to Brussels and the others (about 55 officers) joined the Leuven Police (which by then consisted of about 220 officers, and about 280 total staff, including civilians).
 'There was a perception that the *Gendarmerie* was absorbed by the police' (interview 27). In practice the new organization was designed and personnel needs were determined. All staff had to apply for the new positions internally. About 90 per cent got their desired positions.

2003
Physical co-location of Leuven Police HQ and the local branch of the Rijkswacht, and relocation of the Leuven Police Zone in new buildings on the Phillips Site.

2005
The Zonaal Veiligheidsplan 2005–2008 (local security plan) set out the general context, the contributions from the local police, the resources, and the special projects (PZ Leuven, 2005). This presented quite a detailed statement of planned inputs and standards (for example shift patterns for the police on intervention duties; numbers of district officers in relation to resident populations).

2006
Louis Tobback was re-elected as mayor for a third term of six years (when his term expires in 2012 he will have served for 18 years as Mayor).
 Michiels resigned as Chief of the Leuven Police. He had served for nine years.

2007

Jean-Paul Mouchaers was appointed as new Korpschef. He quickly developed a diagnosis of the problems facing his organization. He wanted to use processes as the main basis for the organization rather than vertical structures. The presence of former Rijkswacht staff was not considered to be a significant influence on the culture. The old cultures were said to be disappearing, partly because there was a high turnover of personnel. There were plans to consult the population (target groups, stakeholders) in forming the elements for a new local security plan. There was a refining of the existing security monitoring process by adding new measures of public perceptions of insecurity. New tasks made their call on police resources and skills, for example the Prosecutor-Generals asked the police to focus on intra-family violence (two directives from the College of Prosecutors General). And there were plans to organize a satisfaction survey among the personnel.

The published monitoring report was still mainly limited to budgetary data. It did not yet include much non-financial management information, particularly with respect to performance outputs or outcomes. The perception was that external communication and information and communication technology (ICT) needed to improve (including the website and the yearly report). There was a need to think in the long run by combining systems of calls, with despatching, geographic information system (GIS) and closed-circuit television (CCTV). This would allow faster and better reactions.

7.8 LEUVEN POLICE: ANALYSIS

The Leuven history manifests a number of significant trends over time.

From Fragmentation to Critical Mass

This was achieved by means of country-wide mergers of municipalities (1976), voluntary coordination (from 1995 on) and merging local branches of the Rijkswacht with Municipal Police organizations into local police forces (2001). Nevertheless this still leaves the Belgian forces much smaller than most English forces (and in England from 2006–2007 the government was engaged in a (failed) attempt to push through mergers to get even bigger forces). On the other hand, England has no direct equivalent of the Belgian national police force – Rijkswacht/Gendarmerie.

There was also a concern for equilibria, for checks and balances between:

- justice and administration;
- central and local;
- specialized and generic policing;
- state power and citizen rights (which resulted, *inter alia*, in the 1991 establishment of Committee P – See chapter 4).)

This trend towards greater coordination and increasing concern for professionalism and quality took well over a decade to unfold (interview 32), and changed over time. For example, in 1988 the choice was not for community policing but for prevention. Later, in 2002, the community policing emphasis was added.

From Informal Common Sense to Formal Professionalism

There was also a shift from a politicized grassroots organization towards greater managerial professionalism. However, this never took the form of a blind belief in models. It was always pursued with a great amount of pragmatism:

> Many models are put forward to make things happen: Initially there was BPZ [Basis Politie Zorg: Basic Police Care] which was translated into six basic functions. Then there is the model of 'Excellent Organisation' with EFQM. Now there is IGP [Informatie Gestuurde Politie: Information Guided Police]. (interview 26)

There is, however, a concern:

> that new models arrive before the previous ones have been implemented, that all these models are top-down (from Brussels), that the consistency of all initiatives is lost, that there is insufficient training. Is there an impact on change, and is this improvement? There is a loss of expertise: nobody knows what a district cob is [*wijkagent*, or local constable]. Informing police actions is not just about numbers, it is about district police transferring their intelligence to other parts in the organization. (interview 26)

Doubts of this kind are certainly not confined to the Leuven Police. Here the Chief Commissioner of another Belgian force:

> A lot of police organizations . . . often have beautiful visions, well sounding mission statements, and a clear concept of what community policing should be. A few more have elaborated strategic planning and policy documents that describe the desired future in more details. However, a systematic and structured approach to make this vision operational and to implement it, is often lacking. (Bergmans, 2005, pp. 14–15)

Despite these anxieties, however, there was a clear agenda that the police needed to be upgraded to professional and modern standards. This included training and quality.

From a Spirit of Competition to a Culture of Collaboration and Coordination

At one time competition between the different police forces was endemic. For example, the Rijkswacht had developed a quality policy around BPZK (Basic Police Care with Quality/BasisPolitieZorgKualiteit) This was a bottom-up type of initiative which included elements such as :

- reception desks;
- involving policemen in the process of improvement;
- abandoning the traditional model that 'officers think, police constables execute';
- recontacting victims;
- shopping days within the police: a 'market' for police projects;
- defining basic police care.

In general the municipal police found this project quite threatening. In the Leuven district the new approach was first implemented in Diest.

Two particular projects in Leuven became part of a conflict with between the Rijkswacht and the municipal police:

- Rijkswacht and students: the proposal to put a police unit on the university campus.
- Rijkswacht and the university hospital (Gasthuisberg) (this included traffic issues since there is a flux of 8000 vehicle movements per day).

In both cases the Leuven Police claimed the authority to perform these functions; Commissioner Michiels had said that there should be no campus bureau for the Rijkswacht, the students were 'ours'. This was a competitive claim (interview 30).

In the earlier part of our period the position of the Rijkswacht was:

- the smaller the local police zones the better (this would strengthen the federal police);
- divide and rule;
- central police has more power when local police are dispersed.

The pressure to move to bigger local units came from the Municipal Police themselves. The mayors were usually united in favour of smaller units.

Eventually, however, a measure of cooperation was achieved. A good Pentagon platform was established, consisting of the Mayor, the Commander of the Rijkswacht, the Municipal Police, the Judicial Police, and the Royal Prosecutor. Their choice was for a one-city police zone in Leuven. There were several reasons for this decision:

- some mayors of the smaller municipalities did not want to join the bigger unit of Leuven (for example Herent);
- there was a tendency within the province to go for smaller rather than larger – there was some disagreement in several smaller municipalities between the Chef de Corps of police and the Mayor.

Stable Political, Administrative, and Police Leadership

While Sussex chief constables usually enjoyed quite substantial periods in post (1968–83, 1983–93, 1993–2001, 2002–06) the longevity of both chiefs of police and political leaders in the Leuven story is very striking.

Ministers of the Interior

Tobback (SP)	Vande Lanotte (SP)	Tobback (SP)	Van den Bossche (SP)
1988–94	1994–98	1998	1998–99

De Witte: Cabinet Tobback	De Witte: Governor of Flemish Braibant
1988–95	1995–

Mayors of Leuven

Mayor Smets	Mayor Van Sina	Mayor Tobback
1958–76	1976–94	1994–

Leuven police chiefs

Chevalier	Ieven	Michiels	Mouchaers
1935–69	1971–95	1995–2006	2007–

This was therefore a story of strong local mayors and police chiefs, embedded in strong elite networks. They had strong connections and ensured participation of local elites in national decision-making. They managed to secure funds, influence mergers (and so on), to the benefit of their communities and organizations. This pattern therefore contrasts with the experience in Sussex. Whilst it is true that most of the Sussex chief constables remained in office for more than five years, their average length of service was considerably less than that for Leuven police chiefs. More significantly, perhaps, for them and for the local politicians, the national government level was more 'distant' ('them and us') in the Sussex case. Furthermore the demands and interventions from central government were more volatile, as different governments and different Home Secretaries came and went.

Continuity and Change over Time

There were important developments in the Leuven story, but also considerable continuities. First, the changes. Obviously, the relationship with the national force changed considerably, largely in the direction of somewhat greater equality and more cooperation. Connected to that, the Pentagon (five-cornered) system of coordination between the Municipal Police, the Judicial Police, the Rijkswacht, the Mayor and the Prosecutor became an important new way of working. And, as in Sussex, each Police Chief (*Korpschef*) brought with him a new style and mixture of skills. There were also bottom-up changes such as the dissatisfaction by local politicians which resulted in a local evaluation in 1994–5, and the fact that in 1999 Leuven volunteered as a pilot project for the merger of Rijkswacht and Municipal Police (there were only five pilots in the whole country). Obviously the fact that the responsible Minister was Tobback – also the Mayor – is important.

Nor should we underestimate the change-promoting effects of external events. As one of our most experienced interviewees said: 'Catastrophies made a convergence of concepts. It is important to know where to go. One needs to be ready when needed' (interview 34).

Then we come to the continuities:

In Leuven there was always a harmonious situation between the population, the university, and the security services. Some things have remained in the Leuven Police Zone:
- in the municipalities around Leuven there are still townhall sections and related police stations;
- the mentality of the *Gendarmerie* is still present: in the division of labour, former *Gendarmerie* people prefer intervention, and the municipal police people prefer district work. (interview 26)

(Although one might question the first part of this claim, given that student riots were at one time commonplace and regular.)

> There is still a difference in discourse between *Gendarmerie* and municipal police. *Gendarmerie* is implementing as good as possible, is very professional, has some averse towards politics; Municipal Police is more critical, has more feeling for politics, and is more problem driven. (interview 26)

7.9   COMPARISONS AND CONCLUSIONS

The two local police stories can be told in different ways. The contrasts are perhaps more 'front stage', but just behind them lie some important similarities.

The three most obvious contrasts are, first, the different structures and scales of police forces, second, the distinctive role of local politicians in the Belgian case and, third, the far greater availability of performance information in the Sussex force. The first contrast can be stated bluntly by saying that, for the people of Brighton, there is and has been only one police force, whereas for the people of the Leuven area there have been many (see Figure 7.2) and even now, after all the structural reforms and mergers of the past three decades, there are still two quite distinct bodies – the Leuven Police and the Federal Police. To take the point further, the Leuven Police as a whole are considerably smaller than just the Brighton and Hove division of the Sussex force. These differences in size have significant implications for the range of specialist units and equipment which a force can support, and for career patterns. In Belgium the specialist units tended to be at national level and it was only after the 2001 merger of municipal forces with the local Rijkswacht that some local forces experienced an injection of highly trained professionalism.

As for the role of local politicians, the English police authorities do contain (seconded) local politicians, but these bodies are seldom considered to be particularly powerful influences on chief constables. An active and prominent member described them in the period before the 1994 Police and Magistrates Courts Act as 'a backwater you put the old stagers on'. The arrival of independent members after the Act produced somewhat more activism (interviews 4, 8) but did not transform the situation. In the one case where the Sussex Police Authority appeared to take a decisive executive action – securing the early retirement of Chief Constable Whitehouse in 2001 – the Authority was evidently acting under considerable pressure from the Minister in Whitehall (interviews 8, 28). Usually the Chief Constable 'still had a lot of discretion and room for manoeuvre' (interview 4). The tightening-up of political control over the police has (1990–2005) come almost entirely from the centre. Whitehall has laid down an ever-tighter net of performance indicators, standards, plans and 'initiatives'. In Belgium, by contrast, local mayors were very much in charge of the local police – not only in setting operational priorities but even sometimes to the point of determining quite junior appointments (interviews 26, 27, 30, 32, 34). This was doubly the case in Leuven, where Mayor Tobback was (is): (1) long-serving; (2) also a national political figure of considerable influence; and (3) particularly interested in police reform, having developed a vision of his own as to the direction in which reform should be heading. (We do not mean to imply that he intervened in junior appointments – although some other mayors certainly did – but simply that Tobback's influence and experience were greater than his counterparts in some other Belgian police zones.) Paradoxically, if the Municipal Police were to gain greater professional autonomy, it had first to be awarded to them by local politicians.

The third contrast – the much greater use of performance information in the English force – shone out from almost every document we encountered. By the end of our period the Belgian documentation was certainly reflecting managerial language, models and concepts, but the amount of information about actual outputs and impacts remained very limited by English standards. Most of the figures in the Belgian documentation concerned more traditional inputs – how many officers were assigned here or there, not what they had achieved. There were some figures indicating local crime trends, but on the whole these were not tied to specific police activities, and certainly not to quantified targets. There was very little comparative data. If one compares, for example, the Leuven local security plan for 2005–08 (PZ Leuven, 2005) with the *Local Policing Plan for Sussex 2004–2005* (Sussex Police Authority, 2004b) the latter contains quantified targets in every section and much more precise information on where resources, both financial and personnel, are being allocated. Nor, during our research, did we ever see in Belgium anything remotely approaching the wealth of performance information contained in the regular monthly *Force Strategic Performance Information* booklet which is distributed to senior police officers and the officers and members of the Sussex Police Authority.

We now turn to some of the similarities. We can mention at least three. First, there is the move towards a more professional service, with more explicit standards and better training (for example Bergmans, 2005). That is evident in both localities, and emerges from most of our interviews with senior police officers themselves. Second, there have been a series of technological changes which have various important effects. For example, the new technologies amplify the demand for professionalism and training – responsibility for expensive specialized equipment cannot be sensibly given to minimally trained, generalist, rank-and-file constables. They also directly affect the ways in which police conduct operations. For instance, if you have CCTV cameras wired up to police headquarters (HQ) (as obtains in both Brighton and Leuven) then you need ways of instantly transmitting the information they bring in back to the operational police on the street. If, like the Sussex force, you acquired an armoured vehicle (for anti-terrorist duties at Gatwick airport) then you can do things which are too dangerous for an ordinary police car or van – and you have to train an appropriate number of police to use such a specialized vehicle. More recently, the fact that all English forces are now equipped with the new Airwave radio communications system means that they can communicate with each other (and other emergency services) across jurisdictional boundaries (interview 36). The third – and perhaps most celebrated – similarity between the Leuven and Sussex stories lies in the recent emphasis on community – or neighbourhood – policing. In both cases our local jurisdictions were echoing national policy and rhetoric. But in both cases the forces we examined seem to have prided themselves in being at the leading edge of the policy wave (interviews 1, 2, 4, 11, 13, 14, 27, 33). They were experimenting with and resourcing neighbourhood and liason schemes of various kinds before many other forces in their respective countries.

Finally, we can ask whether there are any obvious patterns to the two local stories. Here we give only a preliminary answer, because we are reserving a more extended discussion of the whole issue of patterns for Chapter 8. Our preliminary answer is based mainly on our interviews – on how the highly experienced group that we talked to themselves 'read' their local histories. It was striking that there was a substantial degree of agreement – in each locality, though perhaps more in Sussex – about what the main turning points had been. There was a shared retrospective view as to what had been important, even if individual respondants' opinions differed in other respects. This consensus, or quasi-consensus, extended to a few core items, while other items were cited by some but seen as less important by others.

For the Sussex force five issues were regularly cited:

1. The 1984 Police and Criminal Evidence Act. This had obliged the police to be far more systematic in handling suspects (interviews 1, 11, 16, 29).
2. The forced early retirement of Chief Constable Whitehouse in 2001. This had proved traumatic for the whole Sussex force and had led to

bitter internal divisions. Sussex had thought of itself as innovative but was suddenly perceived as a 'failing force'. The new CC (Ken Jones) had brought a distinctive new style (interviews 8, 11, 13, 14, 16, 28, 29).

3. The pressures for local 'partnerships' from the late 1980s onwards (interviews 2, 13, 14, 35).

4. The growth of performance measurement and management from the early 1990s (interviews 1, 4, 16, 28).

5. The general growth of central (Whitehall) intervention (1, 4, 8, 11, 16, 28, 29).

It can be seen that only the second of these – the Hastings Shooting and the later resignation of the Chief Constable – can be construed as primarily 'local'. All the others came principally from central government. And even the Whitehouse resignation eventually involved strong pressures behind the scenes from the Home Secretary. Issues 1, 3 and 4 are all genuine policy changes – intendedly basic shifts with lasting effects.

For the Leuven force there was less of a consensus. On the one hand almost everyone agreed that the 2001 restructuring was a watershed (interviews 26, 27, 30, 31, 32). 'Het werd een fundamentale ingreep in ons politiebestel' (It was a fundamental intervention in our police system) (PZ Leuven, 2005, p. 1). But on the other hand, opinions differed about the significance of some other issues. For example, the earlier (1977) merger was seen as very important by some, but was not mentioned by others. The Dutroux case and escape – a national event but one which affected the reputation of the entire criminal justice system – was seen as important by several respondants, but mainly because it gave the final impetus for a further, deeper restructuring. The 1990 Pinksterenplan was clearly acknowledged as a major step, but again it was a national-level initiative, which provided an opportunity for movement locally. The pattern that did emerge from the Leuven interviews was one of a relatively small group of politicians who occupied a variety of roles at national, provincial and local levels, and who pursued a particular direction of structural reform over almost 20 years. As one insider put it: 'it was a combination of personalities, a long term vision which was not changing, and political opportunities' (interview 32). Thus the pattern we see in the Leuven case is perhaps one of change that takes longer but is driven by a more consistent political vision, and one in which some of the key figures were based in or knowledgeable about the particular circumstances of the locality. In the Sussex case, however, we find a police force which is obliged to react to a series of policies not at all of its own making. Things come down from the centre and must be attended to. Of course, some of these things may be attractive to some senior officers in the local force, and even those which are not popular will nevertheless receive a considered and disciplined response. But there is more 'distance', more of a sense of 'them and us' than we find in Leuven.

8. Reflections on theories of change

8.1 INTRODUCTION

The previous five chapters have revealed both similarities and differences in policy and management in the two chosen services and countries. The differences are great – large enough for us to ditch any naive or mechanistic theories that 'globalization' or 'reinvention' or 'the New Public Management' are sweeping through the world, obliging every government urgently to move in the same direction. Evidently even governments that are geographically adjacent, multiply interconnected and similarly subject to the allegedly homogenizing effects of European Union (EU) membership can behave very differently when it comes to policymaking and management.

The similarities between the countries and services are perhaps more subtle, but no less profound. In rather brutal, bullet-point style we can summarize the details of Chapters 3 to 7 as follows.

Main differences:

- Very different central–local relations. Much greater central–local integration of political elites in Belgium – although at the same time much greater fragmentation of political parties. Also, much more scope for local autonomy from the federal government. Put another way, central government is more dominant and controlling in England.
- Faster pace of both policy and management change in England (for both hospitals and police).
- Greater emphasis on 'management' and less on political bargaining and patronage in England (most marked for the police, but also true for hospitals). However, this difference needs to be understood within an overall growth in concern for management in both countries (see similarities, below).
- Far greater emphasis on target-setting and performance measurement in England (both for hospitals and the police). Output and outcome measurement are more common and more influential than in Belgium.

Main similarities:

- Growing emphasis on management. In both countries both the police and the hospital service were regarded as something to be 'managed' far more in 2005 than in 1965. This applied both at the level of the whole system (for example how many hospital beds of various types were needed for the population) and at the level of individual organizations (for example police budgets and staffs had to be explicitly and actively managed by local police chiefs).
- More explicit national and local plans – for both services, but perhaps particularly for the police, who had few plans at the beginning of the period under study, and had been essentially responsive rather than goal-driven.
- For the police, more specialization, and the creation, in both countries, of other types of cadre within the 'police family', to help with the workload (for example Police Community Support Officers (PCSOs), civilian specialists).
- For hospitals a need to form closer and more explicit relations with primary and secondary health care organizations. Hospitals become less free-standing organizations, more the keystone in the arch of a larger, more integrated system of health care.
- A technological transformation for both hospitals and the police. For both, the explosion of diagnostic technologies have considerably altered professional practice, though at a slower rate for the Belgian police than for their English counterparts, and in a less government-steered way for hospital doctors in Belgium than in the National Health Service (NHS).
- An apparent decline in public trust in the police (and the criminal justice system) – in both countries.

Before we move to more detailed analysis it may be useful to make some immediate and very broad comments on these summary lists. A first reflection may seem rather masochistic for a book on policy: it is that policies (in the sense of specific government decisions and initiatives) do not necessarily seem to have been the most overwhelmingly important elements of change, taking the long view. More significant, in many ways, have been the long-term trends towards specialization and professionalization, trends which have, for the most part, quietly proceeded in the organizational depths, only occasionally rising to the surface as explicit statements of 'policy'. This is not to say that policies are unimportant, but rather that they are only one element in the mix of change. They come and go, succeed and fail, amplify existing trends or perhaps delay and subdue them for a while – but they are certainly not the whole picture. The longer time perspective helps us to see this: a short time frame makes it more difficult to stand back from all the rhetoric and display and media attention around new policies in order to see the big picture. That big picture usually includes other influences – cultural, technological, even demographic – that may be simultaneously at work.

The above analysis is not meant to suggest that long-term organizational, technological and cultural trends are completely unconnected with policies; that (for example) the former are never affected by policies, or that policies are hatched in complete ignorance of or indifference towards external trends. On the contrary, policies quite frequently engage directly with these trends, seeking either to speed them up or slow them down (or in some cases prevent them from proceeding altogether). Thus, for example, there are policies to try to guide the types of medical equipment and speeds at which new medical technologies are acquired by hospitals. These may not be the most publicly and politically salient aspects of hospital policies, but they are important nonetheless. Our point, therefore, is not that the two types of change (policy or long-term external trends) are totally disconnected, but rather that, from a 40-year perspective, many policies come and go, but the trends in organizational specialization, managerialization and technological change look more consequential and less strategically or tactically 'chosen' than are most policy shifts. In short, there is much more than just policy to the stories of change in the hospital and police services.

A second initial observation would be that there does not seem to be any obvious, regular, repeating or cumulative pattern to change, in either country or either service. None of these stories are of a neat cycle of stability followed by punctuation, followed by stability, followed by punctuation – at least not with any regular periodicity. But neither are they tales of steady incremental change, with each service moving step by step along a particular path. Patterns there may be, but of a messier, less predictable kind – we will come back to them in a short while.

A third observation would be that the similarities and differences indicated above seem to derive from different levels or locations in the overall governance and social systems. (The following is not a perfect match, but a rough generalization.) The differences appear to derive mainly from distinctive, high-level, long-lasting features of the national political systems of the two countries. Thus the faster pace of change in England and the greater emphasis on quite 'hard' performance management were both outcomes of the strong, majoritarian, 'law-lite', more centralized, political system in that country, contrasting strongly with the weaker, federal, law-heavy, fragmented nature of government in Belgium. However, the similarities are generated by deeper, perhaps less obvious but extensively international trends in society and technology. Thus the technological changes influencing hospital design, clinical practice and, indeed, the cost of acute healthcare are international and common to at least all advanced countries. They do not force a single solution in every case but they do seem to push hospitals in common general directions. Something very similar can be said of police methods. Or again, the increased emphasis on the need to consider public sector organizations of all kinds as managed entities is part of the huge growth of managerial ideology and of management knowledge throughout the Western world and beyond (Parker, 2002; Pollitt, 1993; Sahlin-Andersson and Engwall, 2002).

Fourth, the specific influences of EU membership in both these sectors seems to have been rather marginal. One can write quite a satisfactory history of the two services in the two countries with hardly any reference to EU policymaking or regulation. Of course there have been some impacts – police cooperation through Europol or the European coordination of pharmaceutical regulation in healthcare – but at no time do these either head the domestic policy agendas or dominate operational management at the local level. The domestic effects of EU membership have, as many writers have observed, varied enormously according to, *inter alia*, the competencies set out in the treaties (for example Scharpf, 1999). We happen to have chosen two sectors where the competencies of the EU institutions are at present very limited. This may not continue indefinitely – for example, as we write (2009), the Commission has produced a draft regulation concerning the right of EU citizens to access health services in countries other than their own – but up to now it would be hard to argue that the EU was a key actor in either hospital policy or police policy.

Next, to reflect more systematically on our findings, we should return to the main questions raised in Chapter 1, namely:

1. What is the nature of multigovernment policymaking and, in particular, what is the evidence concerning the relative autonomy of subnational public authorities?
2. What kind of patterns (if any) can we see in our 40-year period of study?
3. What kind of mechanisms or processes seem best to explain the patterns we believe we can see?

8.2   WHAT IS THE NATURE OF MULTIGOVERNMENT POLICYMAKING AND, IN PARTICULAR, WHAT IS THE EVIDENCE CONCERNING THE RELATIVE AUTONOMY OF SUBNATIONAL PUBLIC AUTHORITIES?

Unsurprisingly, perhaps, the nature of multigovernment policymaking seems to be heavily influenced by the nature of the political system (constitution, electoral system, party system).

One striking difference between the two countries lies in the pattern and processes of elite networks. In Belgium these networks span the federal/regional and local levels, and to a considerable extent they are also cross-sectoral. It is not merely that the mayors know the ministers, it is that the mayors often *are* ex-ministers, and vice versa. This perhaps creates the potential for a kind of informal coordination which is more difficult in England:

> Before the direct elections of the regional parliaments (1995) all members of the community and regional parliaments . . . were also members of the Chamber or the Senate. One week they would sit as a member of the federal Parliament, the other week as a regional/community MP. Through this personal combination of mandates, co-ordination between the parliamentary groups . . . at the federal and sub-federal levels did not pose a major problem. (De Winter et al., 2006, p. 941)

In England the links are more distant and, of course, the greater size of the country means that the elites themselves are bigger and more diversified. On the other hand England does not experience the strong division by language and community that characterizes the Belgian situation. It may be that the Flemish elite finds it easier to coordinate multilevel governmental policymaking than is usually feasible in England, but for the Flemish elite to coordinate with the Walloon elite is another story altogether (De Winter et al., 2006, p. 938).

These differences in elites and the cleavages between elites cast the whole issue of autonomy in a different light. Increasingly, during the period under study, the question in Belgium has become less what autonomy central government will allow to the regions and municipalities, as what federal actions the regions are prepared to put up with. The English assumption of a powerful centre, dictating the terms of multigovernment interactions, is wholly inappropriate across 50 km of water. Here we confirm something that has been noticed by other writers. Klijn, in a general piece on networks and governance observes that:

> [O]ne could argue that the growth of governance networks in the UK differs from that seen in many other countries in that it has a more strongly instrumental/managerial and vertical flavour. (Klijn, 2008, p. 515)

8.3 WHAT KIND OF PATTERNS (IF ANY) CAN WE SEE IN OUR 40-YEAR PERIOD OF STUDY?

8.3.1 'Policies Are Not . . .'

In Chapter 1, section 1.3, drawing on the wider policy literature, we listed a number of things that we thought policy usually was not. Subsequently, in section 1.10, we developed three key features of a historical institution-alist approach:

- History matters.
- Institutions matter.
- Developments over time often exhibit certain patterns.

Here we will revisit that introductory template. First, we will look again at the list of what we thought policy was not, a list drawn from the general public policy literature. We need to check how far our Anglo-Belgian investigations confirm or refute those starting assumptions. Then, second, we will discuss what patterns are discernable in our hospital and police stories.

Our first 'policy is not' statement in Chapter 1 was that policy was not usually 'an instrumental-rational business, with clear goals, objectives, calculations of costs and benefit and so on'. The police and hospital stories show that policies could usually be dressed up in this rational garb, but that in practice there were also usually contradictions, ambiguities, con-flicts and accidents as well. Take 'community policing'. It was certainly instrumental and rational in the sense that politicians and police were responding to public concerns and fears (as amplified by the media). Yet at the same time it was a slippery concept, referring to quite a range of groups and types of location or administrative unit, and to a pot pourri of tech-niques and approaches. 'It is hard to determine what precisely is entailed in community policing or what precisely constitutes the community focus' (Tilley, 2008, p. 40). Furthermore, governments have generally avoided giving explicit guidance on how this top priority is to be balanced against the other 'top priorities' such as terrorism or organized crime. Finally, insofar as a good deal of research showed that routine patrolling of the streets was a pretty inefficient way of using expensive professionals, it was irrational to put more effort into it (Audit Commission, 1996).

Community policing also illustrates our second 'is not': that policy usually is not a neatly staged process leading from formulation to imple-mentation to evaluation. Community policing seems more like a hardy perennial – something that sprouts up suddenly (especially after some race riot or community collapse) and is then formulated and elaborated after its introduction as a headline concept. Subsequently it gradually fades from view until the next prominent local disturbance, at which point it is resuscitated and dressed up again. Evaluations are occasional and fre-quently inconclusive. Nevertheless, it is very hard to be against community policing – it is widely accepted as a 'good thing'.

Our third caveat was that what finally gets done (or left undone) often does not closely match the policy as originally announced. This is certainly not a universal divergence, but it is a frequent one. When we look at the history of the KU Leuven (KUL) hospital we see its founders working with a vision of a particular kind of integrated hospital that would be the leading institution of its kind in Flanders and Belgium. Remarkably, 35 years later, that vision has been broadly realized. Elsewhere, however, divergence is common. The huge post-Scarman police effort in England during the 1980s to improve police–community relations, especially in ethnically mixed areas, did not prevent later racially fuelled urban disorders and neither did it enable the police, in the twenty-first century, to reach their equal opportunity recruitment targets, or to avoid well-publicized tensions within the Metropolitan Police and other forces. To put it generously, cultural change is very slow. In Belgium, we can refer to the government's efforts to moderate the growth of the hospital budgets by increasing the fraction of the cost of hospital visits that patients would have to pay themselves. Instead of causing patients to refrain from seeking unnecessary hospital care, initially it mainly led to a rapid growth in top-up insurance to bridge the gap between what the basic mutuality insurance would pay and what the hospital charged. In both countries we have seen periodic initiatives and policy pronouncements intended to eliminate police corruption but it is clear that, though they may ameliorate the problem, such corruption is actually endemic, always able to take new forms, and is particularly associated with certain roles or tasks (Punch, 2008, pp. 51–3).

The idea that policy simply flows from the head of one great leader seldom finds any purchase in our histories. Even if the Leuven hospital grew from the vision of a small number of medical academics, its realization crucially depended on a wider network of Flemish politicians. Even if Chief Constable Ken Jones vigorously led the Sussex force towards a tighter, more performance-driven approach to policing, he did so with internal and external allies, and (not least) in the knowledge that his approach commanded enthusiastic support from ministers and the Home Office.

Similarly, the idea that policymaking begins at the top and flows down organizational hierarchies does not fit with several important elements in our tale. The new Leuven hospital was born of local enthusiasts, although enthusiasts who were wise enough to do their international homework and evaluate a wide range of hospital design concepts. They went on to persuade the upper reaches of the university and then the Flemish and Belgian political hierarchies. Even in the far more centralized English hospital system there are many instances of local innovations or pilots which attract attention and then get 'rolled out' to other locations. The Royal

Sussex, for example, had a charismatic and politically astute consultant physician, Sir Anthony Trafford, who was able to influence, innovate and 'get things done' locally. Chief Constable Paul Whitehouse of Sussex held out against the use of CS gas for riot control by his force, and actively supported alternatives at a time when most English forces were relying on CS.

A further mis-assumption is that policy debates are just about differences of opinion on a fixed range of issues. We have certainly seen evidence to support the point that comes from the more general policy literature to the effect that issues or problems themselves are conceived in different ways by different participants. Thus the lack of major new hospital infrastructure investment in Brighton and Hove between 1970 and 1997 was seen differently by different actors. From the Ministry's angle, Sussex was simply not as needy as some of the economically and socially deprived areas elsewhere in the country. From the position of the NHS regional administration for south-east England there were other places in the region that were even worse off – Hastings, for example. For the staff and managers of some other hospitals in the area it was a threat of closure or downgrading of their institutions, if Brighton were to get money to build a big new hospital. Local politicians also tended to line up in this rivalrous, territorial way: 'we must not lose Hove General without getting something to replace it in Hove', and so on. For the hospital managers and clinical staff (and patients) in Brighton itself it was an immediate practical matter of leaking roofs and crowded, old-fashioned wards. For some other clinical staff in the area it was an opportunity to move resources out of the acute, hospital sector and into more low-tech, community-based facilities.

Finally – and this may be the assumption that is most painful to abandon – we should not assume, even with the great gift of hindsight, that we can confidently sort past policies into two boxes marked 'success' and 'failure'. Different stakeholder groups will often (although not always) have radically different opinions about what constitutes success. (Of course, this is less surprising if they started out with different views of what the issue was.) Thus, the ministerial 'no' to the development of Holmes Avenue as a new 'hot' site for acute medicine in the late 1980s was a defeat and a failure for the management team at Brighton, but for the Ministry in London it could be construed as the successful application of rational, national principles of hospital planning. On other occasions, however, it is hard to see any 'winners': if one thinks of the sequence of failures in the handling of the Dutroux case in Belgium, culminating in his temporary escape in 1998, the reputations of virtually all the relevant policymaking groups suffered in consequence (Maesschalck and Van de Walle, 2006, p. 999).

8.3.2 What Kind of Patterns?

Having dealt with this list of mis-assumptions – and confirmed that as far as our study is concerned they are such – we can now turn to the question of patterns of change. To provide us with some framework for this discussion we repeat the BEST diagram originally introduced in Chapter 1 – see Table 8.1

Before we dive into the detail of this analysis it is necessary to pause and remind ourselves of the levels at which we have been operating. In Chapters 3 and 4 we described sectoral policies at national levels. In Chapters 6 and 7 we described local policies in an English city and county and a Belgian city and its hinterland. The book has therefore been pitched mainly at what, in policy studies terms, is the middle or meso-level, with a few more detailed, micro-level touches to fill out the local narratives. Other than very briefly in Chapter 2 we have not been much engaged at the macro-level. We have not traced, for example, the changing shape of the welfare state in either country, or in explained overall shifts in the national machineries of government. This has implications for the kinds of theoretical apparatuses which are most appropriate for our enquiry. In short, it has pushed us towards the idiographic end of the nomothetic–idiographic spectrum that was mentioned in Chapter 1, section 1.10. Kay puts the issue like this:

> It may be valid to run historical regressions of regime change on percentage of gross domestic product (GDP) spent to establish general theories that predict with an acceptable degree of accuracy regime or empire shifts over several centuries. Similarly, general propositions may be uncovered at the level of welfare state regimes . . . However, a different scale of perspective is involved when

Table 8.1 *Patterns of institutional change: the 'BEST' schema*

		Result of change	
		Within path/incremental	Radical/transformation
Process of change	Gradual	A. Classic incrementalism *TORTOISE*	B. Gradual, but eventually fundamental change *STALACTITE*
	Abrupt	C. 'Radical conservatism' – rapid return to previous ways *BOOMERANG*	D. Sudden, radical change *EARTHQUAKE* (punctuation)

Source: Developed from Streeck and Thelen (2005), p. 9.

looking at UK health policy over a 20-year period, or at a series of economic policy reforms within a particular government's lifetime. The contextual moves to the foreground in detailed accounts of policy change over time; this is the essence of policy studies. (Kay, 2006, p. 23)

Thus our study is of a more 'granular', contexed kind, and the patterns we may (or may not) find are unlikely to fit the formal and usually highly abstract nature of broad, hypothetico-deductive generalizations. (We will return to this issue in greater depth when we look at doctrines of comparison in the final chapter.)

To come now to the substance, the first, and most important point, is that our Anglo-Belgian comparison has yielded examples of all four types of change, often mutually interwoven. To develop this point, change does not seem to come in one package. More typically, several different types of change may be going on in a given sector during a given period, each layered upon and tangled with the others. This complexity appears to have been true for both sectors and both countries – it thus transcends the important institutional and cultural differences between Belgium and England that we have previously commented upon. Our two-country, two-sector comparison therefore gives no grounds for believing that a particular kind of political system produces one these patterns of change (say Tortoise) while another system produces another (say Earthquake). Both systems produce a mixture of the different patterns indicated in Table 8.1

However, there is a different frequency to the occurrence of change, as between the four categories. On the whole it is the top line – gradual change – which seems most common. Sudden, unreversed, radical change (Earthquake) is the rarest, and we have few examples of it in our study. The most obvious one is the creation of the new university hospital at Leuven, but even that is not a 100 per cent clear case. In its favour one might say that an entirely new, large facility, of an innovatory design, was swiftly built and, when put into operation, employed what were (for Belgium) novel systems of human resource management, and a 'progressive' philosophy of integrated, multidisciplinary care. This is by any yardstick a major achievement, but its position as a pure Earthquake is slightly diluted by two further observations. First, for large hospitals, the move from vision to working reality cannot be particularly fast. The 'big idea' for the new KU Leuven Ziekenhuis dates from the late 1960s and early 1970s, but the inauguration of the hospital did not take place until 1985. Whether one can describe this as 'sudden' is doubtful. Second, the ideas involved, while new for the Belgian hospital scene, were largely (consciously, systematically) taken from the existing, international professional discourse of the time.

The other relatively rare type of change is Boomerang – 'radical conservatism'. Here we might consider the 1989 White Paper and subsequent reforms to the NHS. These were intended to produce a quasi-market, with hospitals competing with one another for contracts from health authorities. There can be no question that this was a major change, and on a far, far greater scale than the new KUL Ziekenhuis. At the time it was perceived by most informed commentators as both radical and risky. In one of Europe's largest and most complex institutions, a 30-year-old system of hierarchical bureaucracy was to be replaced by an untried system of quasi-market competition, hatched in great secrecy by a small group of the then Prime Minister's ideological sympathisers. This went far beyond Hall's first level of change (change in the setting of specific policy instruments) and to the very limit of the second level (shifts in the type of policy instrument) (Hall, 1993). Some argued that it was actually a change in the policy paradigm (level three) although we find that more debatable. Yet what actually happened next? Within a short space of time it became clear that ministers had little appetite for the risks of real competition, so that 'the fierce commitment to the market which accompanied the launch of the White Paper became progressively diluted' (Harrison and McDonald, 2008, p. 93). Then the incoming Labour government of 1997 announced that it would abolish the market (though it never dismantled the fundamental purchaser–provider split, and it later brought in new market-type mechanisms). Therefore this story from 1991–2000 was by no means a wholesale reversion to the *status quo ante*, but it was a kind of return to the broad pattern of local collaboration and bargaining between institutional and professional groups – though structured in new ways, organizationally speaking. The Boomerang curved back part of the way, but not right back to the point of origin. The internal market arrangements had originally given some groups some new levers and tactics, but policy and practice sheared away from the volatility which full-blooded competition would probably have inaugurated

In some ways Stalactite – gradual but eventually fundamental change – is one of the less obvious and more interesting patterns. The steady, small dripping of limed water eventually produces a major, even a spectacular new structure in the cave. One example would be the professionalization of the police (a process that may have gone further in England than Belgium, but which is fundamentally common to both countries). This has had many strands to it, but the end result is a far better trained, more technologically and socially sophisticated police force than would have been imaginable back at the beginning of our period of study. This has multiple implications: 'Professionalization has not been the result of a managed process', but 'an increasingly professionalized workforce will need to be managed differently from the traditional, non-specialist model on which many police human resource practices are based' (Stelfox, 2008, p. 227). So here is a case where significant and widespread change has resulted without it having been driven by a single, consistently articulated government policy. As we said earlier, policy – certainly national policy – has not been the only or sometimes even the main source of change.

Finally we come to Tortoise – classic incrementalism. The evolution of the Belgian hospital system as a whole is one example of this – repeated but on the whole quite small adjustments to policy, comprising a gradual tightening of both planning and financing regimes. Another example could arguably be the development of the hospital system in Brighton and Hove. True, a lot has happened, and many small hospitals have closed. But these closures have tended to be quite long-drawn-out and carefully staged. Meanwhile the final closure of Brighton's second main acute hospital (the Brighton General) has been an extremely elongated process which is not completely over even in 2009. And the build-up on the Royal Sussex site has been cumulative, over several decades.

8.3.3   A more Schematic Approach?

Since the first chapter we have made use of two broad categorizations of policy change – the three levels of Hall, and the fourfold categorization into Boomerang, Earthquake, Stalactite and Tortoise (BEST) which we have ourselves built out of an original schema suggested by Streeck and Thelen. The Hall scheme focuses mainly on the level of the change – small, medium or big, as defined by whether only settings, or instruments or paradigms themselves are altered. Our BEST schema focuses on both the level of change and its modality: has the process been brutal and short (Earthquake) or slow but directional (Stalactite) or meandering and gradual (Tortoise) or fast but short-lived (Boomerang)? The two schemes do not map directly onto each other, except that Hall's level three change would clearly have to be the product of either Earthquake or Stalactite.

It has been clear from the beginning that assigning actual, real-world policies to cells within either of these typologies entails a good deal of judgement on the part of the analyst. Neither scheme fits neatly over all the varieties of specific policies in a messy world. Policies cannot sensibly be displayed like stamps in a stamp album, neatly lined up in rows according to indisputable criteria of date, origin, denomination and so on. There is a question, therefore, of how far we can push such typologies. Whilst they seem tolerably clear and useful at a macro-level or over a long time span, how far can we take them into our meso-world before they lose their discriminatory power and become factors that complicate rather than simplify?

Despite much discussion, we are entirely not sure ourselves what the correct answer to this question should be. In the remainder of this sub-section we therefore make a highly tentative attempt to apply the BEST scheme and the Hall three-level model at a level of greater detail. We will do this at the local rather than the national level, partly because these types of scheme have been less often applied there, so the exercise is more original, and partly because we anticipate that going 'down' to local level may provide a stiffer test for these classifications.

First, therefore, we have to go back to the 'local' chapters – Chapters 6 and 7 – to select key changes for analysis. This is in itself problematic, insofar as we cannot regard our selections as representative of the total population of policies in any statistical sense. This book has never claimed to be able to describe all policies (indeed, it is doubtful if any book could). Thus there are whole areas of hospital policy and police policy which have fallen entirely outside our research. We have not looked at police recruitment policy, for example, nor at police financial management. Neither have we examined hospital safety policies, or the NHS initiatives on junior doctors' working hours – important though all these issues were.

What we did do at local level was to ask which changes had been important, and which things had stayed broadly the same (see Appendix). So if we go back to Chapters 6 and 7 and ask what the important changes seemed to have been, we come up with a list like that in Table 8.2. The capital letter in brackets after each entry signifies our best assessment as to whether the change was B, E, S or T.

How well do these fit into Hall's model and BEST? We can take them one by one.

The double failure to secure a new greenfield site acute hospital for Brighton (mid-1970s and late 1980s) is hard to characterize using BEST. That is because, first, it was a non-change rather than a change – the defeat of local policymaking rather than an achievement. Looked at from a macro-perspective, however, the two rejections were rather different decisions, one from the other. The first was the result of an Earthquake on a national, indeed global, scale. Following the oil price shocks of the early 1970s the British economy wobbled badly, and the government of the day felt itself bound to seek International Monetary Fund (IMF) aid – a nightmare shift of paradigm. One price of that aid was a set of deep cuts to the whole range of public spending programmes. The new hospital at Falmer was just one local example of many casualties in these fiscally fraught times. The second rejection was a result of a more incremental policy. It was the national policy, explicitly pursued from the mid-1970s onwards for many years, to ration NHS new investment at the margin in favour of those parts of the country which suffered the highest morbidity and

Table 8.2   Key local changes

Brighton hospitals	Leuven hospitals
1. 2 x failure to get greenfield site for new hospital (?)	1. Creation of new KUL *Ziekenhuis* (E)
2. Long-term centralization on RSCH site (T)	2. Governance crisis 1998 (S)
Sussex Police	**Leuven Police**
1. PACE, 1984 (E?)	1. 1977 merger of forces (E?)
2. Partnerships policy, from late 1980s (T)	2. 1990 Pinksterplan (S)
3. Growth of performance management, from early 1990s (S)	3. Dutroux events, 1996–98 (E)
4. Growing general Whitehall intervention, from early 1990s (S)	4. 2001 merger of forces (E)
5. Early retirement of Chief Constable in 2001 (?)	5. Professionalization and specialization (S)
6. Professionalization and specialization (S)	

mortality. This was a perfectly rational policy in its own terms, and incremental when viewed from the Olympian perspective of the Department of Health. From a Brighton point of view, however, it meant that it was always going to be hard to make a strong enough case for a single, big new investment. This policy might be thought of as a Tortoise, because it involved a very slow, step-by-step migration towards equalling out the historically unequal distribution of resources within the NHS. (Had it ever reached its goal it might have been recognized as a Stalactite at national level, but that is not an issue we can deal with here.) Yet for Brighton (and other localities) it had a sharp, singular result – not half a new hospital or a quarter of a new hospital, but no new hospital at all. Overall, then, the BEST framework is not particularly helpful here, and neither is Hall's three-level model.

The long-term centralization and reprovision of acute facilities on the Royal Sussex County Hospital (RSCH) site was a Tortoise type of change. It went on, bit by bit, for virtually the whole of our 40-year period. It accelerated in the 1990s, when it had become clear that the alternative of a greenfield site was as good as dead, and when the Private Finance Initiative made the availability of capital somewhat less constrained. In the period 1998–2008 the amount of new investment on the RSCH site has been very considerable, but it would be incorrect to represent this as a deliberate long-term policy all along.

Turning to Leuven, the creation of the new KUL Ziekenhuis must probably be regarded as an Earthquake. Local policymakers seized the moment and created something that had no precedent – a large, brand new, uniquely Flemish teaching hospital. It also qualifies as a level three change in Hall's terms, mainly because it was consciously organized along novel lines – a new concept of a hospital, at least for Belgium.

The KUL finance and governance crisis of 1998 is harder to fit into the BEST scheme. It could be seen as a Tortoise but we would be inclined to label it as more of a Stalactite. This is because there had been two streams of events, each flowing in the same direction over a decade or more, which finally reached a point at which there was a rapid shift in key relationships. The first stream was financial – a cycle of deficits which seemed to be gaining in amplitude and a gradually tightening set of government regulations about reimbursement. The second was political and managerial – the new hospital had gained more and more de facto independence from its parent university, but the latter was beginning to wonder whether this was such a good thing, especially if it was ultimately the university that was going to have to pick up any financial losses. Finally the university asserted its authority and 'made an issue' of what had actually been building up for many years. In terms of Hall's model one would say that 1998 marked a second-level change. There was no change in the paradigm of the hospital as a leading national and international centre but there was a refashioning of the governing instruments.

We now come to the key police developments. The Police and Criminal Evidence Act (PACE) was a central government initiative, a detailed new statute born out of a recent history of embarrassing public reports of the police mishandling suspects and evidence. When it came it was almost immediately decisive. Many senior policemen referred back to it. Nationally and locally, it could be regarded as an Earthquake in the detailed work of the police. In Hall's terms it would be a high level two change (what had previously been partly informal and conventional became specific and statutory). Or possibly it could be said to have been a level three change, insofar as a legal and bureaucratic model was substituted for the previous view of police work as a norm-governed craft.

Partnerships policy is another one which is problematic in terms of our classification schemes. To begin with, it was hard to define, since the terminology was various and it overlapped with a number of other concepts, including neighbourhood policing. Our interviewees tended to divide into those who thought it had been very important and those who did not even mention it. Then it was something where the relationship between inputs and outputs was not particularly clear. Obviously great efforts had gone into discussing it and how it should be organized. But it was much less clear what effects this might have had on actual police operations, and still less on outcomes in terms of public order. It has waxed and waned on local agendas, but had basically grown from the late 1980s onwards and had later become a part of the new national orthodoxy, so that Brighton was one of the police authorities which could claim to be ahead of the field. We therefore classified it as a Tortoise, although we suspect that some of our interviewees (but not others) would have said it was more of a Stalactite – something which accumulated until it was a striking feature of the police landscape. In Hall's terms it is again hard to place. Some might say it was (for England) such a new idea that it should be seen as a paradigm-breaking third-level innovation. Others would argue that it was merely going back to earlier days – righting the balance a bit after the techno-cop period of the 1970s and early 1980s. Certainly it entailed the creation of some new policy instruments (level two).

The growth of performance indicators (PIs) was another much-mentioned change, and one that we would see as a Stalactite. When PIs were first used in the late 1980s they did not seem particularly central to police operations – an interesting new managerial gimmick, perhaps, but not much more. Gradually, however, the framework of PIs grew in scope and sophistication, and the government started to use them more and more for assessing the competence of police forces. By the end of our period they had almost become a way of life. In Hall's terms they are clearly level two – a (once) new policy instrument.

Performance indicators were one element in a wider phenomenon – growing Whitehall intervention in the management of police forces. This movement also involved, *inter alia*, the reshaping of the police authorities in the mid-1990s and the introduction of regular National Policing Plans from 2002. We would classify this as a Stalactite because it involved many different moves over a decade or more in a consistent direction (including some that were diluted or defeated by the police themselves). No single move was in itself an Earthquake, but they accumulated. This process reflected a conscious and deliberate intent that was, to a large degree, shared by the Major Conservative government and its New Labour successor. In terms of Hall's model this succession of measures certainly represented level two change (new instruments) and there is a case for saying that if one compared, say, 2005 with 1975, there had actually been a shift in the paradigm governing relations between the government and its police forces.

The 2001 catharsis of Paul Whitehouse's resignation is another development that is hard to classify. Whilst virtually all our interviewees thought it had been important and traumatic, the deeper question is whether it made a big difference to the way the Sussex police were organized. We are inclined to answer 'Some but not much.' Certainly there was a change in mood and style under Ken Jones, and the use of perfomance indicators came to the fore, but these strike us as changes of emphasis rather than significant changes of policy. The main lines of national government policy continued to be applied within the Sussex force. So it does not qualify as an Earthquake, but neither was it a Boomerang, Stalactite or Tortoise. It was a dramatic event but not one that can be readily fitted into either the Hall model or BEST.

Finally, the long-term, multifaceted processes by which the Sussex Police (and other English forces) became more specialized and professional are probably our best example of a Stalactite. Sometimes this direction was facilitated by central policies (PACE led to a huge training effort for nearly all police) and sometimes it was more a matter of local initiative (setting up a special unit for this or that; developing special techniques for dealing with 'problem estates'). Taken as a whole this process would easily qualify as a Hall level two change and it could be argued that, over three decades, it has almost amounted to a level three shift of paradigm (from a practical, generalist force to a high-tech, specialized force).

The first key change for the Leuven police was the 1976–77 restructuring. This is another issue which is hard to classify. In one way it seems of great consequence – an Earthquake – but in another it appears to be of much smaller importance: just a change to organizational structures which, although big in terms of numbers of forces, had little immediate effect on police cultures or operational practices. Some of our interviewees took this latter view, some the former. We cannot, with any confidence, find a box to fit it.

The Pinksterplan of 1990 is also less than straightforward. We tend to see it as an early and important step in a long process that eventually, with the 'help' of external events, led to the major structural reforms of 1998–2001. We would therefore bracket this with the Dutroux drama of 1996–98 and the 1998 Police Reform Act. They form a set of factors which eventually produced an Earthquake, but only after a Stalactite-like process of negotiations and attempted reforms that stretched back for a decade. Dutroux was an Earthquake that provided the window of opportunity that, in some sense, the reformers had been waiting for. It enabled them to cement their intentions in the new law, which itself became an Earthquake for structural and professional reforms.

Last of all we should refer to the processes of professionalization and specialization which affected the Leuven Police as they did the Sussex Police. These fit quite well to the notion of a Stalactite. As in Sussex, there were many sources, central and local (and occasionally even international) but they tended to flow in the same general direction – towards quality, standards, training, professionalism. It is a process which still continues.

According to Hall's model, it mainly involves level two changes, but there is a judgement to be made about when so many of these have accumulated that the new ensemble can be regarded as a new paradigm.

To sum up this subsection, it seems that neither the BEST nor Hall's three-level scheme work very easily when applied to detailed policy narratives at meso- and lower levels. Most of the key developments which we identified can, with a bit of intellectual effort, be pushed into one of the BEST boxes. Sometimes they fit quite snugly. But in quite a few cases there is some uncertainty about which box is most appropriate, and in one or two it is clear that none of the four boxes fits very comfortably at all. One obvious untidiness about real world changes is that they may change speed over time. For a few years they may Tortoise along, and then speed up during a particular period and subsequently slow down again. To take this point further, the BEST scheme (and its Streeck and Thelen forebear) really only offer a two-speed gearbox – gradual and abrupt. But there is no reason why policies should not proceed like a car in traffic, crawling here, speeding up a bit when the traffic eases, and occasionally, on the open road, travelling really fast. In short the patterns of change are more varied than a simple two-by-two classification can fully capture. We need at least a four- or five-speed gearbox, and the capacity to make gear changes as the conditions in the policy traffic and the wider environment change.

The principal value of the two schemes (and it is considerable) is therefore heuristic – they do help to organize broad ideas and generate useful questions. Trying to use them obliges the user to think hard about what the shape of the policy was, and how best to describe apparent changes of pace. (And they do fit quite a number of episodes, even if they do not fit all.) The performance of BEST (or Hall's three levels) is less impressive when they are deployed as empirical sieves for ordering detailed data and/or generating matrices of policy performance. The problems in this latter role are just too many. One would need a population of all policies in order to establish true representativeness, and that can seldom be achieved. Policies would need to be: (1) readily identifiable; (2) mutually exclusive; and (3) roughly comparable units, so that they could be meaningfully counted. But in fact policies overlap and interact, and different policies have vastly different scopes and weights and lifetimes. And there is the further complication that a T at national level may constitute an E at local level, or a local B may not register as anything important at national level at all.

Thus to apply BEST or Hall's model as the basis for a comprehensive quantitative analysis would be highly problematic. It would be counting together not so much apples and pears as branches, trees and forests. Furthermore the Hall scheme has an additional limitation, from our point of view. It is built to deal with specific policies, whereas, as we have demonstrated, changes in public management quite frequently come about through processes that are less a matter of explicit 'policy' than of a slow, drip, drip of low- and middling-level changes in a certain direction – in other words Stalactites. So, again, the Hall scheme, useful though it is within its intended field of application, will not stretch to cover all the important events that emerged from our Anglo-Belgian narratives.

This mention of 'narratives' is perhaps the right point at which to conclude this subsection. We would suggest that the main insights in the preceding chapters were generated by the approach of analytic narrative, rather than by the application of BEST or Hall's three levels. The latter have been useful props to the narrative, and have prompted us to ask some key questions, but their role has been just that – supportive rather than formative. We shall have something more to say about the role of narrative in the final chapter, but now we must get back to the business of explanation. What has generated the complex patterns which we have observed?

8.4 WHAT KIND OF MECHANISMS OR PROCESSES SEEM BEST TO EXPLAIN THE PATTERNS WE BELIEVE WE CAN SEE?

It is immediately apparent that we need a broad, not a narrow, concept of mechanisms. It needs to embrace not only economic mechanisms such as increasing returns and sunk costs, but also institutional and symbolic processess such as embedded organizational routines and concerns about legitimacy (Pollitt, 2008, pp. 3–44, 146–7; Carter, 2008). Thus, for example, the symbolic value of Flemish autonomy was a crucial sustaining component in the early years of the new Leuven hospital, and the organizational routines introduced by the English police in response to the 1984 Police and Criminal Evidence Act were regarded by many as a deep and irreversible change in the handling of police suspects.

We can immediately notice that, in contrast with a good deal of the theoretical literature on path dependency (for example Pierson, 2004) not all these mechanisms provide 'increasing returns over time'. Indeed, some of them – the symbolism of Flemish autonomy for example – provide an initial boost and may then begin to fade away. We therefore agree with Kay (2006, p. 34) that: 'Increasing returns are sufficient but not necessary for path dependency.'

We should also register the (perhaps unfashionable) opinion that the existence of a law is important – at least in generally law-respecting, stable political regimes such as those of Belgium and England. It really does matter whether something is a legal requirement or just a 'guideline' or set of 'principles of good practice'. A statutory provision has at least three effects, all of which tend to promote stability and continuity. First, it makes it much harder for public officials and professionals to ignore or sideline the requirement. At the very least, it has to be incorporated into their training and 'given the nod' in official communications. Second, it provides those who wish to hold organizations to account with a firm base on which to ask questions: 'This is the law – have you carried it out or not?' Third, because it is a law, and the processes of legislating (in both countries) is lengthy and expensive of political resources, it is hard to replace or modify. The law is something which is expected to remain reasonably stable, and which is usually difficult to change. A guideline, or charter, or a policy expressed mainly in political rhetoric and glossy brochures: all these can be buried or bent more quickly and more easily. There is a difference of degree between our two countries here, insofar as the English political system gives the (one-party) government greater control over legislation and the legislature than is usually the case in Belgium. Yet reversing an existing law is frequently an inconvenient and time-consuming activity even for a British government, so the basic point still applies.

Having got these preliminaries out of the way, we can turn to the core question of 'What are the mechanisms?' A first approximation would be to say that they are of various types: symbolic, legal, technological, financial, organizational and cultural. Just as there is no single pattern of change (see above) so neither can most of the changes we observed be attributed to the working of a single mechanism. On the contrary, the usual situation is one where several mechanisms operate jointly, although some may act over quite short time periods while others accumulate over much longer ones. Thus any simple idea that policy continuity is caused by something called 'path-dependency' and that this means a kind of political paralysis induced by a single powerful mechanism which brings ever-increasing returns for doing the same thing over and over, should be abandoned. We can find no example of this in the evidence we have reviewed in this book. The 'norm', as far as we can tell, is a situation where policy stability is underpinned by a variety of different mechanisms, some waxing and some waning at any given moment in time, some 'hard' considerations of vote or resource counting, others vague but strong cultural notions of 'who we are and how we do business round here', and some rather dull but deeply embedded legal and organizational processes such as budgeting or planning routines.

It may help to illustrate this variety, drawing from the policy narratives of earlier chapters. We can run quickly through the six types suggested above.

Symbolic: we have already mentioned the powerful beacon that

Flemish autonomy provided in the early years of the Leuven hospital development.

Legal: in police reform the unique legal powers of the English Constable have proven a pivot around which other reforms take place. Thus Police Community Support Officers (PCSOs), for example, lack the basic authority to make an arrest, and thus they are not 'proper police'. PACE was important partly because it codified and elaborated what had to happen at and following an arrest. It remains the key legislation a quarter of a century after its enactment (Jason-Lloyd, 2008, pp. 6–7). Politicians know that they meddle with this legal authority (either by reducing it or by spreading it to others) at their peril – the English public may not entirely trust the police with this power to deprive them of their liberty, but they certainly do not want to trust anybody else with it.

Technological: in academic social science two rather extreme positions seem to have become common. The first is that technology is all important, for example that computers 'drive' this and that policy or type of social change and 'will' lead to an 'information society'. The second is its opposite: that all technologies are so heavily mediated through social arrangements that we can treat them as some kind of flexible, socially constructed artefact, entirely dependent for their effects on the social arrangements within which they are deployed. In general terms we find neither of these positions persuasive. Our study of the police and the hospital system shows technological change as playing a central role, sometimes with only dimly foreseen effects. But it also shows the considerable extent to which different organizational and legal arrangements lead to different patterns and purposes of use. Thus, for example, closed-circuit television (CCTV) cameras are used by both Brighton and Leuven Police, but in different ways, using different types of staff and with different legal and procedural constraints. Technologies can creep up on organizations (like email and mobile phones sometimes did) or they can be introduced with fanfares. Either way, they frequently seem to carry longer-term effects on organization and even upon culture. A police example here would be the tremendous growth in forensic science – not only DNA testing but also a wide variety of other techniques. These have led directly to fundamental changes to the ways in which police officers treat scenes of crimes, including the injection of a series of specialist investigators, many of them civilian staff, into the very heart of the police officer's territory – the crime scene itself. They also mean that police officers have to learn the capabilities of these new technologies, and consider how far evidence derived from them is likely to stand up in court. This has been one important element in the increasing professionalization of the police.

Financial: financial procedures are among the more obvious types of mechanism. The continuing inability of the Brighton and Hove hospital authorities ever to win a big enough slice of the tightly controlled NHS capital budget was the single most important reason why no new hospital appeared in the area between 1965 and 2005. This inability can be explained in terms of the particular resource allocation rules in place at the relevant moments when bids were made, and more generally in terms of the existence of a national system that insisted on elaborate comparisons of all bids from right across each region and, indeed, the whole country. The Leuven hospital never had to go through such a nationally orchestrated budgetary trial-by-comparison.

Organizational: organizational routines can act as powerful mechanisms for continuity. Sometimes these routines may actually be embedded in law, which further strengthens their formative power. But even routines that are not prescribed by statute can constrain the rate and direction of change. In interview senior staff at KU Leuven Ziekenhuis were convinced that the medical payment system put in place by Dr Peers in the early 1970s had helped to sustain organizational loyalty and coherence. 'Once the new salary system was accepted, it was a basic turning point' (interview 5)

Cultural: cultural norms are usually self-reproducing and help give an organization or group a sense of its own identity and history. Often they act to reinforce continuity and stability but, in theory at least, it is perfectly possible that an organizational culture could exist that prizes and rewards continuous innovation and change (as was rumoured to be the case at Microsoft). In our study cultural norms were frequently noticeable, and were sometimes emphasized by interviewees. There is, for example, the professional culture of a university teaching hospital, which values research, high skill and technical innovation. One could say that this makes it 'naturally' an ever-changing, expanding, renewing kind of establishment, at least at the micro-level. But this culture also has wider consequences. It means that the staff are constantly developing new treatments, some of which run ahead of the categories in which third-party payers reimburse the hospital for its services. Indeed, this was one component in the financial crisis at KU Leuven Ziekenhuis in the mid-1990s. In the case of the police several of our English interviewees stressed that the 'street culture' of the lower ranks had largely survived the many organizational and technological changes through which the service had gone. They characterized this culture as one which valued pragmatism and a 'can do' attitude and emphasized team loyalties, but combined this with deep scepticism about politicians and 'bosses', plus a fairly jaundiced view of human nature more generally. Most of all, policing was a career, not just a job.

Policy actors are not to be thought of as the passive victims of this array of mechanisms. Some mechanisms may operate 'behind the backs' of some key decision-makers, but for the most part the latter are necessarily aware of the existence of these constraints and incentives. Indeed, part of the definition of a good leader is someone who can effectively combine and 'ride' a set of mechanisms, either to promote or sometimes to ward off change (Wallace, 2007). They cope and they orchestrate. For the deeper kinds of change – Hall's second and third levels – there has to be a collective shift to new ways of conceptualizing and categorizing issues; a conscious rejection of the old rules:

> It is important to note that for a particular policy paradigm to fade and, hence, for institutional change to occur, it is not enough that a single agent comes to recover into consciousness and stop behaving in accordance with it. Rather, the population of agents to which the rule applies must, collectively, stop behaving in accordance with the rule. (Kay, 2006, p. 71)

Thus, in the case of Mrs Thatcher's post-1989 shift to an internal market for the NHS one might say that the original intention was for a definite shift away from the old rule of complex bureaucratic bargaining between hospitals and health authorities, and its substitution by a new rule of efficiency and customer orientation through competition. In the event, however, once ministers became cautious about the consequences of competition, many of the 'agents' in senior NHS positions drifted back to playing the game by a revised version of the old rules.

To conclude this section, it may be worth reflecting on what, in very general terms, we have and have not seen by way of 'patterns'. First, some patterns we have not seen – these are interesting if only because these 'missing' patterns have been mainstays of some of the popular management literature, and occasionally of political rhetoric. Thus, we have not seen:

- Any successful attempts by governments or managements to 'transform the culture' of either hospitals or the police, and instal, within a year or two, a new, designed culture. So one could say there have been no 'Designer Earthquakes', as far as organizational cultures are concerned.
- Any structural reorganizations that have clearly and rapidly transformed the performance of the police or of hospitals on a large scale. So 'Structural Earthquakes' are one thing, but they by no means necessarily lead to 'Performance Earthquakes'.
- Any charismatic leaders who have demonstrably lifted their organization from one state to another within a short period of time.

In short, we have seen no dramatic revolutions, even if the promoters of reform have sometimes claimed that these are about to occur. However, that does not mean that policymaking is a matter mainly for Tortoises. On the contrary, we have seen:

- Long-term cultural change, proceeding incrementally. The growing emphasis on the citizen/patient focus is one good example of this, in both hospital care and policing. Stalactites have turned out to be rather more frequent and important than we anticipated when we began this research.
- Structural reorganizations which have advantaged certain groups or approaches so that, over a course of years, the balance of power and autonomy between different groups within an organization, or between different levels of government, have shifted. On the whole the direction of travel of these shifts has been opposite in the two countries. In England there has been increasing centralization (in both services), while in Belgium there has been increased autonomy for subnational authorities.
- Leaders who have made significant differences to how their staff feel towards their organization, partly by example and partly by visibly endorsing particular policies or styles. Perhaps because of their more clearly hierarchical nature, this phenomenon is more obviously inscribed in the history of police forces, but we can also see the considerable influence of individual leaders such as Dr Peers in the narratives of individual hospitals.

Finally, it should be clearly apparent by now that the search for different kinds of mechanism requires more than one set of methods. Researching long-term cultural change cannot be satisfactorily accomplished using the same tools as are deployed for researching the immediate antecedents of Earthquakes. The role of organizational standard operating procedures cannot be best investigated with the methods we would use for exploring shifts in, say, elite self-perceptions of Flemish autonomy. If we conclude that many types of processes are at work in promoting or inhibiting change, then we must accept the logical consequence that many kinds of research project will be needed to explore these different influences.

8.5 CONNECTIONS WITH LARGER DEBATES IN THE SOCIAL SCIENCES

8.5.1 Introduction

This is not just a comparative study of continuity and change in two public services in neighbouring countries, important though we think that is in itself. It also has a direct bearing on some major contemporary controversies in the social sciences. In particular we believe it sheds some light on the debate initiated by Lijphart (1999) when he suggested that consensual democracies perform better than majoritarian systems, in respect both of representational inputs and of economic and social performance. We also think that it has relevance for the equally important debate about 'input legitimacy' and 'output legitimacy' (Scharpf, 1997). First, therefore, we review these two key debates, and then go on to see what contribution our own study can make to them.

8.5.2 Do Consensual Systems Perform Better than Majoritarian Systems?

After some complex statistical analyses Lijphart concluded that:

> majoritarian democracies do not outperform the consensus democracies on macroeconomic management and the control of violence – in fact, the consensus democracies have slightly the better record – but the consensus democracies do clearly outperform the majoritarian democracies with regard to the quality of democracy and democratic representation as well as with regard to what I have called the kindness and gentleness of their public policy orientations. (Lijphart, 1999, p. 301)

Lijphart was here challenging what he deemed to be the orthodox view, namely that majoritarian governments were more effective because, through their more unified leadership structures, they could make decisions faster and formulate more coherent policies. When he looked at the records of the Organisation for Economic Co-operation and Development (OECD) countries on economic growth, inflation, unemployment, budget deficits and strikes he found no overall evidence of superior performance by the majoritarian states. When he then examined the 'quality of democracy' through various ratings (including the political representation of women, the rich–poor ratio and measures of satisfaction with democracy) he came to the conclusion that the consensus states scored higher. Finally he also found the consensus states to be better placed with respect to 'kinder, gentler qualities' such as high expenditure on social welfare and relatively small prison populations.

Our study of two policy sectors in a majoritarian state and a neighbouring consensus state cannot prove or disprove Lijphart's statistical analyses of many states, but it can throw some additional light on the debate. It suggests, in fact, that Lijphart's way of 'scoring' leaves out some rather important aspects. It is pitched at a high level, and misses out some important practicalities. Most obviously, it omits the question of the efficiency of government. Less obviously, it takes an approach to democratic responsiveness that might satisfy a political scientist but would be less adequate from a public management perspective.

Efficiency may seem a somewhat cold, technical issue – less important than 'kind and gentle' social policies or a principled reluctance to incarcerate any but the most serious criminals. In practice, however, efficiency is both an important everyday issue for citizens and an ethical as well as a technical challenge (Goodin and Wilensky, 1984). It is important for citizens because spending more on social welfare may bring no better results if the money drains away in an inefficient process of policy implementation. And it is an ethical issue because resources spent unnecessarily on a particular service (because of inefficiencies in that service) are therefore unavailable for other needed services (or, indeed, in the form of lower taxes). Such resources are therefore 'wasted'. In our Anglo-Belgian comparison we have seen considerable evidence to indicate that both the hospital service and the police service are less efficient in consensus Belgium than in majoritarian England. There is also evidence to support the contention that many Belgian citizens are aware of the inefficiency of their system, and are unhappy with it for that reason. One of the pivotal political events of the past 20 years – the White March of 1996 – spoke eloquently of a citizenry that had lost confidence in political processes in general and the police and courts in particular. 'The numerous dysfunctions undermined the confidence of the people in their legal system' (Witte et al., 2000, p. 287).

The hospital case is less clear-cut. The trajectories of hospital policies in the two countries reminds us that, important though efficiency is, it is not the only or even necessarily the dominant value in play. Standard input–output ratios, as typically used in the measurement of technical efficiency, fail to capture either the eventual success or failure of the treatment (did the patient get better?) or the quality of the process of care (did the patient feel cared for, listened to and respected during his or her hospital episode?). It is possible that the Belgium system made up for its lower efficiency by higher quality, though we have very little comparative evidence on that. Extracts from a 2007 Eurobarometer survey of citizens do indeed suggest a degree of difference in favour of Belgium, although both countries score above the EU average (see Table 8.3). An earlier, 1993

Table 8.3   Public experiences of hospital care in Belgium and the UK

Country	Very good %	Fairly good %	Fairly bad %	Very bad %
Belgium	29	64	5	1
UK	24	53	12	6

Source: Special Eurobarometer 283 (2007), Table QA3.1.

survey similarly showed Belgians to be more satisfied with their health care system, and also showed quite big differences (in favour of Belgium) of public perceptions of how well run the health care system was (Mossialos, 1997). Such surveys of popular perceptions are not the firmest ground on which to found public policymaking (perceptions may be heavily context-dependent and even volatile), but we have little else to go on.

We now turn to the point about responsiveness. Lijphart focused on responsiveness in the sense of the representation of a spectrum of views in the legislature and, beyond that, the executive. We would not for a moment deny that that is a core issue for any democracy, and on that score the English two-and-a-bit party system and single-party cabinets look fairly insensitive to variety. There is, however, another kind of responsiveness, which also merits attention. That is the day-to-day responsiveness of public services to the immediate and longer-term needs of individual citizens. This 'street-level responsiveness' may go hand-in-hand with traditional party-political representativeness, but there again, it may not. Highly differentiated political responsiveness to voters in terms of elected representatives, party programmes and finely tuned rhetoric may coexist with unresponsive service bureaucracies and/or unresponsive public service professions. It may also coexist with patronage and partiality in the staffing or provision of public services – a lack of impartiality. In these respects consensus Belgium does not seem to perform so well (Brans et al., 2006; De Winter and Dumont, 2006)

8.5.3   Input Legitimacy versus Output Legitimacy?

Here we refer to the seminal work of the leading German scholar Fritz W. Scharpf. In a series of publications dealing with both the institutions of the European Union and national governments Scharpf has drawn a distinction between 'two faces of democratic self-determination'. These he terms 'input-oriented legitimization' and 'output-oriented legitimization' (Scharpf, 1999, Chapter 1). The former refers to a way of thinking in which political choices are legitimate to the extent that they reflect the 'will of the people' – that is, they can be derived from the authentic preferences of the members of a community. The latter sees the legitimacy of choices as depending on results – on whether they 'effectively promote the common welfare of the constituency in question' (Scharpf, 1999, p. 6). This connects with the nature of the political system because it is argued that systems of proportional representation tend to deliver higher levels of input legitimacy, because they promote a more differentiated and variegated pattern of parties, more accurately reflecting the preferences of the wide range of groups that go to make up a modern, 'post-industrial' society. On the other hand majoritarian systems may find it easier to choose and implement coherent, focused policies and programmes that will enhance output legitimacy. Scharpf himself argues that: 'input-oriented authenticity and output-oriented effectiveness are equally essential elements of democratic self-determination' (Scharpf, 1997, p. 19).

These contrasts are, of course, quite close to – although not identical with – those previously discussed in connection with Lijphart's views on the relative performance records of consensual and majoritarian democracies. Scharpf does not insist, as Lijphart does, that consensual regimes have higher 'input legitimacy', but it is not hard to read that message into his argument (see, for example, Scharpf, 1999, p. 14, footnote). Some of the same qualifications that we made about Lijphart can therefore be reiterated. There is a big gap between headline political choices ('the government decides on more competition in health care' or 'ministers go for community policing') and the experience of citizens on the ground. Both the big decisions and the local experiences may contribute in some general way to 'output-oriented legitimization' (or the lack of it) but if there is an obvious disconnect between the two – as there may be – we may expect a growing disillusionment with the political elite. Just such a disconnect – aided and amplified by more and more aggressive mass media – is said by many commentators to have begun in both countries, indeed internationally. However, this is a tricky subject: careful examination of such international survey data as are available suggests that fluctuations in trust levels cannot accurately be depicted as a general decline (Van de Walle et al., 2008)

Scharpf himself is centrally concerned with the differences in patterns of input and output legitimacy at the interacting levels of national governments and EU institutions. He is preoccupied with the problem that a competitive market at the European level may undermine the ability of individual member states to sustain relatively generous welfare states.

Here, however, we have been concerned with a type of difference which his analysis does little to address: that between national-level policymaking and local policy implementation. In effect this complicates his model because it adds a third layer – and one of great importance to most citizens on a day-to-day basis – at which both input and especially output legitimacy is created or destroyed.

Relevant and reliable empirical evidence is hard to come by on this issue. Eurobarometer does have a series of surveys stretching back to the 1970s in which citizens are asked: 'On the whole, are you very satisfied, fairly satisfied or not satisfied at all with the way democracy works in your country?' Extracting from this series (and reiterating the earlier caveats concerning surveys of popular perceptions) we get Figures 8.1 and 8.2.

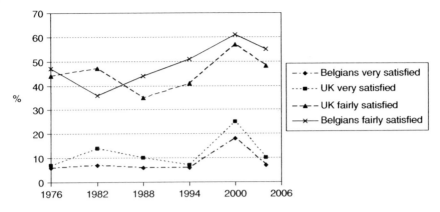

Notes: 'Don't knows' are not shown to avoid crowding the graph.

Source: Eurobarometer: http://ec.europa.eu/public_opinion/cf/waveoutput_en.cfm, accessed 24 September 2008. Selected from Eurobarometers numbers EB6, 17, 30, 41.1, 53 and 61.

Figure 8.1   *How satisfied are you with the way democracy works in your country?*

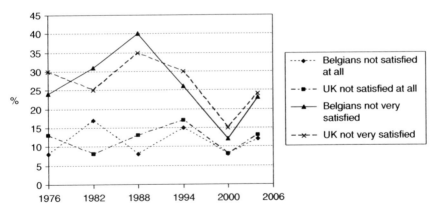

Notes: 'Don't knows' are not shown to avoid crowding the graph.

Source: Eurobarometer: http://ec.europa.eu/public_opinion/cf/waveoutput_en.cfm, accessed 24 September 2008. Selected from Eurobarometers numbers EB6, 17, 30, 41.1, 53 and 61.

Figure 8.2   *How satisfied are you with the way democracy works in your country?*

Unfortunately these graphs tell us little (except, perhaps that many people in both countries were unusually optimistic in the millennial year of 2000 – one suspects the survey was different in some way that year, or that it was conducted during the mass revelry). The table does not suggest either that the inhabitants of one country consistently thought better of their democracy than the inhabitants of the other, or that there has been a precipitous fall in satisfaction over the three decades since the first survey. But even if satisfaction with democracy can be roughly equated with legitimacy, these surveys do not enable us to distinguish between the different sources for such legitimacy discussed above – input and output legitimacy at the level of national policymaking and at the level of local implementation.

Other empirical evidence is less ambiguous. We know that, as far as health services are concerned, neither Belgium nor England have, during the three decades of our study, reduced their absolute or relative public spending on these services. On the contrary, over the period 1975–2005 the percentage of (GDP) devoted to health care has risen in both cases. In Belgium 4.1 per cent of gross domestic product (GDP) in 1970 became 7.6 per cent in 1997 (although this share fell slightly right at the end of this period when the government took special measures to meet the Maastricht criteria for entry to the eurozone) (European Observatory, 2000, p. 27). What is more, the slice of this expenditure devoted to hospital inpatient care also rose. In the UK case the position was as shown in Table 8.4.

Table 8.4   NHS expenditure as a percentage of GDP

Year	% GDP	Real terms (1949 = 100)
1965	3.56	163
1975	4.85	281
1985	4.83	339
1995	5.83	521
2005	7.71	908

Notes:
1.   The third column expresses expenditure in real terms, adjusted by a GDP deflator at market prices, where 1949 – the first year of the NHS – is set at 100.
2   The NHS represents (2003) about 85% of total UK health expenditure.

Source: Harrison and McDonald (2008), pp. 11–12. originally from Office of Health Economics.

Growth has been particularly fast since 2000, when the Labour government announced its intention of raising UK health expenditure as a percentage of GDP 'to the European average'. Hospital spending has more than taken its share of the overall growth. If we look at change between 1997 and 2007 we find that the number of consultants in the English NHS rose by 12 200 (4.6 per cent per annum) and of registrars by 18 850 (10 per cent per annum) (http://www.ic.nhs.uk/, accessed 11 November 2008). NHS hospitals have been a 'growth business'.

None of this means that the European single market will not push national governments into welfare reductions in future, but it does mean, so far as hospitals and health services are concerned, that it has not begun to happen yet. It is possible, of course, that the impacts have for some reason been concentrated in other parts of the welfare state – pensions, unemployment insurance or social care – but it does seem that we can say that Scharpf's concerns about the impact of the single EU market on welfare expenditure is not yet borne out by what is happening in health care.

Next we look at evidence concerning citizens' attitudes towards the civil service. These data raise another question concerning the theories of Scharpf and, more particularly, Lijphart. It is the question of where the civil service (and the public service more generally) fit into their arguments. That is not clear. On the one hand civil servants are not politicians (although in many countries, including Belgium, senior civil servants are appointed within a party patronage system). Therefore one could argue that they play no role in either input or output legitimacy, and are not part of the model. On the other hand the civil or public service is definitely seen by many as part of 'government' or 'the state'. Therefore it could be argued that trust in the civil service would form one component in the aggregate citizen judgement on the legitimacy of the regime. This is a point of some importance because citizen perceptions of the civil service can and do diverge from their perceptions of the political elite. In crude terms they may trust their politicians but not their civil servants, or vice versa (or, of course, they may also trust both, or neither).

Table 8.5 is extracted from the World Values Survey and shows the percentages of those surveyed who declare themselves as having a great deal

Table 8.5 *Confidence in the Civil Service (percentages showing a great deal or quite a lot of confidence)*

Country	1981	1990	1999/2000	Rank in 1999/2000
Belgium	46	42	45	17 (n = 31)
Great Britain	47	46	46	14 (n = 31)

Source: World Values Survey and European Values Survey – see Van de Walle et al., (2008), p. 58.

of confidence or quite a lot of confidence (the two highest categories) in their country's civil service.

Clearly, these figures show no fall in confidence – or rise in confidence for that matter – over what is admittedly only a five-year period. Internationally, they fall in the middle group: much higher than in Italy (scores in the 20s and 30s) or Japan (consistently in the 30s) but significantly lower than in Canada and the United States (50s).

Now we turn to a different survey of trust in the civil service, asking a slightly different question (Table 8.6).

Table 8.6   Trust in the Civil Service (Eurobarometer)

Country	Autumn 1997	Spring 1999	Autumn 2000	Autumn 2001	Spring 2002
Belgium	29	37	41	52	51
UK	46	44	46	45	48

Note: The question to the respondent is whether s/he tends to trust the civil service or not. The figures in the table are the percentage of respondents who tend to trust.

Source: Eurobarometer.

Belgium is unusual among the EU states covered by the Eurobarometer in that it shows a clear trend: upwards. Most other countries do not. Obviously, neither shows any sign of the much-discussed loss of confidence (Van de Walle et al., 2008). Both Belgium and the UK occupy the middle of the EU rank order. Austria, Denmark and Ireland are at the top, Italy is by some margin at the bottom.

We can now summarize this section on the larger theoretical debates initiated by Lijphart and Scharpf. On the whole our two detailed, longitudinal studies do not support these grand theories, although it is always possible that our two countries and policy sectors are exceptions. To begin with, there is no convincing evidence that Belgians have markedly higher confidence in either their consensual democratic arrangements or their civil service than the majoritarian English. More significantly, we suggest that the models used by both Lijphart and Scharpf are deficient, insofar as they fail to recognize the contribution to legitimacy made by a well-regarded public service and a perception that public services are being delivered in a broadly efficient, equitable and reliable manner. Their arguments either miss out altogether or amalgamate what should be a separate level of analysis: the local delivery of public services and the impact this has on citizen attitudes towards the state. This is, in effect, a third component that needs to be added to the two main components that they do discuss – the input legitimacy of electoral arrangements and the output legitimacy of policy selection. It is a more local, experience-based component (and perhaps more stable because of that). It affects output legitimacy (is service delivery efficient?) but also, to some degree, input legitimacy (to the extent that the citizens feel the public servants they deal with are 'responsive' and 'like us'). Unfortunately none of the available international comparative statistics allow us to distinguish between the different possible contributors to trust and legitimacy

As we wrote this book we were pleased to find this argument about the important relationship between legitimacy and citizen experiences with the public services paralleled in recent work by Bo Rothstein. He puts the issue strongly:

> [C]itizens generally come into contact with the output side – with the adminis-tration that is – far more frequently and intensively than they do with the input side . . . public administration is the political system – as citizens concretely encounter and experience it. The character of the administration is therefore decisive for the way in which the political system is viewed. (Rothstein, 2008, p. 18)

Rothstein and Teorell (2008) also stress the foundational role that impartiality plays in generating citizen perceptions of regime legitimacy. They argue that impartiality is even more important than effectiveness or efficiency. This is an interesting argument but one that we have not explored in any direct way in our study. Hypothetically, however, we would expect it to lead to relatively lower ratings for Belgium, since the Belgian system appears to exhibit more extensive and obvious party political patronage than the English (in public sector appointments and promotions, for example).

Finally, we turn to the Scharpf fear that welfare states will be under-mined by the economically competitive logic of the EU single market. Once again, our study of hospitals yields little evidence to support this concern. Public expenditure on health care has actually grown in both countries and, within that total, hospital spending is buoyant.

8.6 CONCLUSIONS

Beyond all the complexity of layered and simultaneous changes, taking place at different speeds, there is perhaps one still larger and more embrac-ing pattern, and that is fidelity to the national policymaking style. To exag-gerate slightly, one might say that the 'big picture' of the 40 years from 1965 to 2005 has been one in which the Belgians and the English policymakers have each become more and more like themselves (rather than more like each other). While specific ideas and techniques may have been picked up in both countries (neighbourhood policing, patient-focused care and so on) the ways in which these ideas and techniques have been introduced have been very different. It is almost as if each country has moved closer and closer to its own policymaking caricature – as if this cultural and procedural element was the most immovable component of the whole complex process of change. So Belgian policymaking in the early twenty-first century was even more opaque, slow-moving, fragmented, bargained and overtly politicized than two or three decades earlier, while English policymaking was even more centralized, hierarchical and managerial.

If we are right about this, there must be a limit to it – a threshold at which each style breaks down and either something else is put in its place or, at the very least, there is a measure of incremental retreat. Furthermore – and speculatively – it could be argued that, right at the end of our period, these 'style thresholds' were beginning to become visible. In Belgium 2007–08 saw a huge national political crisis during which the politicians could not form a government and divisions between the various regions and parties seemed to grow even deeper, with a kind of political paralysis setting in and little progress being made on several crucial issues. Meanwhile in England resistance to centrally dictated performance regimes and endless centrally orchestrated reorganizations and initiatives grew louder and louder. A Cabinet Office paper on public service reform was remarkably apologetic about previous micro-management, Whitehall control and 'giving schools, hospitals, local government and local communities more power and responsibility to decide what is right for their area' (Cabinet Office, 2008, p. 42). Whether these fair words had any subsequent effect is, of course, another question, but the whole tone of this paper spoke of a consciousness that a particular style and approach had been pushed to its sensible limit and beyond.

This idea of some kind of limits currently being approached is perhaps a nice, speculative point at which to conclude our analysis. Alongside the sense of limits, we should also close with the observation that – for Belgium and England – the now classic academic model of policy stability punctuated by rare episodes of radical change just does not fit the facts. On the contrary, change of one kind or another has been constant in both sectors and in both countries. It has been multilayered and untidy, but it has happened. Even in the stereotypically slow-moving Belgium we find big changes in the political system (party fragmentation, decentralization of policy competences) right alongside sometimes agonizingly slow shifts in implemented policies. And at the same time, in hyperactive England, we notice considerable continuities, such as the impartiality of the civil service, the tradition of operational autonomy for the police or the seemingly inexorable growth of the acute health care budget. And last, but not least, some very important changes accumulate gradually, without figuring much on the explicit policy agenda at all. Our long-term view has helped us to see that change takes a multiplicity of forms and has a multiplicity of sources, endogenous and external, of which policymakers are only one. Policy implementation – often ignored or relegated to a minor role by political scientists and legal scholars alike – turns out to be very important. This is no news to students of public administration, or to the millions who use public services, but it is nonetheless a suitable point with which to end the chapter. Formal government policy pronouncements may be the end of complex processes of information gathering and political bargaining, but they are only the beginning of the equally complex business of turning fair words into feasible actions. Studies of change need to pay as much attention to implementation as to formulation.

9. Reflections on doctrines of comparison

9.1 INTRODUCTION

The previous chapter dealt with the substance of our conclusions and further thoughts about our two public services in our two Western European countries. This final chapter deals not with the substance but with the ways in which that substance has been collected, assembled and presented. We have told a pair of intertwined stories (one local, one national) for each country, and we have then compared these pairs, one with another, looking for similarities, differences and general patterns over time. Each has been a complicated narrative, with many different events (for example riots, decisions, changes of government) and influences (for example finance, technology, culture). Each has offered 'thick description' but has also engaged with a range of theoretical issues (the effects of speci-fied types of political and organizational regimes; path-dependency; causal mechanisms; and so on). It is therefore time to ask what kinds of stories these have been, how persuasive and reliable they are, and what kind of explanations they will bear.

This is, in effect, a methodology chapter, but we have not called it that but have chosen instead to title it 'Reflections on doctrines of comparison'. That choice is intended to send two important messages. First, the use of a plural (doctrines) emphasizes that there is no one best way to undertake all international comparisons – no single, stratospheric, gold standard against which all other approaches can be graded. Second, use of the term 'doctrines' suggests that the selection of a methodology by a researcher is not an exclusively scientific activity. Of course it *is* a scientific and technical decision, but not *only* a scientific and technical decision. Epistemological affiliations also frequently have ideological, political or even ethical dimensions to them (Bevir and Rhodes, 2006, pp. 52–5; Hawkesworth, 2005; Lynn et al., 2008; Phillips, 2000, Chapter 11). Both these messages are somewhat controversial (not just recently, but rather perennially so). Nevertheless, we believe that many comparative scholars would more or less share the position that we are about to expound, although certainly by no means all of them would.

Some of those colleagues who would disagree with our position would insist that there is a clear hierarchy of approaches to knowledge acquisition, with something like a scientific laboratory experiment standing at the top, statistical testing of clearly formulated hypotheses against large populations a little further down, and descriptive case studies like ours somewhere near the bottom (Hamm, 1988 offers a particularly clear and well-argued example of this, although it was focused on clinical decision-making rather than policymaking). This hierarchy is still widely taught and practised, especially in the USA, and in countries where US social science is a dominant intellectual import. In subsequent sections of this chapter we characterize it as 'scientific orthodoxy', or the 'variables paradigm'. It is also frequently called 'modernism', especially by its opponents (for example Adcock, 2005; Bevir and Rhodes, 2006). Even if true unreconstructed orthodox positivists are nowadays becoming harder and harder to find, the shadow of their project for an objective science still falls heavily over many labouring social scientists – across a variety of theoretical persuasions.

Since at least the late 1980s, however, others opposed to this paradigm have claimed that there has been a turning

> away from, if not against, the idea of a social scientific practice derived from a model of human behavior abstracted from the physical and/or natural sciences, denuded of the human traits of researchers and researched; and towards a rehumanized, contextualized set of practices. (Yanow and Schwartz-Shea, 2005, p. xii)

Several (rather diverse) groups of these critics have implicitly or explicitly rejected the notion of causality, and have substituted a hermeneutic quest for tracing the ways in which intersubjective meanings are constructed – usually in highly local and specific contexts (Kurki, 2008, pp. 124–36; Yanow, 2005a). A few directly (or, more often, indirectly) deny the possibility of distinguishing truth from falsehood, and incline to the relativist position that no one kind of interpretation is intrinsically better or worse than any other. Some also deny the possibility of learning anything about the external world (reality), claiming in effect that our studies can never get beyond interpretations of texts or text-like media. It should be emphasized that we are writing here only of the radical or 'strong' school of social constructivists, not of the rest of that broad church (Phillips, 2000, Chapters 1 and 11). These radicals are nowhere near as numerous in the field of academic public policy and public administration as are the true or partial believers in the variables paradigm, but they do exist, and are often regarded as rather fashionable, or at least notorious.

In our work we resist both the variables paradigm and radical social constructivism (alternatively, sometimes, 'interpretivism'), as will become clear in what follows. We have pitched our tent in the large, fertile and quite well-populated land that lies between these two poles. Thus our aim for this final chapter is to reflect on the strengths and weaknesses of different doctrines, and explain how our work fits into (or fails to fit into) this large, messy, often impassioned and long-continuing wrangle (for some juicy argumentative extracts see, for example, Lynn et al., 2008; Luton, 2008). To do this we first have to examine some of the general arguments about description and explanation in the social sciences. We can only skate over the surface of this sprawling and vibrant debate, but we do offer a number of references for those who wish to dig deeper (including, as an admirably fresh, clear and concise introduction, Robson, 2002, pp. 3–44). We then move on to the more specific (though still extensive) discussions which arise in the context of international and intersectoral comparisons. Finally, we look more closely at the roles which can be played by case studies and historical narratives.

9.2   SCIENTIFIC ORTHODOXY – THE BIG PICTURE: LARGE N STUDIES OF OBSERVABLE VARIABLES SHOULD BE THE MODEL; SMALL N STUDIES NEED TO SHARPEN UP!

We begin with what is probably still the most orthodox, mainstream position in many university settings and in many parts of the world. We will first describe the central claims of this doctrine and then critique it. In a brief treatment we cannot examine all the subtle variations on this position, but we will try to do it justice by basing most of what we say on one of the most brilliant and widely used texts produced within this approach, King, Keohane and Verba's *Designing Social Inquiry* (1994). For convenience we will refer to this as KKV.

KKV insist that there should be one unified inferential logic that unites all real social science (p. 6). They argue that this logic is often at its clearest in quantitative work, but that it should also apply to qualitative work. It should apply equally to description ('using observations about the world to learn about other unobserved facts') and causal inference ('learning about causal effects from the data observed' – p. 8). They see all the social sciences as being centrally involved in producing generalized, simplified descriptions and explanations. Further, 'our capacity to simplify depends on whether we can specify outcomes and explanatory variables in a coherent way' (p. 10). Note here the emphasis on what can be observed as the basic 'feedstuff' of both description and explanation. Hence the advice 'to make sure a theory is falsifiable, choose one that is capable of generating as many *observable implications* as possible' (King et al., 1994, p. 19). Hence also the need to design research so that it confronts the observable evidence with a limited number of formally stated hypotheses. 'Digging about' or 'immersion' or interpretive speculation are only seen as legitimate as precursors of serious research – they may help to spur ideas or insights that can then be converted into formal hypotheses, so that the real, focused data collection aimed at confirming or disconfirming them can then begin.

One aspect of the KKV approach which has exercised an extraordinarily wide influence is the insistence on seeing the social world in terms of dependent and independent variables:

> Reality as experienced is mentally carved up into conceptually isolated factors, which are, in turn, conceived of as potentially standing in various possible relationships with one another . . . knowledge construction is taken to center around the formulation and evaluation of propositions characterizing these relationships. (Adcock, 2005, p. 58)

The language of variables has become almost second nature to many social scientists, including some of those who would not accept other aspects of the KKV approach. Yet it is also possible to view 'variables thinking' as narrow, mechanical and unrealistic. The eminent sociologist, Andrew Abbott, in an article that looked back at the Chicago School of sociologists, argued that the location of social facts in time and space was crucial to understanding. Yet the dominant 'variables paradigm' often promptly removes them from these locations. He put the matter forcefully:

> [N]ot only do variables not exist in reality, they are misleading even as a nominalist convention. For the idea of a variable is the idea of a scale that has the same causal meaning whatever its context: the idea, for example, that 'education' can have 'an effect' on 'occupation' irrespective of the other qualities of an individual, whether those qualities be other past experiences, other personal characteristics, or friends, acquaintances, and connections . . . The Chicago view was that the concept of net effect was social scientific nonsense. Nothing that ever occurs in the social world occurs 'net of other variables'. All social facts are located in contexts. So why bother to pretend that they are not? (Abbott, 1997, p. 1152)

Whilst we have not ourselves employed the language of 'variables' within the covers of this book, we have sometimes cited others who do operate within this frame. In Chapter 8, for example, we examined the contention of Lijphart that consensual democracies outperformed majoritarian democracies with respect to the quality of democracy (section 8.5).

To illustrate the critique of the 'variables' paradigm we can briefly revisit Lijphart's argument. We will take just one element in his formulation: that consensus democracies are 'kinder and gentler' because they support bigger welfare states. Thus the existence of the political institutions of consensus is taken as the independent variable, and the size of the welfare state as the dependent variable. To test this hypothesis Lijphart looks at two statistical relationships:

- The 'decommodification' scores of consensus versus majoritarian democracies (where decommodification is 'the degree to which welfare policies with regard to unemployment, disability, illness and old age permit people to maintain decent living standards independent of pure market forces'; Lijphart, 1999, p. 294).
- Social expenditure as a percentage of the gross domestic product (GDP).

Both these show quite strong correlations with the status of being a consensus democracy, so Lijphart takes his hypothesis as demonstrated. From a different theoretical and methodological perspective, however, we can see problems with this way of reasoning. These 'variables' are each hugely complex. It is not just that the value of the variable is going up and down, it is that the substance of the variable itself is somewhat plastic. On the one side, consensus democracies (and majoritarian democracies for that matter) are very different among themselves. Consider the many differences between, say, hyper-stable yet modernizing polities like Sweden and Denmark and a fragmented, traditional system such as Belgium. On the other hand 'decommodification', whilst certainly an intriguing concept, is both abstract and complex – and very difficult to measure. The original attempt to quantify it by Esping-Andersen (1990) turned out to be highly controversial, and was strongly criticized (for example in Castles and Mitchell, 1993). Furthermore 'social expenditure', using the Organisation for Economic Co-operation and Development (OECD) definition, is also a tremendous rag-bag of different programmes in each country and, as the OECD itself acknowledges, is not measured in exactly the same way by each member state contributing to the statistics. So 'decommodification' and 'social expenditure as a percentage of GDP' are hardly thermostat-type measures, showing (say) 18 °C in majoritarian states and 23 °C in consensus states. Each political system, each element of 'decommodification' and each budget line of social expenditure is, as Abbot suggests, located in a particular historical, political and institutional context. To take them away from these contexts, aggregate them and then measure the correlations between them is, indeed, a great leap of analysis. It gives us a number, but what does that number mean? It is not a number like temperature, or the number of votes, or the amount of money in your bank account. It is a number measuring academic abstractions of academic abstractions, and in consequence its precise import is hard to locate. Furthermore, the measures themselves tell us nothing about whether the citizens of consensus democracies actually believe that their governments are kinder and gentler (or, indeed, whether the citizens of the majoritarian democracies see their governors as less caring). Still less do they tell us why citizens believe whatever they believe. And even if the hypothesis is true (consensus democracies are kinder and gentler, on average), by themselves the correlations made by Lijphart give us no clue as to why this should be so, or what processes, relationships and perceptions produce this state of affairs.

In her treatise on notions of causation in international relations Kurki describes the underlying problem like this:

> The Humean fixation on observability makes it difficult for them [scholars deeply influenced by the causal philosophy of David Hume – very much including KKV] to deal with certain kinds of questions, notably analysis of social construction . . . it is difficult for Humean approaches to recognize or deal with the fact that factors which 'variables' are trying observationally to measure can be (ontologically) deeply intertwined, co-constituted and inseparable from other causal conditions. (Kurki, 2008, p. 11)

In a recent comparative text Landsman, having sympathetically explained something of the achievements and potential of large N statistical analyses, goes on to identify their limitations. Coming from an author who is basically supportive of the orthodox approach, this is worth quoting at length:

> [T]here are countless topics in political science for which the quantitative comparison of many countries is simply inappropriate. This method of analysis cannot 'unpack' important historical, political and sociological relationships at a lower level of analysis. It cannot be used to analyze discrete moments of political negotiation, consensus building, or the establishment of particular political 'pacts' between elite groups and masses. It cannot be used to examine different political strategies adopted by social movements, trade unions, revolutionary movements, or other forms of collective action. It is not appropriate for 'process tracing' in an effort to establish the links at the domestic level made between actors and their propensity to reform political institutions. It cannot map the inter-subjective meanings and different cultural understandings of political concepts and practices, among other deeper processes of meaning investigated through different methods of comparative analysis. (Landsman, 2008, p. 64)

It will not have escaped the reader's attention that most if not all of the items on the above list are also issues with which our Anglo-Belgian study has been centrally concerned. We have tried to 'unpack' relationships (such as those between central government and the English police forces); to analyse discrete moments (such as the launching of the UZ Leuven project directly after *de splitsing*); to examine political strategies (such as the increasing central control of National Health Service hospitals) and to trace processes (such as the growth of professionalism among the police). We have also pointed to the different cultural understandings of the proper role of politics – for example with respect to local police forces in Belgium as compared with England.

In fact strict adherence to the prescriptions of KKV would have made it impossible to investigate many if not most of the issues we have covered. More generally, '[I]f a sampling logic were applied to all types of research . . . many important topics cannot be investigated' (Agranoff and Radin, 1991, p. 205). For us, measures of suitable 'variables' did not exist or, where they could be conjured up, they would not cover anything like the whole period that we wanted to study. It is true that we could have attempted to collect and build original databases ourselves, but prima facie such an enterprise appeared unlikely to have much success. Even if it had been possible, it would have been a mammoth undertaking, requiring the investment of many person years of research time, for a most uncertain outcome.

None of this should be taken as some root-and-branch opposition to quantification. On the contrary, we have included statistical data in the book wherever it existed and seemed relevant. However, that quantitative material has always been set within a broader analytic narrative that has gone far beyond dependent and independent variables. It has been used in combination with qualitative observations to explore and redefine rather than to test for acceptance or rejection.

9.3   RADICAL CONSTRUCTIVISM: THE SMALL PICTURE: AN EPIDEMIC OF 'INTERPRETIVE MOMENTS'

'Radical constructivism' is the name we have given to the bundle of positions most obviously and fundamentally opposed to the scientific orthodoxy described in the previous section. Its adherents are very various, but share a strong aversion to the idea that social science is about testing preformed hypotheses in order to build up big generalizations that will work across wide expanses of space and time:

Interpretivists diverge from modernist practices of knowledge construction at their most basic step: they are skeptical of the act of conceptually isolating factors, without which it is impossible to even formulate the propositions about recurring relationships to which modernists aspire. (Adcock, 2005, p. 60)

Radical constructivists (interpretivists) often write as though the academic world were still populated by ravening packs of hardline positivists, although in fact that has long since ceased to be the case. They tend to be for interpretation, intersubjectively established meanings, the importance of language, text and contextuality, and definitely for egalitarian and participative relationships between researchers and their 'subjects' (not a term that most radical constructivists would dream of using; Adcock, 2005, p. 61). They tend to be against push-and-pull notions of causation (and some are against causation altogether) and big theories (such as pluralism or corporatism): 'there are no law-like generalizations' (Bevir et al., 2003, p. 202). They are also against any thought that we can directly observe social reality in order to decide what it is 'really' like (we can only interpret the perceptions of others about what they think of social reality, and attempt to identify what meaning these perceptions have for different individuals and groups in different places and at different times). On this last point, some profess themselves uncertain about the existence of any external reality: 'Taking an agnostic position on that means one is content to say (or at least resigned to acknowledge) that "I don't know" whether an objective reality exists' (Luton, 2008, p. 216). They oppose the model of social science as a dispassionate enterprise distant from and above everyday life, where researchers 'objectively' examine the social world. They are uncomfortable with the idea that there are 'material' factors which condition or cause decisions and actions, preferring to look for ways in which ideas themselves 'constitute' actions: 'An interpretive approach explains actions and practices by beliefs, and it explains beliefs by traditions and dilemmas' (Bevir and Rhodes, 2006, p. 20). They are also uneasy with the idea that 'science' develops a technical language of its own that is supposed to be more precise and analytic than everyday speech (it is therefore paradoxical that the texts produced by radical constructivists are frequently extremely abstruse, if not downright opaque – see, for example, Burrell, 1997; Yanow, 2005b). They tend to use ethnographic methods or intensive textual analysis, approaches which, by themselves, mean that large-scale (international, intersectoral) studies are a practical impossibility.

A flavour of radical constructivism can be had from examining one of the most popular and widely-cited early works in this genre, Guba and Lincoln's *Fourth Generation Evaluation* (1989). For example Guba and Lincoln say that:

> Phenomena can only be understood within the context in which they are studied; findings from one context cannot be generalized to another; neither problems nor their solutions can be generalized from one setting to another. (Guba and Lincoln, 1989, p. 45)

They also argue that their own kind of evaluation research has no special legitimacy or status – it is 'simply another construction to be taken into account in the move towards consensus' (p. 45). We see here some of the characteristics referred to above: social reality is 'constructed' by each of us and there is no special method or language of construction which is 'better' than any other. It therefore behoves the researcher to be modest about his or her 'findings', and not to regard them as superior to the interpretations of policy practitioners or, indeed, everyday citizens. The evaluator, in Guba and Lincoln's vision, becomes a kind of negotiator, going round all the stakeholders in a given situation and seeking to facilitate sufficient inter-subjective agreement to serve as a basis for a consensus solution.

Some radical constructivists are happy to abandon all claims to objectivity (or rather to deny that the idea of objectivity makes any sense). Others, however, seek to hang on to that criterion, but do so by substantially redefining it:

> A fact is a piece of evidence that nearly everyone in a given community would accept is true [and]
>   We define objectivity as evaluation by comparing rival stories using reasonable criteria. Sometimes there might be no way of deciding between two or more interpretations, but this will not always be the case. (Bevir and Rhodes, 2006, p. 28)

We trust that it is clear that our Anglo-Belgian comparison does not fall into this camp. Ideas are certainly important to our analysis (the idea of Flemish autonomy; the idea of neighbourhood policing) but so are material factors that can only be reduced to 'beliefs, traditions and dilemmas' by a huge and quite artificial effort (factors such as limited finance, leaking roofs, DNA testing and racially motivated riots). We want and need a concept of causation that will in some way embrace these kinds of factors as well as just 'beliefs'. Of course the leaking roof or the budgetary shortfall has to be 'perceived' and 'believed in' by the relevant actors, and in that trivial sense may be reduced to beliefs, but to treat them primarily or exclusively in that way strikes us as perverse. Nor are we content with Bevir and Rhodes's attempts to rescue objectivity. One does not have to go very far back in time to find quite large communities where most people believed that people with black (or yellow, or brown) skins were intrinsically less intelligent than people with white skins. Or that society was arranged by multiple divinities in a hierarchical series of castes. Did or does that make these beliefs objective 'facts'? As for establishing the truth by comparing stories, that might be an interesting approach, but everything clearly hangs on what the 'reasonable criteria' are. One wonders what the radical interpretivists do when they face a situation in which different individuals or groups cannot agree on what the 'reasonable criteria' should be? As Pawson and Tilley waspishly comment on the Guba and Lincoln proposals:

> We find it difficult to imagine, for instance, the development of a 'joint construction' of the claims and concerns of neighbourhood watchers and neighbourhood burglars, since they begin with uncommonly different assumptions about the legitimacy of this particular way of making a living. (Pawson and Tilley, 1997, p. 20)

None of this is to deny the importance of 'interpretation' (which, as Bevir and Rhodes point out, we all do all the time anyway). Nor is it to contradict the suggestion that ideas and beliefs themselves may act as powerful 'causes', and certainly deserve our systematic study. It is simply to suggest that one can be constructivist and interpretivist without throwing the baby out with the bathwater (Kurki, 2008, pp. 168–77; Pawson and Tilley, 1997, pp. 18–29, 55–82).

9.4   CRITICAL REALISM

Our own paradigm falls between these poles and is usually labelled 'critical realism'. Critical realists hold that social structures and material factors have a 'real' (ontological) existence, and that they can play a part in causation. Yet at the same time they are to a degree – but not to a radical degree – 'social constructivists':

> [W]hile critical realists see interpretive methods as central to their analyses, they are also skeptical of those interpretive and hermeneutical approaches that assume that actors' perceptions or quoted reasons are the sole and a trustworthy source of analysis. (Kurki, 2008, p. 170)

They crucially differ from the orthodox approach 'because prediction is not necessary for causal accounts, nor are regularities a necessary or a sufficient condition of causation' (Kurki, 2008, p. 169). Instead they embrace a wider and more varied notion of causation:

> We can conceptualise causes as 'constraining and enabling' rather than just as 'pushing and pulling' and recognize that the social world is made up by the complex interaction of various different types of cause. (Kurki, 2008, p. 240)

This plurality of types of cause is intended to produce a 'holistic' explanation: 'contra many reflectivists [radical constructivists] we have to recognize that rules, norms and discourses do not, on their own, provide holistic explanations' (Kurki, 2008, p. 237). Equally, '"social (structural) positions" are not just "ideational understandings" that agents possess, but real material positions that carry material as well as formal "constraints and enablements"' (Kurki, 2008, pp. 229–30). So being a Chief Constable or a hospital Chief Executive is not just a question of how one is seen and understood. It also puts the incumbent in a position where they can issue orders, spend money and launch concrete activities. These powers are, to a critical realist, causal. Their users certainly have their own ideas, beliefs and reasons. And the use of these powers may well have to be negotiated, just as the conditions under which other stakeholders regard the exercise of such powers as justified may be both complex and changeable. But they are powers – causal powers – nonetheless.

Kurki goes back all the way to Aristotle to find a typology which captures the variety of causes she believes characterize critical realist accounts (2008, pp. 210–34). She finds four main categories:

- Material causes. Social structures are real and have real effects. Tenants are in a specific relation to their landlord and cannot just choose to think or behave in some other way (unless they want to lose their accommodation). Hospital chief executives have to stay within or close to their budget ceilings (or find a quite exceptional justification for not doing so), otherwise the institutional structure (governments, supervisory boards) will ensure that they are disciplined or removed. The advent of forensic DNA testing leads to old crimes being solved that could not previously be closed for lack of acceptable evidence – the changing technology, although by no means the 'sole' or 'final' cause, conditions what can be achieved at a given moment. As one Chief Constable said in interview 'no cars were stolen in the nineteenth century'.
- Formal causes. Individuals are constrained and enabled by ideas, rules, norms and discourses which surround and pre-exist them and which are difficult to escape or avoid. Like material causes, they condition actors rather than actively bringing about specific effects. We heard, for example, that during the 1970s there was a strong norm in Belgian federal politics to the effect that, if one of the two main regions (Flanders, Wallonia) received major federal support for a project, then the other region was entitled to something similar. There was thus a rough parity between financial support for the new Flemish UZ Leuven, and support for the new

Francophone medical facilities at Louvain-la-Neuve and Woluwe St Pierre.

- Efficient causes. Efficient and final causes are the 'extrinsic' or 'active' types of cause. Efficient causes are the prime forces for change, the actions of agents such as voting, handcuffing a burglar, carrying an injured person to safety. However, 'efficient causes, and hence agency, must always be linked to the material form of causality in the sense that agents' movements and actions are taken within a material environment' (Kurki, 2008, p. 225). Thus (say) doctors at the Royal Sussex County Hospital (RSCH) performing an operation to save a road accident victim may 'cause' the saving of that patient's life, but they are only able to do so because of the prior material existence of a purpose-built operating theatre with suitable equipment, supporting staff, and so on.

- Final causes. This is a more controversial category, which is not used by many critical realists (who, in effect, find the other three categories enough for an explanation). It comprises the intentions of the actors – the reasons why they do what they do. 'If we accept final causes we can . . . give intentionality the fundamental role that it deserves in social explanation' – this is not to downgrade the other types of causality but to conceive a range of always mutually dependent processes that lead to an outcome (Kurki, 2008, p. 226). In our interviews with the founding fathers of the Gasthuisberg hospital it was hard to doubt their passionate intention to create a modern, high-class teaching hospital, just as, in our interviews with senior Sussex police officers one could clearly hear their determination not to expose their junior officers to violence and abuse without proper protection and training.

One does not have to follow precisely this typology to accept the general point that critical realism embraces a more catholic and diverse concept of causes than either the orthodox variables paradigm or the radical constructivists (who are sometimes not sure if they have any time for 'causes' at all).

In another, influential formulation, Pawson and Tilley (1997) present critical realism in a slightly different, though complementary way. They stress that realist explanations of policy outcomes depend on the interactions between specific mechanisms and particular contexts. So it is misguided just to look for mechanisms which have worked (such neighbourhood policing or closed-circuit television (CCTV) in car parks) – mechanisms sensibly cannot be divorced from their contexts (which is a problem for the variables paradigm, which tends to divorce variables from their contexts). Furthermore, contexts are complex. Pawson and Tilley's analysis of mechanisms brings out a number of features that will already sound familiar to those who have read the earlier parts of this section:

> [W]e would expect 'program mechanisms' (i) to reflect the embeddedness of the program within the stratified nature of social reality; (ii) to take the form of propositions which will provide an account of how both macro and micro processes constitute the program; (iii) to demonstrate how program outputs follow from stakeholders' choices (reasoning) and their capacity (resources) to put these into practice. (Pawson and Tilley, 1997, p. 66)

If you glance back at our account of the creation of the Gasthuisberg campus of UZ Leuven in Chapter 6 we hope you will agree that we: (1) showed how the programme was embedded in the complex reality of the then Belgian political system; (2) provided propositions concerning how money and staff and buildings were assembled, and rival projects seen off; and (3) illuminated the reasoning of the 'founding fathers' concerning what they were about.

9.5   POROUS PARADIGMS IN PRACTICE

We have now set out two 'polar' paradigms, plus our preferred in-between one (they are summarized in Table 9.1). In a moment we will move on to the more specific issues of comparisons, case studies and narratives. For clarity, however, we should insert a brief but very important caveat. It is that in practice academics writing on public policy and administration are constantly straying over the boundaries between these philosophically distinct perspectives. These boundaries are therefore porous. Interpretivists will slip into talking of independent variables or the orthodox hardliners will begin to interpret what the actors in their studies might be thinking. Often this is done unconsciously, in the sense that the academics concerned are focused on the topic of their study and reach for any insight or piece of evidence that may be at hand, without worrying too much about exactly how it has been generated and what its epistemological underpinnings might be. At other times academics will quite explicitly and consciously position themselves as occupying 'mixed' positions (indeed, it could be argued that critical realism is itself a mixed position, insofar as it insists on the importance of contextual interpretation and analysis whilst at the same time searching for ways to get closer to the underlying reality which it presumes is 'just out there'). Thus it is not unusual, for example, to find quite hard-nosed quantitative researchers emerging from their multiple regression analyses in order to proclaim that 'there are multiple perspectives on social phenomena and . . . one's own data are likely to

Table 9.1   Three paradigms: a summary

	Scientific Orthodoxy	Radical Constructivism	Critical Realism
Main activity	Testing causal hypotheses derived from general theories	Inductively exploring multiple, socially constructed meanings	Looking for explanations of how key processes operate within specified contexts to produce particular outputs
Typical methods	Statistical testing or relationships between dependent and independent variables	Interpretation of language and texts. Egalitarian and participative research processes.	Thick descriptions, but disciplined within broad theoretical or conceptual frameworks
Ambitions	Big generalizations about stable, cause-and-effect relationships between variables	Local understandings. Sometimes arriving at inter-subjective, consensual interpretations through participative discussion	Small and medium-sized generalizations applicable across a limited number of clearly-specified contexts

provide only a partial (though potentially important) approximation of those perspectives' (Andrews et al., 2008, p. 327). Similarly, interpretivists will sometimes claim that their approach can develop operational concepts and generalizations (though not 'law-like' ones) and can suggest strategies that might be useful for practitioners (Bevir et al., 2003). It would be wrong therefore, to treat our three paradigms as hard billiard balls, capable only of cannoning off each other. They are more soft-edged than that, although when driven hard enough quite likely to cause damaging collisions (Lynn et al., 2008; Luton, 2008; Andrews et al., 2008).

9.6   COMPARISONS

Orthodox adherents of the variables paradigm have no fundamental problem with international comparisons, as Lijphart's monumental analysis of 36 democracies testifies (Lijphart, 1999). He offers us, for example, a 'correlation matrix of the ten variables distinguishing majoritarian from consensus democracies in 36 democracies, 1945–1996' (Lijphart, 1999, p. 244). The more the better, as long as one can get decent data for the specified variables. It does not matter that no one could be an 'expert', in a thick description sense, of 36 countries – as long as the correlation matrix can be filled the orthodox view is that conclusions can be drawn.

Comparisons of smaller numbers of countries are, from this perspective, more difficult but still potentially valuable. Orthodox researchers are still in the business of specifying hypotheses that connect independent and dependent variables, but the problems of holding all other things equal become more challenging. A number of orthodox texts discuss small N comparisons in terms of two techniques which were originally proposed in the mid-nineteenth century by John Stuart Mill: the 'most similar systems design' (MSSD) and the 'most different systems design' (MDSD). With MSSD one looks at countries which share many features in terms of (potentially) independent variables but nevertheless produce one or more outcomes (dependent variables) that differ. In short, how can one explain similar countries producing different outcomes? MDSD, by contrast, compares different countries (for example developing and developed, or dictatorships and democracies) which produce some similar outcomes (Landsman, 2008, pp. 70–82 gives a useful summary).

Radical interpretivists, on the other hand, are often very suspicious of large-scale comparisons of organizations, governments or societies (Adcock, 2005, pp. 61–3). They are more comfortable with small-scale, local studies, where 'thick description' and the intensive analysis of local language, meanings and beliefs can be accomplished. Adcock (2005) suggests that there have been two ways in which 'interpretivists' have nevertheless tried to make comparisons. First, they have focused on 'problems' of a kind that seem to have fairly widespread occurrence (the example of political legitimation is given; we could add from this study the problem of the ever-growing cost of acute health care). Then they have compared the different ways in which different societies or governments have responded to these problems, drawing on contextual differences to help explain the diversity. Second, some interpretivists have suggested that there are general movements in history, diffusing across different societies, and have then examined how these have taken different forms in different places. 'Rather than envisioning a general movement in history sweeping away peculiarities [they] envision it as interacting with particularities in each society so as to produce a variety of outcomes' (Adcock, 2005, p. 63)

With respect to this same issue of large-scale comparisons, critical realism again comes somewhere between the ease of the orthodox and the uncomfortableness or denial of the radical constructivists. On the one hand, as mild constructivists, critical realists are cautious about how far across space and time it is plausible to make comparisons. '[I]nstitutions and their effects can only be understood in particular spatio-temporal contexts' (Kay, 2006, p. 22). So there would be a reluctance, for example, to compare hospital policy in Belgium with hospital policy in China. On the other hand, realist theories, concepts and metaphors do have some portability – they are not strictly confined to one spatio-temporal location. What is important is to try to ensure that the respective contexts being compared are carefully analysed and, if possible, are not wildly different. It is in this sense a more holistic approach than the variables paradigm. That is one reason why we chose two countries which were similar in many socio-economic respects but which were obviously different in the one important element of their political systems. The orthodox comparativist would no doubt say that this was an MSSD if we wanted to make socio-economic conditions our independent variable, but an MDSD if we wanted to make the type of political system our independent variable. Unfortunately for our methodological purity in this sense, we wanted to look at both at the same time (as well as at a whole range of 'outcomes') and we did not want to start off by defining them as variables incorporated in specific hypotheses. We wanted to tell the stories as fully as we could, and then look for patterns, not make up the story beforehand and then check to see whether bits of what actually happened fitted the plot (or not). It is interesting that a recent mainstream English comparative text like Landsman (2008) does not even mention this possibility, despite the fact that this is what many researchers in the fields of public policy and management are actually doing. Like KKV, Landsman sees small N basically as a problem, not an advantage:

> [C]omparative scholars will always face a trade-off between the scope of countries included in one study and the level of abstraction and strengths of the inferences that result from the number of countries that are compared. Unlike the global comparison of many countries in which sample sizes are maximized for increasing variation in the variables of interest, comparing few countries involves significant and intentional choices, any one of which may limit the inferences made possible. The problem of selection bias looms large, the choice of most similar and most different cases can appear at times arbitrary . . . and the inclusion of negative cases, while laudable, may nonetheless not have exhausted all cases that ought to be considered when analyzing particular outcomes of interest. (Landsman, 2008, p. 81)

The overall conclusion, however, is that if one analyses not just an abstract variable like 'decommodification' or 'transparency' but rather looks in detail at the mechanisms and the social frameworks in which they are embedded, then realist comparison is entirely feasible. One may have to abandon the orthodox ambition to make generalizations about all the countries in the world, or even about any large number of countries, but those generalizations were in any case likely to be pitched at a very high level of abstraction. 'Universal mechanisms of change may exist but they are unlikely to yield an intelligible account of specific spatio-temporal contexts' (Kay, 2006, p. 23). Indeed, some of the most widely publicized and ambitious international comparisons, the World Governance Indicators from the World Bank, show very clearly what the dangers and limitations of this kind of high-level, large N comparison can be (Pollitt, 2009). Critical realists will look at smaller numbers of cases, but in more depth, and with the specific ambition of understanding contexts as well as mechanisms. Pawson and Tilley (1997, p. 22), focusing on specific policies, put the point in characteristically vigorous fashion: 'Social initiatives are . . . begged, stolen and borrowed the world over, and the notion that this process is devoid of learning beggars belief'. This rallying cry to realists, it should be noted, could be directed with equal force against both the orthodox and the radical constructivists.

9.7   CASE STUDIES

Now we can turn from general epistemology and ontology to the more specific question of case studies. The present book consists of four case studies at two different levels: national and local. A crude orthodox critique would be to say. 'Only four cases, what can you prove with such a small sample?' But KKV themselves are considerably more sophisticated than this. They are by no means opposed to small N case studies. Indeed, they make an important point (with which we wholly agree) namely that:

> Although case-study research rarely uses more than a handful of cases, the total number of observations is generally immense. It is therefore essential to distinguish between the number of cases and the number of observations. (King et al., 1994, p. 52; see also Rueschemeyer, 2003)

Where we part from KKV, however, is in relation to the restrictions they place upon the functions and methods of case studies. In essence, whilst appearing supportive, they also insist that small N case study research must be conducted on the same basic principles as statistically driven large N research. We prefer what Robson (2002, p. 5) refers to as a 'flexible' approach and, within that, we see a wider range of roles for case studies than do KKV. Orthodox social science requires a 'fixed' approach: 'their hall mark is that a very substantial amount of pre-specification of what you are going to do and how you are going to do it, should take place before you get into the main part of the research study' (Robson, 2002, p. 4). In flexible designs, although there is certainly plenty of planning, 'much less pre-specification takes place and the design evolves, develops and . . . "unfolds" as the research proceeds' (Robson, 2002, p. 5). We certainly operated flexibly, finding and following up some issues that we were quite unaware of when we first planned our research, and adding to our conceptual repertoire as we went along. However, 'flexible' does not mean 'shapeless' or 'anarchic' – we spent quite a lot of time choosing our countries and services and defining what kind of focus and data to go for. Furthermore, at the micro-level we were reasonably meticulous with our interviews, providing each person we approached with a summary of the project in advance, then interviewing according to a carefully devised schedule of questions, and finally sending the interviewees copies of our interview records for them to correct or amplify (see the Appendix for details).

However, the amount of prespecification or flexibility is only one of the restrictions which are applied by the orthodox school. For the main they also see case studies as having a limited range of functions. First, they have some value in testing existing hypotheses – a single well-chosen and well-specified case (chosen and specified in relation to a defined population of cases to which the relevant hypothesis is supposed to apply) can seriously damage an unreliable hypothesis by showing that it is not confirmed. (Note, though, that the situation is far more complicated with probabilistic hypotheses, where one or two counter-cases do not dislodge the original hypothesis; Mahoney, 2000. For probabilistic hypotheses, therefore, case studies tend to lose even this function.) Second, they allow that in-depth case studies may sometimes serve as useful preliminaries to hypothesis formation. Thus, in a relatively unexplored field, a detailed case may lead the researchers to see what they think may be a causal relationship, which can then be incorporated in a formal hypothesis that can subsequently be tested on a suitably defined large N population.

As for the radical constructivists, their attitude to case studies is arguably paradoxical. On the whole they do not use the term, presumably because it is tainted with 'positivist' and orthodox connotations. Yet a great deal of their own work is what other social scientists would call 'case studies', often quite small and local ones. At any event, the radical constructivists provide us with no set of prescriptions specifically aimed at case studies. Their methodological guidelines tend to be universal, in the sense that they are held to apply to all scholarship, not just to certain subtypes.

In the territory between these two poles the past decade or so has witnessed a surge of writing about case studies, the main outcome of which can be said to be a much wider appreciation of the range of achievements which can be hoped for from this form of research (Blatter and Blume,

2007, 2008; George and Bennett, 2005; Gerring, 2007; Mahoney, 2000; Rueschemeyer, 2003; Yin, 2003). Blatter and Blume (2008) have advanced a particularly cogent 'map' of where case studies have made and can make a contribution. They write of three main approaches to 'case studying', each linked to a different epistemology.

First, 'co-variance', which looks to confirm or falsify correlations between dependent and independent variables. This comes from the 'variables paradigm' we discussed above, and the function of the case is to show whether and how the postulated independent variable(s) produces the (dependent) outcome(s).

Second, 'causal process tracing', which aims to follow the mechanisms that lead from prior conditions and interventions through to outcomes. This holds out the potential to 'get behind' the statistical correlations of the orthodox school and see into the 'black box' where this follows that and then leads on to something different. It embraces a wider notion of 'causes' than the 'variables paradigm' would normally allow (Kurki, 2008, Chapter 6). If a researcher is using a case or cases to trace processes then the kinds of observations he or she will be pursuing and collecting will be those which show quite detailed steps that lead from cause to consequence. For example, we might be interested in the details of how the adoption of the Resource Allocation Working Party (RAWP) formula for the distribution of financial resources between National Health Service (NHS) districts across the UK meant that it was very hard for Brighton ever to receive a large increment to its budget, because there were always other districts – mainly geographically very distant ones – which were calculated as being 'more deserving'. It is unlikely that the original architects of the RAWP formula ever looked at the particular case of Brighton, but their principled formula nevertheless had this consequence. Central government could not make an exception of Brighton, however persuasive its pleas, because once the whole issue was embedded in a centralized, national system, any 'special deals' would call forth demands and protests from the many other districts that could argue that they too had a strong case for reasons that lay outside the formula.

Third, 'congruence analysis', where the researcher is comparing, on the one hand, a set of expectations that can be deduced from theories and concepts with, on the other, whatever empirical findings emerge from the case or cases. This is not the same as the formal hypothesis testing of the variables paradigm because it is undertaken with what Robson (2002) would no doubt term greater 'flexibility'. Here theory is treated as an interpretive framework (mild constructivism) but not as one which totally or almost entirely determines empirical 'findings' (radical constructivism). The case study is at its most powerful when a plurality of theoretical expectations can be tested against it. When used in this mode, the most valuable observations are not those which would best enable process tracing, but rather those which help the researcher to discriminate between two or more competing theories. In our case we found the theoretical expectation that the fragmented and consensual Belgian political system would be slower and less decisive confirmed in the case of police policy at the national level, but disconfirmed as far as hospital policy at the local level was concerned. This usefully drew attention to another dimension of the contrast between the two different political systems – that even if the fragmented and consensualist Belgian system was slower-moving overall, its unpredictability and lack of national 'standardization' meant that local breakthroughs and projects (such as the new UZ Leuven) stood a better chance than in the grindingly bureaucratic NHS. There were perhaps more 'interior windows of opportunity' than in a more majoritarian and centralized system. However, in the light of Blatter and Blume, we could undoubtedly have done more to try out a wider range of rival theoretical models than we actually did.

We therefore see the Blatter and Blume reappraisal of case studies as being of considerable relevance to the analyses conducted in this book (which include both some elements of process tracing and some congruence analysis). They show that a wider appreciation of the nature of theory coupled with a more plural concept of causation makes the small N problems identified by the orthodox look less important and less constraining.

9.8 HISTORICAL NARRATIVES

Whilst our account may have been 'critical realist' and 'mildly constructivist' a large part of it could also be described as 'narrative'. We describe and explain by telling stories and, because these stories cover 40 years, we can begin to think of them as historical narratives. Histories, of course, can take many forms – some can be theory driven and others can be virtually theory-free, at least in any overt sense – but most involve narrative (Pollitt, 2008, pp. 32–40). In almost every case the sequence of events is deemed important. Some later things can happen only because some earlier things have already happened. Diachronic comparisons reveal arrows as well as cycles (Pollitt, 2008, pp. 51–9). In our study, for example, the rapid construction of the new UZ Leuven on the Gasthuisberg would have been unlikely unless it had been immediately preceded by the momentous political events of *de splitsing*. And the considerable infrastructural investment in the RSCH site in the 2000s would have been unlikely if the New Labour government had not previously reshaped the Public Finance Initiative policy so as to enable considerable new public sector investment to take place largely 'off-books' as far as public expenditure was concerned. On the other hand we also found cycles and oscillations, such as the recurrent in-year budget crises in the Brighton health authority during the 1970s and 1980s, or the oscillations between national-level special units and local neighbourhood policing within the English police service since the mid 1980s.

Good historical narratives are usually characterized by traditional historical fieldcraft skills: meticulous attention to primary sources, concern for detail and *verstehen* (empathy) for the meanings given to events by the participants themselves. We also prize these and hope to have applied them at least in our local stories where, in both Brighton and Leuven, we sifted through a great deal of primary source material and took considerable pains to see that we had accurately rendered the views of our interviewees (see the Appendix).

But what is it that narratives are doing for our descriptions and explanations? Some, in the orthodox camp, would like to reshape narratives so that they will more directly and narrowly serve the purposes of hypothesis testing. Büthe, for example, argues that:

> To be useful as a test of a deductively sound model, a narrative should be structured by the model's identification of actors, their preferences etc, so as to minimize the ad hoc character of the empirical account. (Büthe, 2002, p. 490; see also Pollitt, 2008, pp. 151–3)

This would result in 'a story, Jim, but not as we know it'. It would be a highly stylized, preformed plot, with a carefully preselected list of characters. It would be vigorously opposed by many mainstream historians, but even more by the radical constructivists, who want all narratives to be 'decentred', not told from one point of view with one hypothesis to be tested, but to be exploratory and conjectural (Bevir and Rhodes, 2006)

> An interpretive approach encourages us to foreswear management techniques and strategies but . . . to replace such tools with learning by telling stories and listening to them. (Bevir et al., 2003, p. 200)

Our own, critical realist take on narratives is slightly different. We agree that, useful though it may be for followers of the variables paradigm, we do not want to preform narratives into specialized vehicles for testing hypotheses deduced from general theory:

> We reject here the notion that narratives should be conceived as 'testing' the model, on the grounds that to do so would inevitably render the narrative a 'just so' story where features of the world that are essential and causal in this

context are ignored because they do not have, nor could they have, a place in the general model because of the irreducible complexity that characterizes policy processes. (Kay, 2006, p. 63)

On the other hand we want go beyond any radical constructivist view that all we have to do is listen to the various stories from the actors involved in the events, place them side by side, and search (somehow) for their (multiple) meanings. We want a narrative to do more work than this, and we are very willing to admit that that means that we, as authors, are actively reshaping the evidence that comes from primary sources. We are trying to find explanations, and we are perfectly willing to use theories as and when they seem helpful in ordering and making sense of what we read and hear:

> In historical narratives, theoretical models are used but they are local or con-textual, and sometimes limited to one specific, temporally distinct event within the narrative. Theory is always subordinate to the evidence. The burden of the narrative is to weigh competing models, concepts or metaphors and show that one is the most appropriate in view of the evidence. (Kay, 2006, pp. 61–2)

This means, of course, that our narratives often have loose ends, and that they seldom confirm or falsify in orthodox, binary fashion. Instead they are used in an analytic dialogue with the evidence, strengthening this interpretation a little and weakening that one. They present a synthesized assessment of the relative appropriateness of a series of explanations for this unique body of evidence rather than the (dis)confirmation of the applicability of a general hypothesis to a theoretical instance.

9.9 CONCLUSIONS: WHAT DO WE THINK WE HAVE BEEN DOING?

So what kind of Anglo-Belgian comparison has this been? To dress it up in formal terminology, we might say that it has been a comparative, historical-institutionalist and mildly constructivist account set within a critical realist paradigm. (Incidentally, we do occasionally share the impatience of those colleagues who perceive these sometimes lengthy parades of philosophical labels as tiresome, since the wordiness often does little more than provide elaborate underpinning for empirical researchers to go on doing what good social science scholars have done for decades anyway. That is one reason why we have placed this chapter at the end of the 'main business' of the book rather than having required those who were interested in the substance of policy to wade through an ontological and epistemological marsh before they could get started on Belgium and England.)

Certainly our study has not been a KKV-style orthodox 'scientific' study of observable variables. In particular it has not been shaped around the formal testing of one or more defined hypotheses. And although it has used plenty of statistics these have played a supportive rather than a decisive role: it has not been first and foremost a quantitative analysis. The first tasks we set ourselves (Chapter 1, section 1.1) were in fact those of description rather than explanation. They were to:

- Compare public policymaking in Belgium and England.
- Compare two major public services, hospitals and the police.
- Compare shifts in national policies with what was actually happening in two specific localities.
- Compare developments over time (diachronic comparisons over four decades).

It was clear from the outset, however, that description was neither a simple nor a theory-free task. Our own attempts necessarily employed concepts and categories drawn directly from theory – most notably the distinction between a majoritarian and a consensus political regime, but also concepts of centralization and decentralization, managerialism and so on. We have a sneaking sympathy with Bruno Latour's point that 'if your description needs an explanation, it's not a good description' (although we would not go along with much of the rest of Latour's 'Actor Network Theory') (Latour, 2007, p. 147).

Theory has therefore figured as an input to description (as is often said, there are no wholly theory-free facts or, to put it another way, no truly naive descriptions). But there has also been a theoretical output. This has mainly come in an inductive manner, not through the kind of hypothetico-deductive processes that are pursued by the orthodox 'variables paradigm' type of social science. Various theoretical insights and possibilities have thus emerged from our historical analyses, and can be tested by further research. Just five may be offered here as illustrations:

- The insight that the mechanisms keeping a policy in place or an organization on a particular historical path are quite varied and need not be of the 'constant positive returns' type that path-dependency theorists originally concentrated on (see also Kay, 2006, p. 35).
- The conclusion that some of the main classifications of change (the Hall three-level model and the work of Streeck and Thelen) work well as heuristic devices but fail fully to allow for the variety of types

of change at the meso-level and cannot safely be used for quantitative hypothesis testing on 'populations' of policies.

- The insight from our long-term perspective that certain policies seem to cycle or oscillate – especially in the form of shifts from centralization to decentralization and back again (in both the hospital system and the police), or between the police as crime fighters and the police as protectors of public order in the community.
- The suggestion that changes in 'outcomes' in our two public services seem to have been determined as much by developments in the socio-technological environment as by formal shifts in public policy. Changing policies are just one ingredient in the mix of public service change.
- The further suggestion that the main driver of path-dependency in the ways in which policies get made has been the very slowly changing political system, whereas the main driver of changes in the substance of operational practices has been the generally more rapid developments in society and technology.

In short, we would claim that the activity of description, often seen as a very poor academic cousin to the noble practice of explanation, is actually rather a challenging and fruitful endeavour.

Coming to explanation, we would claim to have provided explanations for both similarity and difference, continuity and change. We have done this within the multicausal paradigm of critical realism. Obviously these explanations are more or less provisional and subject to revision in the light of further evidence, but in some cases we believe them to be reasonably robust. Thus we have proposed, for example, that the different political systems have made a big difference both to how decisions have been taken and to what decisions have been taken. Yet at the same time we have suggested that changes in society and technology, including the ever-increasing internationalization of professional communities of discourse surrounding the police and (especially) health care, have generated the material and formal causes of an observable degree of convergence in professional practices. These professional networks seem – at least in our two sectors – to have been far more potent influences than the more written-about international agencies such as European Union (EU) institutions or the OECD.

We have also identified a number of processes that have contributed to stability in specific aspects of particular policies. The top-down, national process of distributing NHS revenue and capital budgets according to measures of mortality and morbidity was for a long time a prime mechanism in preventing a major new investment in the Brighton hospital system. The intensive interactions of the Flemish Christian Democratic elite were an ongoing material and formal cause of the successful implementation of the Gasthuisberg plan over the period from the late 1960s up to the late 1980s, when things began to change as this particular political 'pipeline' started to leak.

Of course we are not claiming that our research design was perfect. As Blatter and Blume (2008) make clear, there is much work still to be done in building up a set of clear guidelines on how to proceed with cases that are aimed at process tracing or congruence analysis. Certainly we have not even strictly followed the advice which does exist – with hindsight there is a good deal of tightening up that we could and should have attempted.

These methodological arguments will never be finally settled. What is more, the practicalities of a substantial research project almost inevitably mean that, however pure one's initial design and philosophy (whether it was 'fixed' or 'flexible' in a Robsonian sense), compromises have to be made along the way. Hindsight is a wonderful thing, and there is nothing we would like to do more than start over again, knowing what we now know, to investigate the hospital system and the police in England and Belgium, Sussex and Leuven. But we cannot do that, of course, both because we probably could not find the time and the money, but also because the people and organizations concerned will have themselves moved on. We must therefore rest our case here, hoping that we have provided an account which is clear, plausible, evidenced, contextualized and – even – interesting.

Appendix: The Brighton–Leuven Project

The project was conceived as a study of long-term (1965–2005) local policy and organizational change in two complex public services (hospitals, police) in two countries (Belgium, England). The fieldwork was carried out in Leuven and Brighton from 2006 to 2008. It provides the basis for Chapters 6 and 7 of this book, and elements of it are deployed in some of our other publications.

Sources are a crucial feature of any historical account. In this case we had generous access to both persons and papers, although the nature of the documentation differed somewhat on either side of the Channel. We wish to express our deep appreciation to the many senior figures who gave us their (often hard-pressed) time and attention.

One reason for choosing the period since the mid-1960s was that a good proportion of the key decision-makers were still alive and potentially available for interview. For example, we were able to interview all the hospital chief executives for both the Brighton and Leuven hospitals for virtually the whole period, plus a good number of other senior figures. We were also able to interview a cohort of senior police officers, with careers that stretched back to the 1970s. In all we conducted 36 interviews with the key players and observers, using a standard schedule of questions (see below) but departing from that if the respondent wanted to lead us onto new or different issues (or if we ran out of time – one interview took 3.5 hours to deal with just four questions). We focused on top management (the top three levels in the respective organizations) but also interviewed key local politicians who had played significant roles with respect to hospital and/or police services. Some of these had also played national roles.

Records of these interviews were usually sent to the respondents so that they could correct any mistakes and add further thoughts if they so wished. The culture of research interviewing differs somewhat between the two countries. The majority of the Brighton interviewees were willing to have their opinions attributed to them by name, but that would not be so usual in Belgium. Therefore in this book we have simply indicated the interviews by code numbers, adding a few words about the source where the understanding was that we could do so.

We also examined a large number of documents. In Leuven we were able to see speeches and policy papers, consultancy reports and a number of retrospective accounts produced for the 75th anniversary of the foundation of the university hospital in 2004. On the police side we saw some internal police documents plus a number of public policy papers and one local police history. In Brighton the documentation was more extensive, both for hospitals and police. Hospital board minutes and planning documents were available back to 1993. A full set of the monthly local *Health Bulletin* was analysed back to that journal's foundation in 1967. Police annual reports – in occasionally changing formats – covered the whole period, and contained a wealth of detail including annual crime and police activity statistics. The Brighton newspaper, *The Argus*, has an archive which enabled us to track down reports on the hospital and the local police force going back to 1985. The far greater public documentation for the Brighton case probably reflects a number of factors. In the case of the hospital it is significant that the Royal Sussex County Hospital (RSCH) is a unit within a publicly accountable National Health Service, whereas Leuven University Hospital is a non-profit foundation, subject to government regulation but not a direct part of the state apparatus, even if it treats and relies upon public patients largely paid for through the Belgian national health insurance system. However, the greater availability of public documents and the greater detail they contained also applies to the police services, where local police plans in Belgium do not carry anything like the wealth of performance information that has become standard in English police plans, and there is no trail of annual public reports stretching back into the 1960s.

SCHEDULE OF INTERVIEW QUESTIONS

1. Over what period did you serve at [X]?
2. What positions did you hold?
3. During that time, what were the most important changes, from a senior management perspective?
4. What pressures or possibilities gave rise to these changes?
5. During that time, what things stayed essentially the same (stable), from a senior management perspective?
6. Why did these stay the same – why didn't they change?
7. How far did the approach and methods of working of the senior management team remain the same, or change?
8. Which were more important, local influences or national policies?

9. Were there tensions or contradictions between local pressures and national policies and, if so, how were these resolved?
10. What about changes in context and environment, rather than changes in policy: were there important longer-term trends in the environment that impacted on the management of [X]?
11. How far would you say [X] was able to choose and pursue its own strategy, or was it more a case of being forced to go down certain paths?
12. What would you say was the most important lesson you personally learned about the management of change?

FUNDING AND SUPPORT

In 2004 one of us (Pollitt) was awarded the Hans Sigrist International Prize in recognition of his previous comparative public management research. The Hans Sigrist Foundation is connected to the University of Berne, Switzerland. The prize money paid for most of the research that was carried out in Brighton. At the same time, the organizational support and base for this research was provided by the Institute of Public Management at the Katholieke Universiteit Leuven (KUL). KUL awarded Pollitt a Senior Research Fellowship from 1 September 2005 until 31 August 2006, and from October 2006 he became a tenured professor there. Bouckaert was Director of the Institute throughout the period of the project.

In Brighton Pollitt made arrangements to work with Professors Sue Balloch and Michael Hill of the Health and Social Research Policy Centre and with Professor Peter Squires, Professor of Criminology – all at the University of Brighton. He remains warmly grateful to all of them for their generous advice and support, and for the offer of a working base at the University's Falmer site.

References

Abbott, A. (1997) 'Of time and space: the contemporary relevance of the Chicago School', *Social Forces* 75: 4, pp. 1149–82.

Adcock, R. (2005) 'Generalization in comparative and historical social science: the difference that interpretivism makes', in D. Yanow and P. Schwartz-Shea (eds) (2005) *Interpretation and Method: Empirical Research Methods and the Interpretive Turn*, Armonk, NY, M.E. Sharpe, pp. 50–66.

Agranoff, R. and B. Radin (1991) 'The comparative case study approach in public administration', *Research in Public Administration* 1, pp. 203–31.

Allen, D. (1979) *Hospital Planning: The Development of the 1962 Hospital Plan*, Tunbridge Wells, Pitman Medical.

Andrews, R., G. Boyne and R. Walker (2008) 'Reconstructing empirical public administration: Lutonism or scientific realism?' *Administration and Society* 40:3, pp. 324–30.

Arthur, B. (1994) *Increasing Returns and Path Dependence in the Economy*, Ann Arbor, MI, University of Michigan Press.

Association of Chief Police Officers (1990) *Setting the Standards for Policing: Meeting Community Expectations*, Strategic Policy Document, London, ACPO.

Audit Commission (1990) *Effective Policing: Performance Review in Police Forces*, London, HMSO.

Audit Commission (1993) *Helping with Enquiries: Tackling Crime Effectively*, London, HMSO.

Audit Commission (1996) *Streetwise: Effective Police Patrol*, London, HMSO.

Bache, I. and M. Flinders (eds) (2004) *Multi-level Governance*, Oxford, Oxford University Press.

Ballantine, J., J. Forker and M. Greenwood (2008) 'The governance of CEO incentives in English NHS hospital trusts', *Financial Accountability and Management* 24:4, pp. 385–410.

Barclay, G. and C. Tavares (2003) *International Comparisons of Criminal Justice Statistics 2001*, issue 12/03, London, Home Office paper.

Baumgartner, F. and B. Jones (1993) *Agendas and Instability in American Politics*, Chicago, IL, University of Chicago Press.

Baumgartner, F. and B. Jones (eds) (2002) *Policy Dynamics*, Chicago, IL and London, University of Chicago Press.

BBC News (2005) *Interview with Peter Coles*, *Panorama*, 20 July, http://news.bbc.co.uk/2/hi/programmes/panorama/4701921.stm, accessed 15 April 2008.

Bergmans, D. (2005) 'Police and gendarmerie reform in Belgium: from force to service', paper presented to the Geneva Centre for the Democratic Control of Armed Forces international conference Democratic Horizons in the Security Sector, Ankara, 3 February.

Bevir, M. and R. Rhodes (2006) *Governance Stories*, London, Routledge.

Bevir, M., R. Rhodes and P. Weller (2003) 'Comparative governance: prospects and lessons', *Public Administration* 81:1, pp. 191–210.

Billiet, J., B. Maddens and A-P. Frognier (2006) 'Does Belgium (still) exist? Differences in political culture between Flemings and Wallons', *West European Politics* 29:5, pp. 912–32.

Blanplain, J. (2004) 'Oud-directeur Jan Blanplain en Gasthuisberg: "Mijn opdracht waas een haalbaarheidsstudie voor behoeften van Leuven"' Lxxven 75, 10 September, p. 9 (a newspaper produced on the 75th anniversary of the founding of UZ Leuven).

Blatter, Joachim (2007) 'Case study', in *The Sage Encyclopaedia of Qualitative Research Methods*, Sage, Thousand Oaks, CA.

Blatter, J. and T. Blume (2007) 'Beyond the co-variational template: alternative directions in case study methodology', paper presented at the Conference of the American Political Science Association, Chicago, IL, 30 August–2 September.

Blatter, J. and T. Blume (2008) 'In search of co-variance, causal mechanisms or congruence? Towards a plural understanding of case studies', *Swiss Political Science Review* 14:2, pp. 315–56.

Bovaird, T. and K. Russell (2007) 'Civil service reform in the UK, 1999–2005: revolutionary failure or evolutionary success', *Public Administration* 85:2, pp. 301–28.

Brans, M., C. De Visscher and D. Vancoppenolle (2006) 'Administrative reform in Belgium: maintenance or modernization?' *West European Politics* 29:5, pp. 979–98.

Brighton and Sussex University Hospitals NHS Trust (2005), 'Minutes of the Strategic Finance and Planning Group', 23 September, (http://www.bsuh.nhs.uk, accessed 16 January 2006.

Brighton Health Bulletin (1980) '"Absolute misery", but cuts go ahead', No. 59, February, p. 2.

Bruggeman, W. (1986) 'Naar een vernieuwde statistiek bij de regiliere politiediensten in Belgie' (Towards renewed regular Belgian police service statistics), PhD thesis, Brussels, Vrij Universiteit Brussel.

Bulletin (1991) 'MP challenges single-site hospital plan', No. 246, April, p. 2.

Burrell, G. (1997) *Pandemonium: Towards a Retro-organization Theory*, London, Sage.

Büthe, T. (2002) 'Taking temporality seriously: modeling history and the use of narratives as evidence', *American Political Science Review* 96:3, pp. 481–93.

Butler, Y. (2000) 'Managing the future: a chief constable's view', in F. Leishman, B. Loveday and S. Savage (eds) *Core issues in policing*, 2nd edition, Harlow, Pearson Education, pp. 305–20.

Cabinet Office (2008) *Excellence and Fairness: Achieving World Class Public Services*, London, Cabinet Office.

Canadian Institute for Advanced Research (1997) 'CIAR estimated health impacts of determinants of health on population health status', http://www.hc-sc.gc.ca/hppb/regions/ab-nwt/pdf/pop-health_e.ppt.

Carter, C. (2008) 'Identifying causality in public institutional change: the adaptation of the National Assembly for Wales to the European Union', *Public Administration* 86:2, pp. 345–61.

Castles, F. and D. Mitchell (1993) 'Worlds of welfare and families of nations', in F. Castles (ed.) *Families of Nations: Patterns of Public Policy in Western Democracies*, Aldershot, Dartmouth, pp. 93–128.

Colebatch, H. (1998) *Policy*, Buckingham, Open University Press.

Collier, P. (2006) 'In search of purpose and priorities: police performance indicators 1992–2004' *Public Money and Management* 26:3, pp. 165–72.

Cumberledge, J. (1985) quoted in *Brighton Health Bulletin*, No. 188, January, p. 3.

Davies, A. and R. Thomas (2008) 'Dixon of Dock Green got shot! Policing identity work and organizational change', *Public Administration* 86:3, pp. 627–42.

Delarue, D. (2001) *Algemeen politiemanagement: managementtechnieken et concepten voor de politie* (General police management: management techniques and concepts for the police), Brussels, Politiea.

Department of Health, Welsh Office, Scottish Home and Health Department, and Northern Ireland Office (1989) *Working for Patients*, Cm. 555, London, HMSO.

Deschouwer, K. (2006) 'And the peace goes on? Consociational democracy and Belgian politics in the twenty-first century', *West European Politics*, 29:5, pp. 895–911.

De Somer, P. (1985) Speech at Plechtige inhuidiging van het Universitaire Ziekenhuis op de gasthuisberg te Leuven, Leuven, Katholieke Universiteit Leuven, pp. 3–9 (inauguration ceremony for the Leuven University Hospital).

De Winter, L. and P. Dumont (2006) 'Do Belgian parties undermine the democratic chain of delegation?' *West European Politics* 29:5, pp. 957–76.

De Winter, L., M. Swyngedouw and P. Dumont (2006) 'Party system(s) and electoral behaviour in Belgium: from stability to Balkanisation', *West European Politics* 29:5, pp. 933–56.

Dunleavy, P., H. Margetts, S. Bastow and J. Tinkler (2006) *Digital Era Governance: IT Corporations, the State and E-Government*, Oxford, Oxford University Press.

Dye, T. (1972) *Understanding Public Policy*, Englewood Cliffs, NJ, Prentice Hall.

Eeckloo, K., G. Van Herck, C. Van Hulle and A. Vleugels (2004) 'From corporate governance to hospital governance: authority, transparency and accountability of Belgian non-profit hospitals' board and management', *Health Policy* 68, pp. 1–15.

Elias, N. (1992) *Time: An Essay*, Oxford, Blackwell.

Ericson, R. and K. Haggerty (2002) 'The policing of risk', in T. Baker and J. Simon (eds) *Embracing Risk: The Changing Culture of Insurance and Responsibility*, Chicago, IL and London, University of Chicago Press, pp. 238–72.

Esping-Andersen, G. (1990) *Three Worlds of Welfare Capitalism*, Princeton, NJ, Princeton University Press.

EUICS Consortium (2005) *The Burden of Crime in the EU: A Comparative Analysis of the European Survey of Crime and Safety*, Gallup Europe, Belgium, EUICS Consortium.

European Observatory on Health Care Systems (2000) *Health Care Systems in Transition: Belgium*, Copenhagen, European Observatory on Health Care Systems.

European Sourcebook of Crime and Criminal Justice Statistics – 2006, 3rd edition, Den Haag, Wetenschappelijk Onderzoek en Documentatiecentrum.

Evening Argus (1991) 'Medics hospital election pledge', 8 May, p. 13.

George, A. and A. Bennett (2005) *Case Studies and Theory Development in the Social Sciences*, Cambridge, MA, MIT Press.

Gerring, J. (2007) *Case Study Research: Principles and Practices*, Cambridge, Cambridge University Press.

Goodin, R. and P. Wilensky (1984) 'Beyond efficiency: the logical underpinnings of administrative principles', *Public Administration Review* 44:6, pp. 512–17.

Guba, Y. and E. Lincoln (1989) *Fourth Generation Evaluation*, London, Sage.

Hall, P. (1993) 'Policy paradigms, social learning and the state' *Comparative Politics* 25:3, pp. 275–96.

Hamm, R. (1988) 'Clinical intuition and clinical analysis: expertise and the cognitive continuum', in J. Dowie and A. Elstein (eds) *Professional Judgement: A Reader in Clinical Decision Making*, Cambridge, Cambridge University Press, pp. 78–105.

Harrison, S. (1988) *Managing the National Health Service*, London, Chapman & Hall.

Harrison, S. and R. McDonald (2008) *The Politics of Healthcare in Britain*, London and Los Angeles, Sage.

Hartley, J. (2005) 'Innovation in governance and public services: past and present', *Public Money and Management* 25:1, pp. 27–34.

Hartley, J., M. Fletcher and C. Strachan (1990) 'Hospital closures and the future of hospital services in Brighton', *Bulletin*, No. 244, February, p. 3.

Hawkesworth, M. (2005) 'Contending conceptions of science and politics', in D. Yanow and P. Schwartz-Shea (eds) *Interpretation and Method: Empirical Research Methods and the Interpretive Turn*, Armonk, NY, M.E. Sharpe, pp. 27–49.

Hay, C. and D. Wincott (1998) 'Structure, agency and historical institutionalism', *Political Studies* 46, pp. 951–7.

Heclo, H. (1972) 'Review article: policy analysis', *British Journal of Political Science*, 2, pp. 83–108.

Hensher, M. and N. Edwards (1999) 'The hospital of the future: hospital provision, activity, and productivity in England since the 1980s', *British Medical Journal* 319, pp. 911–14.

Hill, M. and P. Hupe (2002) *Implementing Public Policy*, London, Sage.

Hogwood, B. and L. Gunn (1984) *Policy Analysis for the Real World*, Oxford, Oxford University Press.

Home Office (1998) *Ministerial Priorities, Key Performance Indicators and Efficiency Planning for 1999/2000*, London, Stationery Office.

Home Office (2001) *Police Task Force Numbers: Report and Recommendations*, London, Research Development Statistics, Home Office, 18 December.

Home Office (2004) *National Policing Plan 2005–08: Safer, Stronger Communities*, London, Home Office.

Hough, M. (2008) 'Crime statistics', in T. Newburn and P. Neyroud (eds) *Dictionary of Policing*, Cullompton, Willan Publishing, pp. 65–7.

Howlett, M. and M. Ramesh (2003) *Studying Public Policy: Policy Cycles and Policy Subsystems*, Oxford, Oxford University Press.

Hunter, D. (2006) 'The National Health Service 1980–2005', *Public Money and Management* 25:4, pp. 209–12.

Ieven, R. (1976) *Een voorstel voor de organisatie van de Leuvense-politie na de fusie van gemeenten Leuven, Kessel-Lo, Heverlee, Wilsele*, December, unpublished document.

IPZ Leuven (1997) *Veiligheidscharter IPZ Leuven*, Leuven, 24 April, unpublished document.

James, P. (2006a) *Looking Good Dead*, London, Pan.

James, P. (2006b) *Dead Simple*, London, Pan.

James, P. (2007) *Not Dead Enough*, London, Pan.

Jason-Lloyd, L. (2008) 'Arrest', in T. Newburn and P. Neyroud (eds) *Dictionary of Policing*, Cullompton, Willan Publishing, pp. 6–7.

John, P. (1998) *Analysing Public Policy*, London, Pinter.

Jones, K. (2008) 'Association of Chief Police Officers (ACPO)', pp. 7–8 in T. Newburn and P. Neyroud (eds) Dictionary of Policing, Cullompton, Devon, Willan Publishing.

Joye, V. (2003) 'Ziekenhuzen aan het infuus' (Hospitals on the drip), *Knack* (Flemish magazine), November, pp. 52–8.

Kay, A. (2005) 'A critique of the use of path dependency in policy studies', *Public Administration* 83:3, pp. 553–71.

Kay, A. (2006) *The Dynamics of Public Policy: Theory and Evidence*, Cheltenham, UK and Northampton, MA, USA, Edward Elgar.

King, G., R. Keohane and S. Verba (1994) *Designing Social Inquiry: Scientific Inference in Qualitative Research*, Princeton, NJ, Princeton University Press.

Kingdon, J. (1995) *Agendas, Alternatives and Public Policies*, 2nd edition, New York, Harper Collins College Publishers.

Klijn, E-H. (2008) 'Governance and governance networks in Europe', *Public Management Review* 10:4, pp. 505–25.

Kurki, M. (2008) *Causation in International Relations: Reclaiming Causal Analysis*, Cambridge, Cambridge University Press.

Landsman, T. (2008) *Issues and Methods in Comparative Politics*, 3rd edition, London and New York, Routledge/Taylor & Francis.

Latour, B. (2007) *Reassembling the Social: An Introduction to Actor-Network-Theory*, Oxford, Oxford University Press.

Leppard, D. (2008) 'Police to get 10 000 Taser guns', *Sunday Times*, 23 November, p. 1.

Lijphart, A. (1984) *Democracies: Patterns of Majoritarian and Consensus Government in Twenty-one Countries*, London, Yale University Press.

Lijphart, A. (1999) *Patterns of Democracy: Governance Forms and Performance in 36 Countries*, New Haven, CT, Yale University Press.

Lindblom, C. (1959) 'The science of muddling through', *Public Administration Review*, 19:3, pp. 79–88.

Lindblom, C. (1979) 'Still muddling, not yet through', *Public Administration Review*, 39:3, pp. 517–26.

Loveday, B. (2000) 'New directions in accountability', in F. Leishman,

B. Loveday and S. Savage (eds) *Core Issues in Policing*, 2nd edition, Harlow, Pearson Education, pp. 213–31.

Luton, L. (2008) 'Beyond empiricists versus postmodernists', *Administration and Society* 40:2, pp. 211–19.

Lynn Jr., L., C. Heinrich and C. Hill (2008) 'The empiricist goose has not been cooked!' *Administration and Society* 40:1, pp. 104–9.

Maesschalk, J. (2002) 'When do scandals have an impact on policymaking? A case study of the police reform following the Dutroux scandal in Belgium', *International Public Management Journal*, 5:2, pp. 169–93.

Maesschalk, J. and Van de Walle, S. (2006) 'Policy failure and corruption in Belgium: is federalism to blame?', *West European Politics*, 29:5, pp. 999–1017.

Mahoney, J. (2000) 'Strategies of causal inference in small-N analysis', *Sociological Methods and Research* 28:4, pp. 387–424.

March, J. and J. Olsen (2006) 'Normative institutionalism', in R. Rhodes, S. Binder and B. Rockman (eds) *The Oxford Handbook of Political Institutions*, Oxford, Oxford University Press, pp. 3–22.

McKinsey's (1998) 'Naar een transparent en efficient beheer eerste diagnose en voorstel van aanpak' ('Towards a transparent and efficient management: first diagnosis and proposal of approach'), unpublished management consultancy report on UZ Leuven.

McLaughlin, E. (2007) The New Policing, London, Sage.

Ministry of Health (1962) *National Health Service: a Hospital Plan for England and Wales*, Cmnd. 6502, London, HMSO.

Mintzberg, H. (1979) *The Structuring of Organizations*, Englewood Cliffs, New Jersey, Prentice Hall International.

Moran, M. (2003) *The British Regulatory State: High Modernism and Hyper-innovation*, Oxford, Oxford University Press.

Mossialos, E. (1997) 'Citizens' views on health care systems in the member states of the European Union', *Health Economics* 6:2, pp. 109–16.

Moynihan, D. (2008) *The Dynamics of Performance Management: Constructing Information and Reform*, Washington, DC, Georgetown University Press.

National Health Service Management Inquiry (1983) *Report* ('The Griffiths Report'), London, Department of Social Security.

National Health Service Management Inquiry (1989) *Report* ('The Griffiths Report'), London, Department of Health and Social Security.

Newburn, T. and P. Neyroud (eds) (2008) *Dictionary of Policing*, Cullompton, Willan Publishing.

Neyroud, P. (2008) 'Association of Chief Police Officers (ACPO)', in T. Newburn and P. Neyroud (eds) *Dictionary of Policing*, Cullompton, Willan Publishing, pp. 7–8.

Nowotny, H. (1994) *Time: The Modern and Postmodern Experience*, Cambridge, Polity Press.

OECD (2007) *OECD Reviews of Human Resource Management in Government: Belgium*, Paris, OECD.

Olsen, J. (2009) 'Change and continuity: an institutional approach to institutions of democratic government', *European Political Science Review* 1:1, pp. 3–22.

Osborne, S. and K. Brown (2005) *Managing Change and Innovation in Public Service Organizations*, Abingdon, Routledge.

Parker, M. (2002) *Against Management: Organization in the Age of Managerialism*, Cambridge, Polity.

Parsons, W. (1995) *Public Policy: An Introduction to the Theory and Practice of Policy Analysis*, Aldershot, UK and Brookfield, US, Edward Elgar.

Pawson, R. and N. Tilley (1997) *Realistic Evaluation*, London, Sage.

Peers, J. (1985) Speech at Plechtige inhuidiging van het Universitaire Ziekenhuis op de gasthuisberg te Leuven, Leuven, Katholieke Universiteit Leuven, pp. 10–25 (inauguration ceremony for the Leuven University Hospital).

Peers, J. (1994b) 'Vijftig jaar ziekenhuiswezen in Belgie', *Tijdschrift voor Geneeskunde* 50:1, pp. 17–24.

Peters, B. (1989) *Comparing Public Bureaucracies: Problems of Theories and Method*, Tuscaloosa, AL, Alabama University Press.

Phillips, D. (2000) *The Expanded Social Scientist's Bestiary: A Guide to Fabled Threats To, and Defenses Of Naturalistic Social Science*, Lanham, MD, Rowman & Littlefield.

Pierson, P. (2004) *Politics in Time: History, Institutions and Social Analysis*, Princeton, NJ, Princeton University Press.

Politie PZ Leuven (1996), 'Nota over de algemene organisatie en werking van het politiekorps van Leuven', Leuven, 2 May, unpublished.

Politie PZ Leuven (1997) *Veiligheidscharter IPZ Leuven*, 24 April.

Politie PZ Leuven (2001) 'Nota over de algemene organisatie en werking van de lokale politie PZ-Leuven in het raam van het pilootproject', 1 April, unpublished.

Politie PZ Leuven (2005) 'Zonaal veiligheidsplan 2005–2008', 5388, PZ Leuven, unpublished.

Pollitt, C. (1985) 'Measuring performance: a new system for the National Health Service', *Policy and Politics* January, pp. 1–15.

Pollitt, C. (1993) *Managerialism and the Public Services*, 2nd edition, Oxford, Blackwell.

Pollitt, C. (2007) 'New Labour's re-disorganization: hyper-modernism and the costs of reform: a cautionary tale', *Public Management Review* 9:4, pp. 529–43.

Pollitt, C. (2008) *Time, Policy, Management: Governing with the Past*, Oxford, Oxford University Press.

Pollitt, C. (2009) 'Simply the best? The international benchmarking of reform and good governance', in J. Pierre and P.W. Ingraham (eds) *Public Sector Administrative Reform and the Challenges of Effective Change*, Montreal and Toronto, McGill-Queens University Press.

Pollitt, C., J. Birchall and K. Putman (1998) *Decentralising Public Service Management*, Basingstoke, Macmillan.

Pollitt, C. and G. Bouckaert (2004) *Public Management Reform: A Comparative Analysis*, 2nd edition, Oxford, Oxford University Press.

Punch, M. (2008) 'Corruption (police)', in T. Newburn and P. Neyroud (eds) *Dictionary of Policing*, Cullompton, Willan Publishing, pp. 51–3.

PZ Leuven (2005) *Zonaal veiligheidsplan 2005–2008* (Zonal security plan, 2005–2008), Leuven, PZ Leuven.

PZ Leuven (2006) *Protocols en samenwerkingsakkorden vanaf 24-04-1996*, (Protocols and co-operation agreements from 24-04-1996) Leuven, 1 June.

Reiner, R. (2000) *The Politics of the Police*, 3rd edition, Oxford, Oxford University Press.

Robson, C. (2002) *Real World Research*, 2nd edition, Blackwell, Oxford.

Rothstein, B. (2008) 'Creating political legitimacy: electoral democracy versus quality of government', QoG Working Paper 2008/2, Quality of Government Institute, University of Gothenberg.

Rothstein, B. and J. Teorell (2008) 'What is quality of government? A theory of impartial government institutions', *Governance* 21:2, pp. 165–90.

Rubin, I. (2000) *The Politics of Budgeting: Getting and Spending, Borrowing and Balancing*, 4th edition, New York, Chatham House.

Rueschemeyer, Dietrich (2003) 'Can one or a few cases yield theoretical gains?' in J. Mahoney and D. Rueschemeyer (eds) *Comparative Historical Analysis in the Social Sciences*, Cambridge, Cambridge University Press, pp. 305–36.

Sabatier, P. (ed.) (1999) *Theories of the Policy Process*, Boulder, CO, Westview Press.

Sahlin-Andersson, K. and L. Engwall (2002) *The Expansion of Management Knowledge: Carriers, Flows and Sources*, Stanford, CA, Stanford Business Books.

Salter, B. (2006) 'Governing UK medical performance: a struggle for policy dominance', *Health Policy* 82, pp. 263–75.

Scarman, Lord (1981) *The Brixton Disorders 10–12 April 1981: Report of an Inquiry*, Cmnd. 8427, London, HMSO.

Scharpf, F. (1997) 'Economic integration, democracy and the welfare state', *Journal of European Public Policy* 4:1, pp. 18–36.

Scharpf, F. (1999) *Governing in Europe: effective and democratic?* Oxford, Oxford University Press.

Schön, D. (1999) *The Reflective Practitioner: How Professionals Think in Action*, Aldershot, Aldgate.

Sheehy, P. (1993) the *Report of the Inquiry into Police Responsibilities and Rewards*, Cm. 2280, London, HMSO.

Special Eurobarometer 283 (2007) *Health and long-term care in the European Union*, Luxembourg, European Commission, December.

Steen, T., C. Van den Berg, F. Van der Meer, P. Overeem and T. Toonen (2005) *Modernising Governments in Other Countries: International Comparisons of Change in Central Government*, Den Haag, Ministry of the Interior (Programma Andere Overheid).

Stelfox, P. (2008) 'Professionalization', in T. Newburn and P. Neyroud (eds) *Dictionary of Policing*, Cullompton, Devon, Willan Publishing, pp. 227–8.

Streeck, W. and K. Thelen (eds) (2005) *Beyond Continuity: Institutional Change in Advanced Political Economies*, Oxford, Oxford University Press.

Sussex Police (1980) *Sussex Police Annual Report 1980*, Lewes, Sussex Police Printing Department.

Sussex Police (1981) *Sussex Police Annual Report 1981*, Lewes, Sussex Police Printing Department.

Sussex Police (1982) *Sussex Police Annual Report 1982*, Lewes, Sussex Police Printing Department.

Sussex Police (1983) *Sussex Police Annual Report 1983*, Lewes, Sussex Police Printing Department.

Sussex Police (1984) *Sussex Police Annual Report 1984*, Lewes, Sussex Police Printing Department.

Sussex Police (1985) *Sussex Police Annual Report 1985*, Lewes, Sussex Police Printing Department.

Sussex Police (1986) *Sussex Police Annual Report 1986*, Lewes, Sussex Police Printing Department.

Sussex Police (1987) *Sussex Police Annual Report 1987*, Lewes, Sussex Police Printing Department.

Sussex Police (1988) *Sussex Police Annual Report 1988*, Lewes, Sussex Police Printing Department.

Sussex Police (1989) *Sussex Police Annual Report 1989*, Lewes, Sussex Police Printing Department.

Sussex Police (1990) *Sussex Police Annual Report 1990*, Lewes, Sussex Police Printing Department.

Sussex Police (1992) *Sussex Police Annual Report 1992*, Lewes, Sussex Police Printing Department.

Sussex Police (1993) *Sussex Police Annual Report 1993*, Lewes, Sussex Police Printing Department.

Sussex Police (1995) *Sussex Police Annual Report 1994/5*, Lewes, Sussex Police Printing Department.

Sussex Police Authority (2003) Joint Annual Report of the Sussex Police Authority and the Chief Constable of the Sussex Police 2002/3, Chichester, Sussex Police Authority.

Sussex Police Authority (2004a) Joint Annual Report of the Sussex Police Authority and the Chief Constable of the Sussex Police 2003/4, Chichester, Sussex Police Authority.

Sussex Police Authority (2004b) *Local Policing Plan for Sussex, 2004–2005*, Lewes, Sussex Police Authority.

Sussex Police Authority (2005) Joint Annual Report of the Sussex Police Authority and the Chief Constable of the Sussex Police 2004/5, Chichester, Sussex Police Authority.

Tange, C. (2004) 'Evaluating the police: apolitical, professional and scientific issue – 25 years of experience evaluating the police in Belgium', *European Journal of Crime, Criminal Law and Criminal Justice* 12:3, pp. 232–50.

Team Consult (1988) *Les services de police en Belgique: rapport au Ministre de l'Intérieur*, PGR, Brussels, INBEL.

Team Consult (1995) 'Evaluatie van de werking van het Korps van Leuven' (Presentatie Nr. 4, 20 Januari) ('Evaluation of the workings of the Leuven police corps'), unpublished report.

Test Gezondheid (2005) 'De reputatie van ziekenhuizen: artsen aan het woord', No. 69, Oktober/November, pp. 12–16.

The Argus (1995) 'Down but not out!', 12 April, p. 1.

The Argus (2005) 'Sussex NHS vows to improve', 28 July, p. 1, http://archive.theargus.co.uk/2005/7/28/201527.html, accessed 1 June 2006.

Thelen, K. (2003) 'Insights from comparative historical analysis', in J. Mahoney and D. Rueschemeyer (eds) *Comparative Historical Analysis in the Social Sciences*, Cambridge, Cambridge University Press, pp. 208–40.

Thompson, J. and H. Rainey (2003) 'Modernizing human resource management in the federal government: the IRS Model', Washington, DC, IBM Endowment for the Business of Government.

Tilley, C. (2006) 'Why and how history matters', in R. Goodin and C. Tilley (eds) *The Oxford Handbook of Contextual Political Analysis*, Oxford, Oxford University Press, pp. 417–37.

Tilley, N. (2008) 'Community policing', in T. Newburn and P. Neyroud (eds) *Dictionary of Policing*, Cullompton, Willan Publishing, pp. 40–41.

Tobback, L. (1989) *Op nieuwe sporen: vier toespraken over politiebelied*, (On new tracks: four speeches about police policy) Brussels, INBEL.

Tuohy, C. (1999) *Accidental Logics: The Dynamics of Change in the Health Care Arena in the United States, Britain and Canada*, Oxford, Oxford University Press.

UZ Leuven (2000) 'Strategisch Plan UZ Leuven 2000', Lueven, unpublished.

Van den Bulck, J. (2002) 'Fiction cops: who are they and what are they teaching us?' in H. Giles (ed.) *Law Enforcement, Communication and Community*, Amsterdam, John Benjamins Publishing, pp. 107–27.

Van den Bulck, J. and K. Damiaans (2004) 'Cardiopulmonary resuscitation on Flemish television: challenges to the TV effects hypothesis', *Emergency Medicine Journal* 21, pp. 565–7.

Van Outrive, L. (2005) *La nouvelle police belge: désorganisation et improvisation*, Bruxelles, Bruylent.

Van Outrive, L., Y. Cartuyvels and P. Ponsaers (1992) *Sire, ik ben ongerust. Geschiednis van de belgische Politie, 1794–1991*, Leuven, Kritak.

Van de Walle, S., S. Van Roosbroek and G. Bouckaert (2008) 'Trust in the public sector: is there any evidence for a long-term decline?' *International Review of Administrative Sciences* 74:1, pp. 47–64.

Wallace, M. (2007) 'Coping with complex and programmatic public service change', in M. Wallace, M. Fertig and E. Schneller (eds) *Managing Change in the Public Services*, Malden, MA and Oxford, Blackwell Publishing, pp. 31–5.

Whipp, R., B. Adam and I. Sabelis (eds) (2002) *Making Time: Time and Management in Modern Organizations*, Oxford, Oxford University Press.

Whitehouse, P. (2001) 'Determined and courageous in fighting crime', *Policing Sussex 2001*, p. 5 (local police newspaper).

Wildavsky, A. (1979) *Speaking Truth to Power: The Art and Craft of Policy Analysis*, Boston, Little, Brown & Co.

Wildavsky, A. (1986) *Budgeting: A Comparative Theory of Budgetary Processes*, revised edition, New Brunswick, NJ, Transaction Books.

Witte, E., J. Craeybeckx and A. Meynen (2000) *Political History of Belgium: From 1830 Onwards*, Brussels, VUB Press.

World Health Organization Europe (2006) *Highlights on Health in the United Kingdom, 2004*, Copenhagen, WHO Regional Office for Europe.

Yanow, D. (2005a) 'Thinking interpretively: philosophical presuppositions and the human sciences', in D. Yanow and P. Schwartz-Shea (eds) *Interpretation and Method: Empirical Research Methods and the Interpretive Turn*, Armonk, NY, M.E. Sharpe, pp. 5–26.

Yanow, D. (2005b) 'How built spaces mean: a semiotics of space', in D. Yanow and P. Schwartz-Shea (eds) *Interpretation and Method: Empirical Research Methods and the Interpretive Turn*, Armonk, NY, M.E. Sharpe, pp. 349–66.

Yanow, D. and P. Schwartz-Shea (eds) (2005) *Interpretation and Method: Empirical Research Methods and the Interpretive Turn*, Armonk, NY, M.E. Sharpe.

Yin, R. (2003) *Case Study Research: Design and Methods*, 3rd edition, London, Sage.

Zerubavel, E. (2004) *Time Maps: Collective Memory and the Social Shape of the Past*, Chicago, IL and London, University of Chicago Press.

Index

1998 Crime and Disorder Act 114, 115

accounting system changes 6
accreditation for doctors, Belgium 46
achievement, monitoring of, in English
    hospitals 40
acute hospital, greenfield site
    failure to secure for Brighton 147
Airwave radio communications system
    132
Anglo-Belgian parallel trends 98
animal rights against live animals for
    export
    partial ban on exports 110
Anti-Social Behaviour Orders
    (ASBOs), 1998 56, 112
Area Health Authorities, England 39,
    82
    see also District Health Authorities;
    Regional Health Authorities
armed protection for VIPs 106
Ashley, James, police shooting in
    Hastings, 1998
    drugs raid 110
assaults on nursing staff 100
Association of Chief Police Officers
    (ACPO), 1990 50
    Setting the Standards for Policing:...
    54
Audit Commission 50
    Helping with Enquiries: Tackling
    Crime Effectively 55
autonomy of Belgian hospitals 48
autonomy of subnational public
    authorities, evidence 138–53

Banditism Commission, Parliamentary
    Committee of Enquiry into
    Nivelles Gang, 1988 63
Basic Command Units (BCUs) 111
beds in English hospitals, 1987–2006
    37–8

Belgian health care system,
    organizational chart 36
Belgian hospitals development 34–7
    disadvantages 98
    federal-level planning 72
    policy, 1965–2005 43–8
    Rijkswacht/Gendarmerie 50, 64, 99,
    118, 121, 125, 130
    military character 61
    national reach of 68
Belgian police organization since 2001
    118–19
    police aims to achieve 66
Belgian regime 22–31
Belgian state intervention in contracts
    and agreements 46
Belgium
    federal and decentralized system
    24
    public policymaking and
    management 1, 61
Belgium, main police forces 61
BEST diagram and 'typology' 18, 20,
    143–4
    value of applying 152–3
Best Value (BV) regime, police
    consultation of public 56
Birch, Roger, Chief Constable, Sussex
    Police, 1983
    annual report Sussex Police, 1992, on
    crime escalation,
    drugs and moral standards 108
    policing style and community
    consent 104
Blunkett, David, Home Secretary
    Home Office Police Standards Unit,
    2001 56
BOB (Bijzondere Opsporings Brigade)
    guard and investigation brigade
    119
'*BOOMERANG*' change, return to
    former policy

British government's periodic emphases on 'bobbies back on the beat' 19
BOOMERANG, EARTHQUAKE, STALACTITE AND TORTOISE (BEST) 18, 146–7
    patterns of change 146
Brabant killers (Nivelles Gang), 1982–5
    robbers in armed attacks 62
Brighton and Hove
    police merger, 2001 111
    research on local perspective, hospitals 81
Brighton and Leuven hospitals
    professional management 99–100
Brighton General Hospital 85–92
Brighton Health Authority 82
Brighton Health Care Trust 91
Brighton hospitals, current spending 89
    key local changes 148
    list of major restructurings 91–2
    medical school 2001, link to Brighton universities 90
Brighton Hospital story, 1965–2005 85–92
Brighton–Leuven project, interviews and documents 195–7
Brighton, multilevel governance 11–12
Britain and Belgium, similarities and differences 22–3
    policymaking similarities and differences 71–80
British civil service and policymaking, reforms 25–6
British Crime Survey, 1988 58
    decline of public confidence in police 54
Brixton riots 53
budgetary control in hospitals, England 33
budget category changes 6–7
budgeting in 'advanced' Western states 18
'bullying culture' under New Labour 90
burglaries, increase in, 1980 103

capital for Brighton hospitals 87
car speeding in rural lanes of Sussex 102

case studies 186–9
    England and Belgium 12
causal process tracing 188
causation 175, 178, 180–81
Cellules Communistes Combattantes (CCC), 1984–5
    terrorist bombings, Belgium 62
central and local power, Leuven 126
central government more dominant in England 114, 135, 158
central–local relations of political elites in Belgium 135
change, consequence of strategic action 17
change, gradual, 'stalactite' change
    professionalization of police 145–6
change management 5–8
changes in crime figures 57–8
change, theories of 135–69
Chief Constable, Sussex Police, 1987–99 annual reports 106–8
child welfare services 38
civil servants and ministers, Belgium 24–5
civil service
    citizens' attitudes, Belgium and Britain 165
    role in policy making 27
Clarke, Kenneth, Home Secretary
    police organization re-structuring, 1993 55
classic incrementalism
    development of hospital system at Brighton/Hove 146
    evolution of Belgian hospital system 146
clinical audit, mandatory 34
closed-circuit TV (CCTV) 31
Cluster's Law 44
Codes of Practice of police 53
Commission for Health Improvement (CHI) 41–2
Commission for Social Care Inspection, merger, 2005 42
Committee P, monitoring Belgium's police forces, 1991 51, 63, 66, 126
'community policing', England and Belgium 30–31, 126, 140
community relations, need for more proactive, with police 60, 69

Community Support Officers 114
comparison across space and time 1–2, 185
  of hospitals sector and police 8
competition as selection system 42
competition between police forces, Belgium
  bottom-up initiative elements 127
competitive elements in hospital system under Labour and Conservative governments 43
confidence in police
  England and Belgium 77
congruence analysis 188
consensual democracies versus majoritarian systems 159–61, 174–5
consensus decision-making in hospitals 39
consensus states (Belgium)
  Lijphart's statistical analysis of efficiency 159
constitutional reform in Belgium 23
constitutions of countries 15–16
continuities over time in Leuven 129
co-payments introduction, Belgium Royal Decree, 1993 46
corruption of police 51, 68
courts, instruments in fight against crime 73
Crime and Disorder Act, 1998 56
crime
  change in categories 58
  detection league tables, 1995 110
  high media coverage 10
  increase in, 1968–1982 104
  influences on 77
  investigation, DNA analysis 9
  levels higher in England than Belgium, 1988–2004 76–7
crime victims and police support 77
criminal acts, number of, in Belgium 67–8
criminals, active targeting of 109
critical realism 179–85, 190, 193
criticism of doctors and police 9
Crossroads Bank for Social Security, Belgium 1990
  e-government in social sector 46
Crown Prosecution Service (CPS) 54

cultural mechanisms
  professional culture of university teaching hospital 156
  'street culture' of some police 156

Data Protection Act, 106
deaths in police custody, government report on growing number 52
decommodification scores 174
demilitarization of federal police, Belgium 72
democratic self determination 161–7
De splitsing (splitting), national political crisis
  Belgium 83, 84, 92, 93, 97, 122
detection rate in Sussex Police 112–13
De Witte, Lode, Governor of Flemish-Brabant 63, 64, 122, 123, 128
diachronic comparisons 1
Diagnostic-Related Group (DRG) system
  hospital pharmaceutical expenditure 47
district bureaus, establishment of, 1996 123
District Health Authorities 40
District General Hospital (DGH) 38
District Management Teams 39
DNA testing 31
doctors in Belgium, self-employed 35
doctors, tighter guidance and regulation by managers 34
Dutroux Affair, Belgium, 1996-7, 64, 133, 142, 151
  unrest over criminal justice system 29
  'White March', public demonstration 64
Dutroux, Marc, paedophile and killer escaped briefly from custody, 1998 64

Edmund-Davies report, increase in police pay 52
efficiency and effectiveness, ratio of inputs to outputs 78
efficiency, less in Belgian than English police force 160
efficiency savings 80
  England versus Belgium 79

elite networks, Belgium and England
     139
emergency calls, rapid rise, 1980 103
England
     Area Health Authorities 39
     public policymaking and
          management 1
     no national police force 101
     similarities to Belgium 10–11
English hospitals 32–4
     market-type mechanisms, increased
          use 72
English hospitals policy, 1965–2005
     rationalization drive 37–43
ethnic equality in police force 116
ethnic minorities, urban disorder and
     police riots, London, 1980s 28, 54
Euro 2000 Football finals, Belgium
     international security concerns 65
Eurobarometer, satisfaction with
     democracy 163
Eurobarometer, trust in Civil Service,
     Belgium/Britain 162–63, 166
European Council of Ministers 54
European Observatory on Health Care
     Systems, 2000 35, 43
European single market
     European Union membership,
          marginal influence 138
     government welfare reductions 165
Europol Organization, Maastricht
     Treaty 54
expansion and specialization, Belgian
     police 61
expenditure rises for hospital
     pharmaceuticals, Belgium, 1996 29

federal-level hospital policy, Belgium
     92
Federal Security Plan, Belgium, 2000
     65
fee-for-service payment of providers,
     Belgium 43
financial mechanisms, NHS capital
     budget 156
financial support for Brighton
     hospitals 87
financial targets 89
fire service, and origin of police,
     Leuven 120

fiscal crisis in 1976 and 1980s, National
     Health Service 39
Fisher Report on police
     rights violation of teenage boys
          charged with murder 52
Flemings and Walloons, conflict 24,
     83, 92
Flemish autonomy 153, 155
Flemish Brabant province,
     Leuven, administrative capital 116
Flemish Christian Democratic elite
     interaction 94, 96, 194
football hooligans, Heysel Stadium,
     Brussels, 1985
     deaths and injuries 62
foot patrol, efforts to direct more
     officers, 103–4
Force Crime Strategy, 1994 109
form filling by police 31
Foundation Trust (FT) 42
Francophone students, Thursday riots
     in Leuven, 1975 121
Francophone (Walloon) university,
     Louvain-la-Neuve, 83, 93
funding needs, Leuven 125
funding of Sussex police, 2002–03
     112

Gasthuisberg plan 194
Gatwick airport, Sussex, special police
     unit 102
Gendarmerie
     district staff merger with Leuven
          118
     municipal police differences 129–30
gender equality in police force 116
general practitioners in medicine 38
geriatric ward, indefensible nursing
     practices 100
     TV documentary on Brighton
          hospitals 90
governance networks, different in
     England 139
government influence
     Leuven and Sussex, comparison
          130–31
government initiatives, impact of, on
     police 113
government intervention in hospital
     system 30, 31, 48–9

government pressure for hospital economies, England 37
governments, declining public trust in 5
Gow, Ian, Conservative MP for Eastbourne
    murder by IRA bomb 108
Greater London Council, police monitoring 104
    in Brighton, 1987 107

Hall three-level model 146–7
    value of applying 152–3
Hans Sigrist Foundation, University of Berne, Switzerland 197
Hastings hospital, priority capital 87
Hastings Shooting, retirement of Paul Whitehouse 133
    considered a loss to force 111
    police investigation of Sussex police 111
headline crimes, failure to solve 68
health care
    comparisons, England and Belgium 74, 75
    expenditure, rising 30 164–5
    insurance, Belgium, 1960s 44
    provider, free choice of 43
health care as federal responsibility, Belgium 35
Healthcare Commission, merger, 2005 42
health care public spending, limits to growth of
    international problem 98–9
health insurance system 35
health matters, high media coverage 10
Health Supervisory Board, England, government policy 40
help from public for police 104
Her Majesty's Inspectorate of Constabulary (HMIC)
    Matrix of Police Performance Indicators, 1987 54
Heysel Stadium, Brussels, football hooligans,
    international criticism of Belgian policing 62
hierarchy emergence, 1979–90, England 33

high-profile crime fighting
    political and media pre-eminence 73
historical institutionalism 13–15
historical narratives 189–91
HM Inspectorate of Constabulary 50
Home Office Circular 114/83
    Manpower, effectiveness and efficiency on the police service 105
Home Office Police Standards Unit 50
Home Office power, performance-driven culture 113
Hospital Act, 1963 ('Cluster Law'), Belgium 44
Hospital Act 1973, Belgium 28, 45
hospital care, Belgium and England
    public experience figures 160–61
hospital funding in Belgium 36–7
hospital pharmaceutical expenditure
    Diagnostic-Related Group (DRG) system 47
Hospital Plan for England and Wales, 1962 86
    new hospital building 38
hospital reform in England 1985–95 29
hospital run by Christian institution, Leuven 94
hospitals 1, 8, 80–100
    admissions minimization, Belgian objective 45–6
    beds, fall in number, Leuven 95
    Belgium moratorium on new hospital beds 72
    health care organizations and 136
    national reforms 32–49
    patient co-payments for visits to doctors, increase in 72
    reduction in waiting times, England 72
    'trusts', self-governing public corporations 33
hospital services, 1960s, Belgium/England comparison 28
hospitals in Belgium, lack of professional management 73
hospital spending, limiting measures 99
hospital stays, falls in 1965–2005, England 37
hospital trust chief executives
    clinical responsibility, no training 41

Hove (Holmes Avenue) development 87–8
Hulpagenten, Belgium, 'community support officers' 69
'hyper-innovation' and 'hyper-modernism' in Britain 23

Ieven, Ray, head of Leuven Police 1971
organised shooting training, reduction of riots 121
impartiality of civil service, England 169
increased autonomy, Belgium 158
increase in recorded crime 1965–2005, England 60
information and communication technologies (ICTs) and police 9
innovations and change 6
input legitimacy 162
of electoral arrangements 167
reflecting will of people 161
institutional change, patterns of, 'BEST' schema 18
insurance for healthcare, Belgium 44, 75
integration of police personnel, Leuven 123
intensive training of police, need for 69
internal market for NHS, efficiency through competition 157
international comparisons 183–6
international crime 73
International Monetary Fund (IMF) aid 147
Internet connection, public service 7
'interpolice zones', coordination between local forces, 1995 64
Interpolice Zones, Leuven 119
interviews with hospital chief executives 85
IRA bomb attack, Grand Hotel Brighton
Conservative Party Conference, 1984 105
Bognor Regis and Brighton, 1995 110

James, Peter, crime novels set in Brighton 102

Jones, Ken, Chief Constable, Sussex Police, 2002
emphasis on performance indicators 111, 115
new style leadership 133
Judicial Police, Belgium 50, 61, 123
justice and administration, Leuven 126

Katholieke Universiteit Leuven (KUL) 92–7
de splitsing (splitting up) 83, 93
finance and government crisis, 1998 149
formal inauguration, 1985 94–5
knowledge construction 173
major structural reform, 1997 budgeting and decision-making 96
strong position, training Flemish doctors 93
Ziekenhuis, Leuven, new 144
Earthquake type change 149

Labour Government, 1997
Abolition of market (White Paper, 1989) 145
Labour Party Conference, Brighton, policing, 1997 110
Labour victory, Greater London Council (GLC), 1981
Police Committee 52
legal mechanisms
Police and Criminal Evidence Act, 1984 28, 52, 113, 132, 153, 155
Police Community Support Officers (PCSOs), 2002 155
legal requirements or guidelines 154
length of service of chiefs of police, political leaders 128–9
Leuven, ancient Flemish city 82
area and population, map 117
comparison with Sussex 130–34
hospitals, key local changes 148
multilevel governance policy 11–12
one-city police zone 128
PilotPoliceZone (PPZ), 2000 124
similarities to Sussex 131–2
Leuven City Security Charter 1997, priorities for Leuven 124

Leuven Hospital Story, 1965–2005 92–6
Leuven interviews
consistent political vision, longer-term changes 133
Leuven police, (De Leuvense Politie) 101, 116–20, 151
analysis 125–30
Leuven Police Zone, mergers, 2001 124
liberal democracies 23–6
life expectancy statistics 75
linguistic cleavages in Belgium, Flemish and French, some German 24
local case studies, Brighton and Leuven 12
local changes, key in hospitals 148
local communities, instruments in fight against crime 73
need for police connection 60
Local Criminal Justice Boards 114
local issues and neighbourhood approach for police 69
local 'partnerships', pressure for, Sussex 133
local policies, versus national 11
local zones for police, establishment of, 2002 65

Maastricht criteria, European Single Currency 47
majoritarian states (England), Lijphart on 159, 161, 174
managerialism in Belgian police and hospitals 66, 72–3
managerial power, growing emphasis 136
in English hospitals and police 30, 33, 74, 115, 135
managerial professionalism, Leuven, doubts about 126–7
managers, no clinical training 34
mayoral influence on local police, Leuven 128, 129, 131
mechanisms to explain patterns 153–8
medical expertise 'as bargaining counter' 34
medical profession, resistance to competitive market 33, 41

merger of Municipal Police forces of Leuven, Heverlee, Kessel-Lo and Wilsele
1976–7, dog section and motor-cycle section 122
merging and regrouping hospitals, Belgium, 1989 45
micro-management, Cabinet office paper 168
miners' strike, England, 1984–5 28
left-wing criticism of police 53
miners striking, Belgium 1986
violent suppression by Gendarmerie/Rijkswacht 63
minimization of hospital admissions, 1985–95, Belgium 29
Ministers of the Interior, Leuven 128
Ministry of Public Health and Environment, 1980 36
merger with another Ministry, Belgium, 1995 47
moratorium on opening of new hospital beds
Belgium, 1982 44–5
Mouchaers, Jean-Paul, Korpschef, 2007
consultation on local security plan 125
multicultural and multi-ethnic communities 9
multigovernment policymaking, nature of 138–53
multilevel governance in Belgium and England 1, 97–8
multiparty Belgian political system 10
multiplication of specialist national bodies, police in England 72
municipal police and fire service integration, Leuven 120
Municipal Police, Belgium, 50–51, 61, 117, 119, 121, 123
mergers, 1976–77 122, 124
position on size of units, Leuven, one-city police 128
strike, 1982 62
murder of Stephen Lawrence, London
criticism of police handling 55
Macpherson Inquiry report, 1999 56

mutualities' health-care expenditure,
    Belgium 47

National Alliance of Christian
    Mutualities, Belgium, 44
national and local plans 136
National Crime Squad, 1998 55–6
National Criminal Intelligence Service,
    1997 50, 55, 72
National DNA Database 50
National Health Service (NHS), 1948
    7, 28, 32, 33, 37, 91
  Brighton hospitals, part of 86
  central control of manpower 40
  expenditure as percentage of GDP
    164
  free at point of access 75
  laundry, domestic and catering
    services
    compulsory competitive
      tendering, 1985 40
  Management Board, creation of
    government policy 40
  professional managers 32, 115
  restructuring as 'internal market',
    1989 41
  spending restrictions for Brighton 99
  'tripartite' basis 38
  trust status 41
National Institute for Clinical
    Excellence (NICE) 34, 48
  regulatory body 41
National Institute for Sickness and
    Invalidity, Belgium 35 (INAM/
    RIZIV) 43–4
national league tables for police,
    pressure to improve position 109
national level policymaking, local
    policy implementation 162
national performance measurement
    system
  Belgium, 27, 30
  England, 27, 30, 57
National Police DNA Database 114
national police force, absence of, in
    England 50
  Belgium (Rijkswacht/Gendarmerie)
    50
  performance indicators, Home Office
    Circular 17/93 55

National Policing Improvement
    Agency 50
National Policing Plan (NPP), annual
    requirement 29, 150
national political crisis, 2007–2008,
    Belgium
  party and regional divisions 168
national reforms 22–31
  Belgium and England 71–80
National Reporting Centre, 1972,
    England 52
National Union of Socialist
    Mutualities, Belgium 44
Neighbourhood Policing Teams,
    Sussex, 2004/05, 111–12
Neighbourhood Watch, growing
    enthusiasm of public 105
  Sussex, 1987 107, 114
'New Deal' for junior doctors 89
New Labour government 1997–2005,
    73
  're-disorganization' 33–4
  stronger Whitehall grip on hospitals
    90
  strengthening of hospital managers
    29
Newman, Sir Kenneth, Commissioner
    for Metropolitan Police, 1982
    53
New Public Management (NPM)
    reforms 16

'Octopus Agreement' May 1998
  integrated police force proposal
    64
oil price shocks, 1970s, British
    economy 147
operational autonomy for police,
    England 169
Operation Bumblebee, anti-burglary
    initiative 109
Order of Physicians, Belgium,
    registering doctors 35
Organisation for Economic Co-
    operation and Development
  health care expenditure 47–8
  records, performances in 159
organizational mechanisms, medical
    payment system at KUL 156
output legitimacy 161–7

Parliamentary Committee for Home
 Affairs
 report on growing number of deaths
  in police custody 52
partnerships policy 149–50
patients, active role in own care 100
patterns of institutional change 143–6
pay increase, 1979, English police 72
Pentagon platforms
 move against fragmentation and
  non-communication 67
performance indicators (PIs) in English
 force, 1982
 District Health Authority (DHA) 40
 English police and hospital systems
  27, 150
 high level compared with Belgium
  131
 Regional Health Authority (RHA)
  40
 Sussex force 130
performance measurement, England
 90, 133, 135
 in English hospitals 33
performance-related pay (PRP),
 resistance from police unions, 55
personnel management systems,
 Belgium 25
physical violence of citizens in UK 9
Pinksterenplan, (Pentecost Plan) 1990,
 66, 133, 151
 emphasis on community policing,
  29 63
police
 accountability 53, 109–10
 changes in England and Belgium,
  comparison 70
 co-operation across the EU 54
 corruption and complicity, Belgium
  64, 141
 corruption in England 28, 141
 discontent with, in Belgium 62
 national reforms 50–70
Police Acts, 1964, 1976, 1996, 1997 51,
 52, 55–6
Police and Criminal Evidence Act
 (PACE), 1984 28, 52, 113, 132,
 151
 central government initiative 149
 codification of police powers 53

deep change in handling police
 suspects 153
training requirements 105–6
police and fire service separation in
 1935 120
police and hospital policies, overview
 26–31
Police and Magistrates Courts Act,
 1994
 Home Secretary's role strengthening
  55
 local authority role weakening
  55
police areas in England, larger than in
 Belgium 101
police–community relations, England
 53, 141
Police Community Support Officers
 (PCSOs) 69, 112, 136, 155
 'plastic police' 57
Police Complaints Board, 1976,
 England 52, 111
police force amalgamations, Belgium,
 1970s 61–6, 118, 122, 123, 125–6
police force structures and sizes,
 Leuven/Sussex 130
Police Function Act, Leuven 1992
 coordination of tasks 123
 functions of Municipal police/
  Rijkswacht 63–4, 119–20
police, local jurisdictions, Brighton and
 Leuven 101–34
police manpower, 1987 annual report,
 Sussex Police 106–7
Police National Computer, 1969,
 England 52
police numbers in England,
 unreliability of statistics 59
police numbers in Belgium 68
police officers on streets, popular
 demand 114
police pay increases, England 52
police performance indicators,
 1985–95, England 29, 55, 56, 57,
 60, 108
police policy, British and Belgian,
 1965–2005 51–61
 monitoring, seen as 'politicization of
  police' 52–3
police, probity in doubt, 1988/89 54

Police Reform Acts, 1998, 2002 27, 56, 59, 64–5, 151
police services 1965–85, comparison, Belgium /England 28
high-tech operations 31
reduction in Belgium 28
police specialization 136
police statistics, selected, England and Belgium 76
police training in Leuven 120–21
police training in technology 31
Policing Improvement Agency, 2004 72
Policing in Sussex, 1990
public opinion survey, University of Sheffield team 108
policing, traditional 'beat', prevention of, by other duties 105–6
policy activism for police, debatable good 4, 75
policy aspects 3–4, 7
policy instruments, changes in levels 71
policymaking as 'bright ideas', England 40–41
policymaking for English hospital system
government intervention increasing 43
political control over police, Sussex, tightening 131
political systems of England and Belgium 10–11, 16, 23–6, 137
politicians, local, role of, in Leuven 130
politicization of public service 27
popular culture, hospitals and police 10
powers, devolution of, in Belgium to Wallonia, Flanders, Brussels 24
Primary Care Trusts, 'independent treatment centres' 42
Princess Royal Hospital, Haywards Heath 88, 90
prisoner transportation contract 55
Prison Policy, Belgium, 2000 65
private health care expenditure Belgium in 2000, lowest rate 47
private security industry 66, 73
probation services 73
professionalization of local police 60, 72
proportional representation system 161

Prosecution of Offences Act, 1985 54, 106
public health insurance, compulsory in Belgium 34–5, 43
public order breakdowns, England 31
public policy change, levels of examples in National Health Service (NHS) and police 7
public policymaking and management Belgium and England 192
public reporting of crimes, variable 58
Public Service Agreements (PSAs), England 30, 57
public trust decline in police and criminal justice system 136

Quality of Service (QOS) initiative 54

radical conservatism 145
radical constructivism 176–9, 183, 187, 191
rainbow coalition in Belgium, 1999 liberals, socialists, environmentalists 65
rationing of NHS investment 147–8
recorded crime, tables of, England and Wales, 1965–2002
statistics, unreliability of 59–60
reforms, intensity of, Belgium and England
comparisons over time 71
Regional Directorates of Health and Social Care, 2001 42
Regional Health Authorities, England 38, 40, 89
Regional Offices of NHS 42
regulation by central government, increase in England 60
resignation of Ministers of Justice, Belgium 64
resistance to centralised reorganisation, England 168
Resource Allocation Working Party (RAWP), 1976 188
allocation of NHS revenue funds 89
resource allocation, health authorities 39
respect for authority, loss of, in population 116

revenue monies to northern England
more poverty and sickness 89
Rijkswacht and Municipal
Policemergers
local police forces 125
Rijkswacht District, Leuven 119, 127
Rijkswacht/Gendarmerie 50, 64, 99,
118, 121, 125, 130
entente with Leuven police, 1968
after *de splitsing* (splitting up)
121
military character 61
national reach of 68
Rijkswacht/Gendarmerie, 1960s
Central Bureau for Investigation
(CBO) 61
Surveillance and Detection Branch
(BOB) 61
rival images of police 114
Royal Commission on the National
Health Service ('Merrison report')
1979 39
Royal Decree No. 47, Belgium, bed
approvals and process criteria 45
Royal Sussex County Hospital (RSCH)
82, 87, 88
budgetary overspend 83
ill-treatment of elderly patients 83
main development events 86
Tortoise type change 148
'undercover' BBC TV documentary
on 83

Safer and Stronger Communities Fund
114
satisfaction level with own country's
democracy 163
scandals and disasters, Belgium, 1980s,
1990s 51
Scarman Report, 1981,
police–community relations 53
Sussex Chief Constable finds
unnecessary 104
Scharpf, Fritz W.
on input-oriented and output-
oriented legitimization 161
Serious Organised Crime Agency
(SOCA) 50, 59, 114
Sex Discrimination Act, 1975, women
in police force 103

social and technological change
effects of, on police 116
impacts on management of hospitals
100
social expenditure 174
social habits and norms, changes in 9
social sciences, controversies in 13,
158–67, 172–3
South Yorkshire Police Authority
attempted disbanding of certain
police units 53–4
spatio-temporal contexts 185
Special Intervention Squad (SIE/
DYANE), Belgium, 1970s
dealing with hostage-taking 61
specialist skills in policing 60, 69
speciality-based divisions within
hospitals, England 38
specialized and generic policing,
Leuven 126
Special Operations Unit, 1986, Sussex
106
stability of Belgium 23
Stadswachten (town watch), Belgium
69
stakeholder groups, different opinions
142
'stalactite' change, gradual change 18
'star system' for British hospital trusts
'stars' for performance 42
state power and citizen rights, Leuven
126
Statutory Performance Indicators
(SPIs) 57
stereotypes of Belgium from British
perspective 22–3
St Gasthuisberg site, Leuven, hospital
rebuilding project 94
strategic action, in institutional
contexts 17
Strategic Health Authorities 42, 92
street crime, violent, England 31
suspect packages searches, Sussex
police 106
Sussex interviews 133
Sussex map 103
Sussex Police 101, 112–116
active in community liaison 116
active in neighbourhood-based
policing 116

distance of national government
changes of Home Secretaries 129
merger of five forces, 1968 102
national trends resisted
pepper sprays instead of CS gas
113
unmarked cars for armed response
114
Organizational Monitoring Unit
performance indicators 108
specialization and professionalism
151
urban centres, Brighton, Hastings
102
Sussex Police Annual Report 1984
terrorist attack on Grand Hotel,
Brighton 105
Sussex Police Standard
service standards expected by public
109
targets and minimum service levels
110

target lengths-of-stay, Belgium 46
target-setting emphasis in England 135
targets system, England 30
'taser' guns, for English police forces 69
Team Consult report, 1995
recommendation of decentralized
district teams 123
technological changes, hospitals and
police 9, 136–7
closed-circuit TV (CCTV) 155
demands on hospitals 100
forensic science, DNA testing 155
professional training, needed for 132
terrorism fears 73
terrorist activities, appeals against
convictions
'Guildford Four', 'Maguire Seven',
'Birmingham Six' 54
Terry, George, Chief Constable, Sussex
Police 103–4
Tobback, Louis, socialist minister,
Belgium 1987
development of police policy 63
Mayor of Leuven 117, 121, 123–4
Vice-Prime Minister, 1997 124
trade unions in police, Belgium and
England 51

traffic increase, addition to police tasks
109, 127
Trafford, Sir Anthony, consultant
physician, Royal Sussex
influential innovator 142
trust in police, higher in Britain than
Belgium 77–8
TV series about hospitals and police
10

UK, centralized state, domination of
local authorities 24
UK political system, majoritarian and
adversarial 23
'Unit beat policing' (UBP), 1967
car patrolling instead of foot patrols
52
University Hospital Leuven (UZ
Leuven) 95
best and biggest teaching hospital in
Belgium 83, 94, 96
contrasting factors in growth of
Leuven and Brighton 96
financial crisis 93
stable compared with NHS 96
university hospital, special
characteristics 95
urban disorder, Handsworth, Brixton,
Broadwater Farm 54

value for money (VFM), police
concern with measured efficiency
53
Van Sina, Mayor 1982, 1988 122
Vesalius Acts, 2005, integration of
police personnel 65–6
Vlerick Business School, Belgium
training of senior police officers 66

Wallonia, autonomous region of
Belgium 10
welfare states 162
and competition of EU single
market 167
Whitehall control, growth of 133, 168
in management of police forces 150
Whitehouse, Paul, Chief Constable of
Sussex Police
alternatives to CS gas for riot control
142

annual report 1993, standards of
    service expected by public 109
forced early retirement, traumatic for
    Sussex force 132–3
Whitehouse, Paul, Chief Constable of
    Sussex Police
resignation, effect of 150–51
White Paper, *Working for Patients*,
    1989 33, 91–2

hospital competition for contracts
    145
restructuring of National Health
    Service 41

Zonaal Veiligheidsplan, 2005–2008
    (local security plan)
detailed statement of plans
    124